AF521829

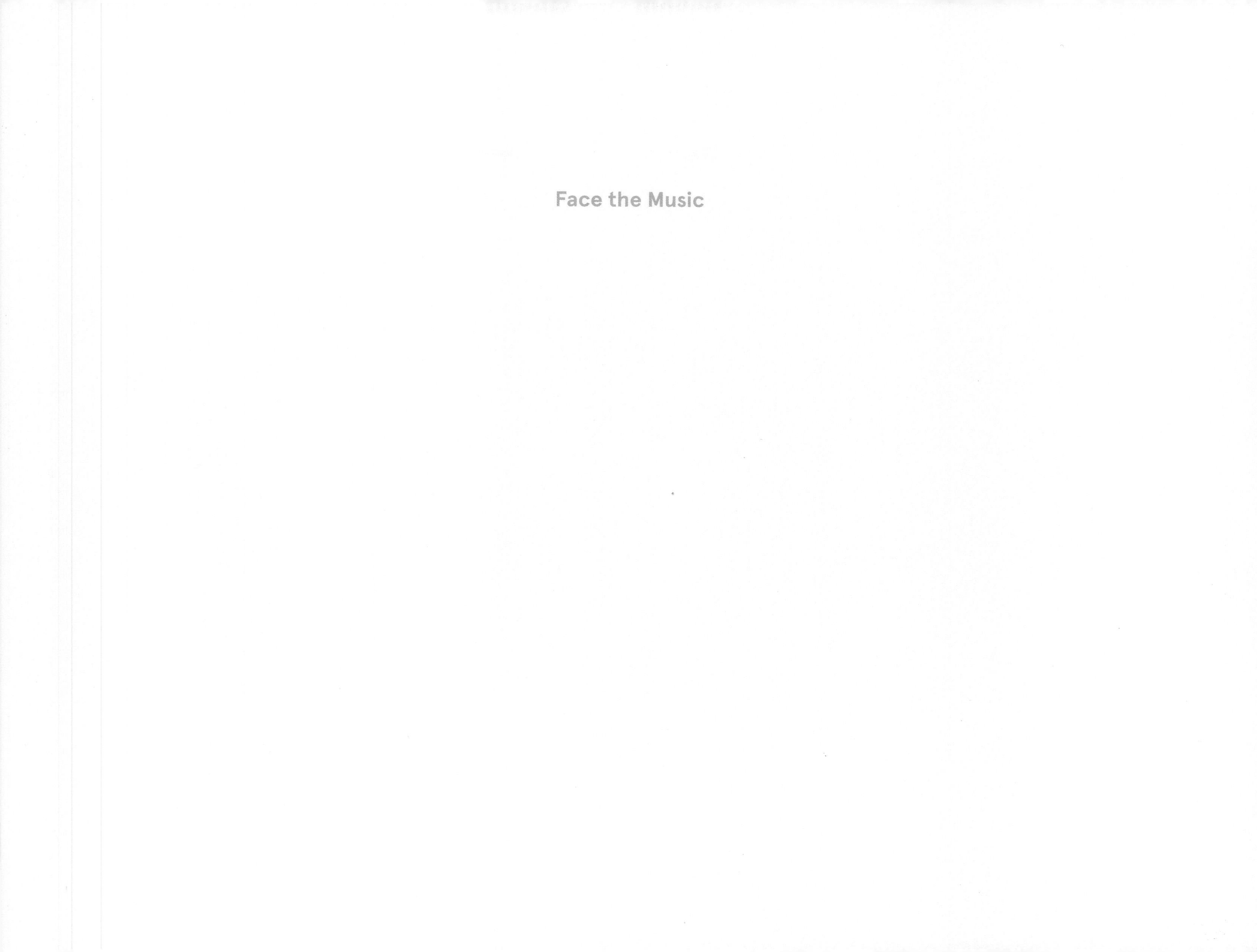

Face the Music

Forty-one Artists
Face the Music

Foreword by Daniel J. Levitin
Notes by Joel Selvin

FACE THE MUSIC

Richard Ehrlich

Steidl

FOREWORD

Daniel J. Levitin

Photography and music are complementary art forms. Both can represent forms of reality that feel more real than reality itself. Consider portrait photography. In real life, emotions unfold over time and we see the dynamic and complex unfolding ripple across a person's face, across their eyes, mouth, cheeks, and forehead. The photographer can freeze this movement to capture a single fleeting image, a thin slice of time so short that the human eye and brain never get to register it the way the camera does. Playing with time in this way gives us access to micro-expressions and an otherwordly view of one another, a window into the complexity and depth of our emotional life. The whole process recontextualizes our experience of human emotions and that is, to many ways of thinking, the quintessence of what art is all about.

In music, a brief moment of emotion can be elaborated, stretched out over time. The burst of joy that doesn't seem to last long in real life can be extended in song to any arbitrary length.

Here, these two art forms come together in a unique and moving way. In Richard Ehrlich's portraits we see the ineffable, we experience the private moments of intense concentration, joy, inspiration and awe that some of the world's greatest musicians experience while listening to their favorite music. The subjects' comfort with the photographer is apparent, and one of the great achievements of this project. Their expressions reveal something of their inner mental musical life rarely seen before by anyone. There is Verdine White playing air bass; Ringo Starr contemplating the drum fills of "Come Together;" Rosanne Cash, whose mind seems to be teeming with activity, forging musical connections as we eavesdrop. Graham Nash looking positively delighted and taken over by the spirit of Jerry Lee Lewis' "Great Balls of Fire." Emmylou Harris looking like the terrestrial projection of an angel. Quincy Jones' musical wit, charisma, and deep knowledge of musical tradition and history peers through his warm smile.

To play music well, you have to have listened to music well, to know what has come before, what people tried and what may or may not have worked. And the very best musicians have listened to lots of music. The specialness of the images collected here is that we get to see, in these wonderfully expressive portraits, musicians doing something that they spend countless hours doing in private. Ehrlich is a true artist. Join me in this novel adventure that brilliantly and artfully brings together two distinctly modern and complementary art forms.

PREFACE

Richard Ehrlich

"Musical sound has direct access to the soul. It finds there an echo, for man 'hath music in himself.'"

Wassily Kandinsky, "On the Spiritual in Art"

"Music is what feelings sound like out loud. I sing songs that speak from my heart. They tell my story, how I feel."

Georgia Cates, *Beauty from Pain*

To pose the question: Can one capture in photographic portraiture the intense and profound inner depth of feeling and emotion while listening to one's favorite music?

In 1872, Darwin published the seminal treatise "The Expression of the Emotions in Man and Animals," which intersected with the dawn of photography. While the study of physiognomy, until recently, had limited scientific acceptance, it provided the impetus for linking portraiture and emotion. If "the face is the window to the soul," capturing a rhapsody of emotions through facial expression provides a unique entry into each artist's inner being.

Recent computer-generated studies analyzing facial expressions have demonstrated that faces are organs of emotional communication, and by some estimates, we transmit more data in our expressions than we do through speech itself.[1] Fleeting facial microexpressions transmit extremely complex as well as nuanced feelings. The book you hold before you validates the original premise that a portrait can capture and convey a complex depth of feeling while listening to music.

Of related interest, a recent neurobiological study found that the sense of smell is derived from electrical impulses and spikes that the brain mathematically translates into specific smells. Simple mathematics.[2] No doubt cognitive neurophysiology will unearth similar cell biology to explain experiencing music but it may never fully capture nor substitute for the compelling ecstasy and transcendence one experiences listening to Bach, Beethoven, Quincy Jones or Herbie Hancock.

The forty-one artists in the project were requested to select between one and four favorite pieces of music while being photographed. It is fascinating to note that with few exceptions, they chose music of other musicians rather than their own, with the three exceptions perfectly comprehensible.

The selections of many artists were also fascinating and surprising: Witness Roger Daltrey choosing Edith Piaf's "Non, Je Ne Regrette Rien;" Esperanza Spalding: Shostakovich; Sir Graham Nash:

"Be-Bop-A-Lula;" Rosanne Cash: The Decemberists' "This is Why We Fight;" Herb Alpert: Pavarotti's "Nessun Dorma;" Lani Hall: Bill Evans; Mickey Hart: Gyuto Monks.

Other choices were easily understandable: Ringo listening to "Come Together;" Herbie Hancock to Miles Davis; Kenny Burrell to Duke Ellington.

This five-year project provided a wealth of memorable moments: Spending the day with Dave Brubeck and Iola, his wife of nearly seventy years, noticing Bach's music atop his grand piano; being fascinated by his long graceful fingers, mirrored in his iconic portrait by Yousuf Karsh hanging on the wall; Wayne Shorter exuding an aura of calm, grace and mystery; Herb Alpert listening to Pavarotti with eyes closed and lost in reverie; Herbie Hancock, Michael Bublé, Rosanne Cash, LeAnn Rimes—all crying, revealing the profound depth of emotion they were experiencing; Lars Ulrich's exuberant and emotional facial expressions to "Rage Against the Machine;" Iggy Pop shouting out Link Wray's "Rumble."

Music, painting, photography—as art forms—share a common nexus for experiencing feeling, and are inextricably linked in contextualizing human emotion. This project helped redefine the profound and transcendent influence music has on human emotion. Its transformative sublimity is conveyed in an elegant synthesis of facial expression.

The phenomenology of musical perception encompasses music as "the only language with the contradictory attributes of being at once intelligible and untranslatable" and as "the supreme mystery of the science of man."[3]

As Nietzsche proclaimed in his *Twilight of the Idols:* "Without music, life would be a mistake."[4]

1. Raffi Khatchadourian, "We Know How You Feel," *The New Yorker*, January 19, 2015.
2. Jo Craven McGinty, "Scents of Smell Rooted in Math," *Wall Street Journal*, May 8, 2015.
3. Claude Lévi-Strauss: *The Raw and the Cooked*, New York 1969, p. 18.
4. Friedrich Nietzsche: *Twilight of the Idols*, Mineola 2004, p. 7.

HERB ALPERT at home, Malibu, California, May 31, 2011

Giacomo Puccini – *Nessun Dorma* (from *Tosca*, sung by Luciano Pavarotti)

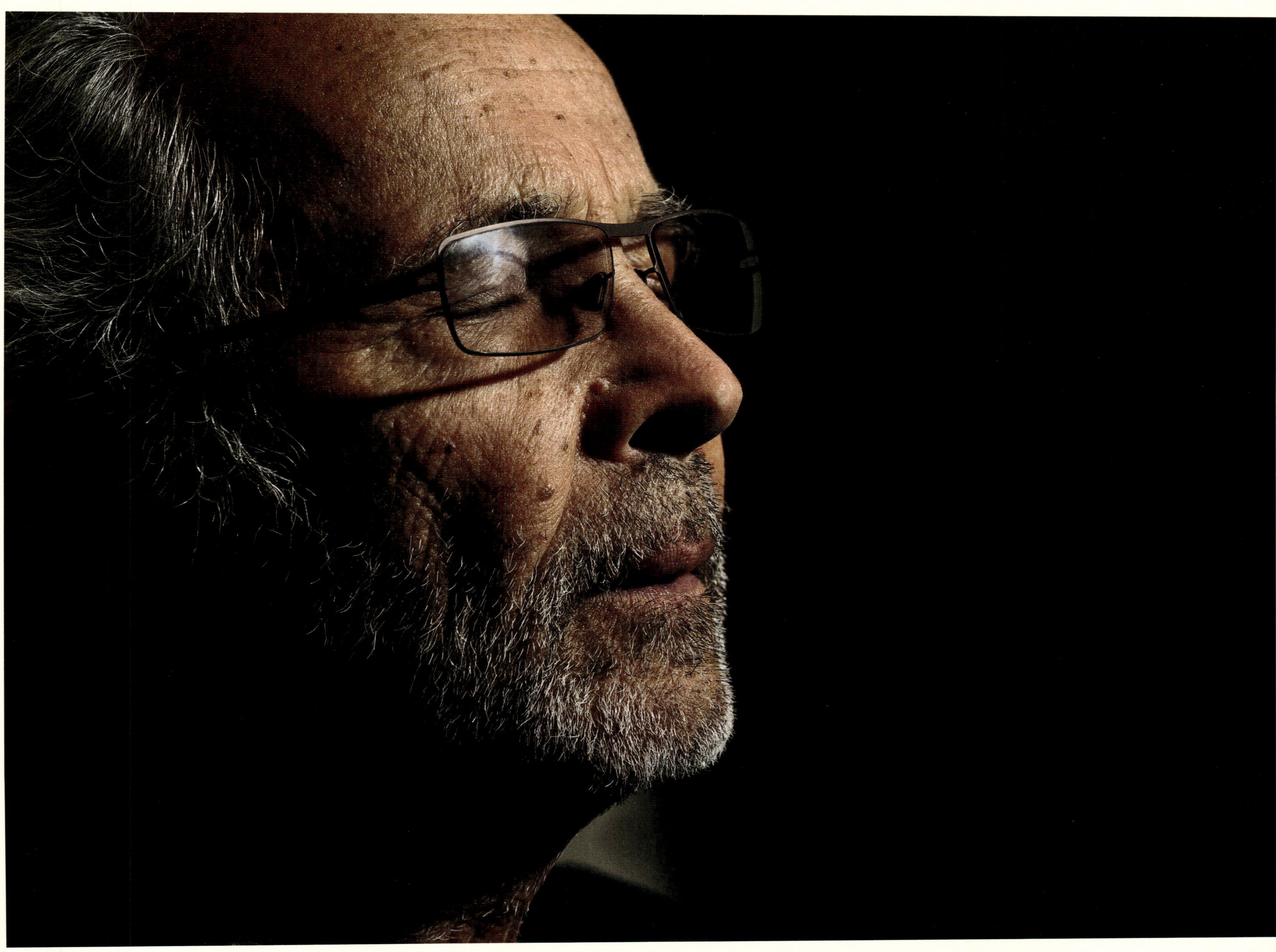

Herb Alpert used to like to practice trumpet in the reverberant men's room at A&M Records, the former Charlie Chaplin film studios in Hollywood that Alpert bought after selling the first fifteen million records for the label he founded with partner Jerry Moss. A weekend trip across the border, where Alpert encountered a mariachi band at a bullfight, inspired him to add a little crowd noise and some shouts of "Olé!" to a perky little instrumental he had been recording called "Twinkle Star." He changed the name of the song to "The Lonely Bull" and released the single on their own label—named A&M after the last names of the two partners, Alpert and Moss. The 1962 top ten hit was the first of a long line of hits by Herb Alpert and the Tijuana Brass, who sold more records than The Beatles during the peak year of 1966. While A&M grew to become one of the great independent labels of the record industry, Alpert maintained a workmanlike approach to his craft, consistently making polished, stylish music. His "Rise" was a number one hit in 1979. He is also an artist and his abstract expressionist paintings and sculptures have been widely exhibited. Despite his immense success as a recording artist—and he is the sole musician in the history of the pop charts to have a number one record both as a vocalist ("This Guy's in Love With You") and an instrumentalist—he has always remained a hardworking, dedicated musician and artist with aspirations not tied to the pop charts.

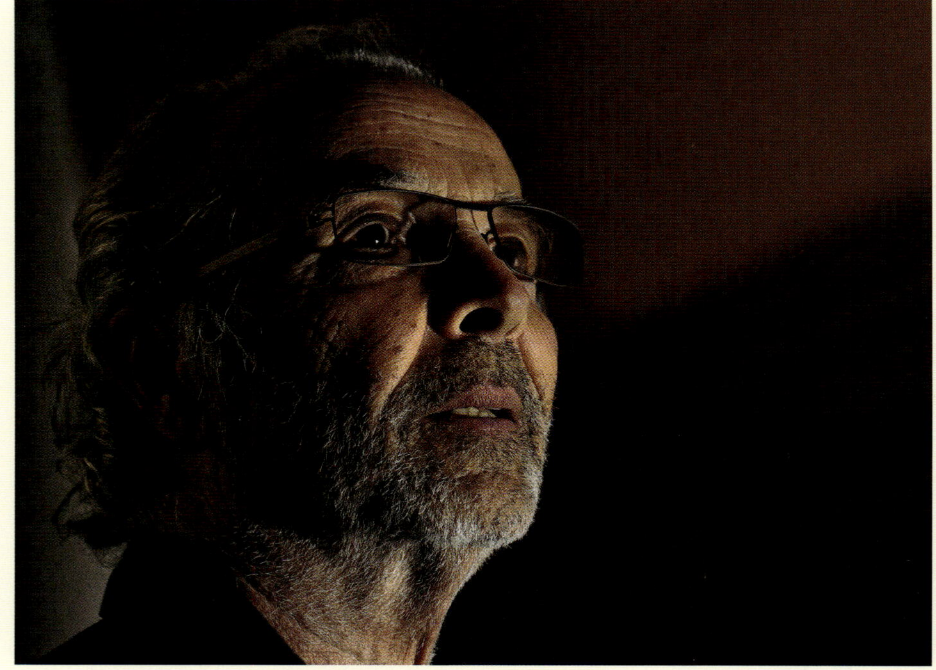

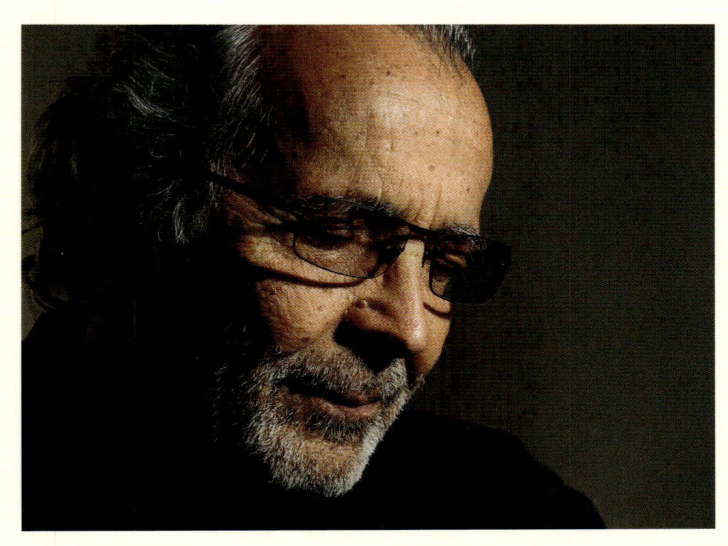

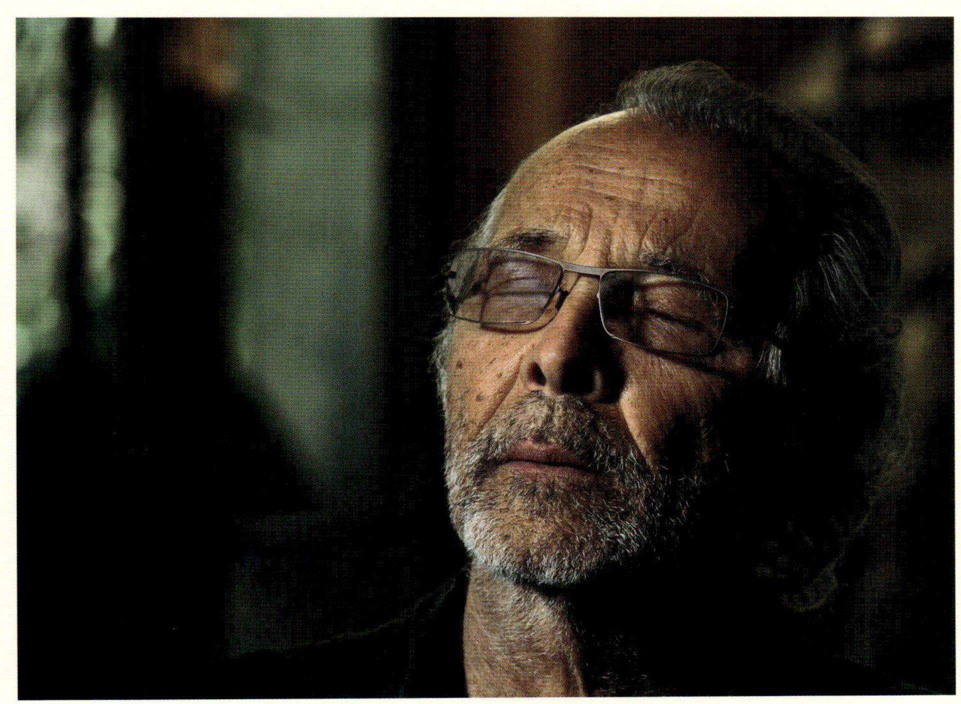

DEE DEE BRIDGEWATER at home, Los Angeles, California, January 19, 2015

Nina Simone – *Four Women*
Nancy Wilson – *Guess Who I Saw Today*
Miles Davis – *Bitches Brew*

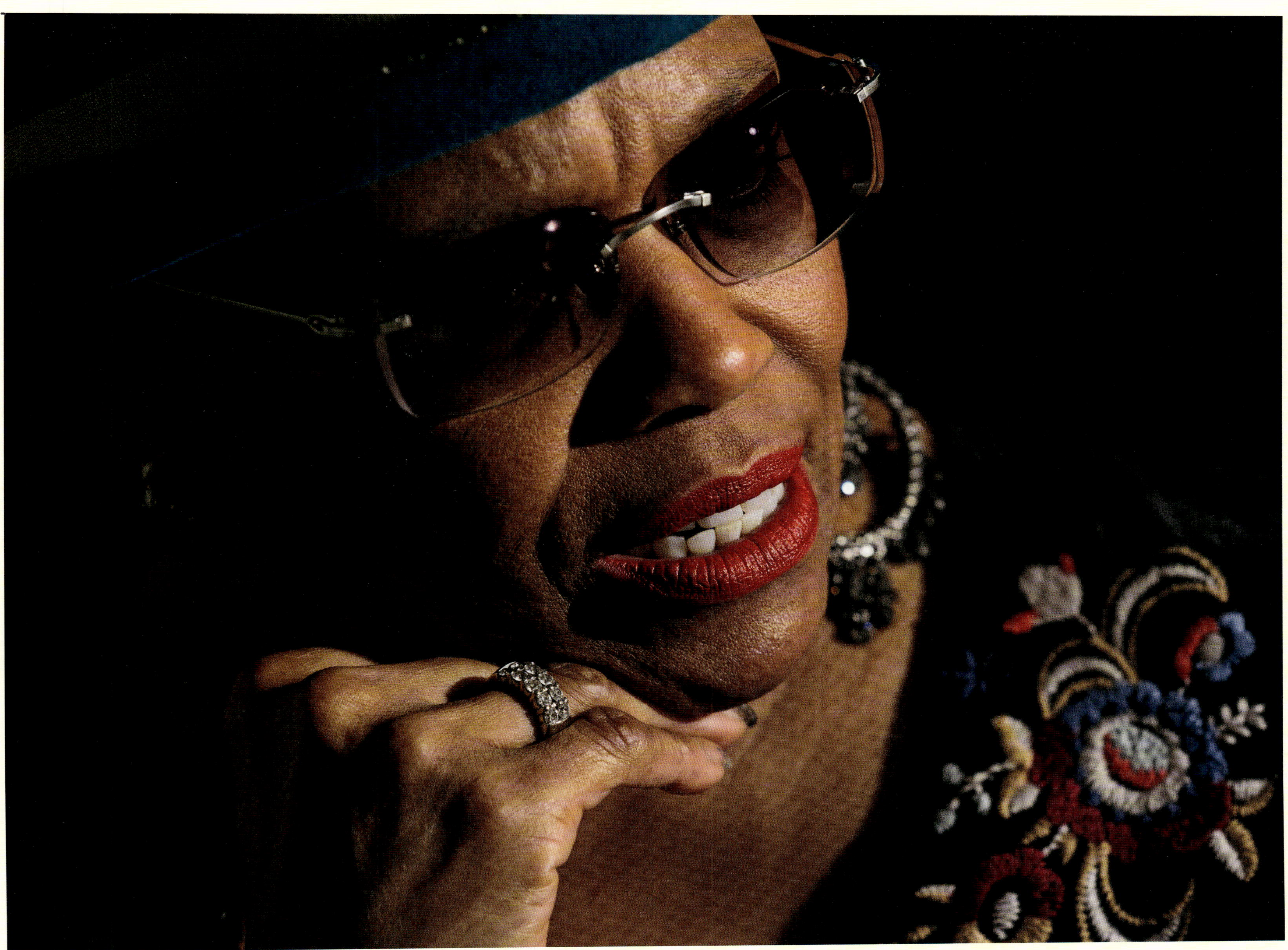

Something of a late bloomer in her professional life, jazz vocalist Dee Dee Bridgewater had to move to Paris, France, to be truly appreciated, even after an estimable career that included her Tony-winning work as Glinda the Good Witch in the 1975 groundbreaking Broadway musical *The Wiz*. Raised in Flint, Michigan, she toured the Soviet Union as a teenager with her college jazz band on a cultural exchange mission. She moved to New York shortly after marrying trumpeter Cecil Bridgewater, who went to work with Horace Silver whose wife became the vocalist with the Thad Jones/Mel Lewis Orchestra for four years. After a dead-end detour into dance music at the height of the disco era, Bridgewater went to France in 1985 to tour with a musical, Duke Ellington's *Sophisticated Ladies*, and returned the next year to play Billie Holiday in the musical *Lady Day*. Her 1989 album *Live in Paris* re-established her on the jazz scene in this country, and four years later she made her Horace Silver tribute record, *Love and Peace*. Her 1997 Ella Fitzgerald tribute, *Dear Ella*, won the Grammy Award for Best Jazz Vocal Performance. Her 2005 album *J'ai Deux Amours* was her first album of French music. For more than twenty years, she was the host of the NPR program "JazzSet with Dee Dee Bridgewater." She divides her time between homes in Los Angeles and Paris.

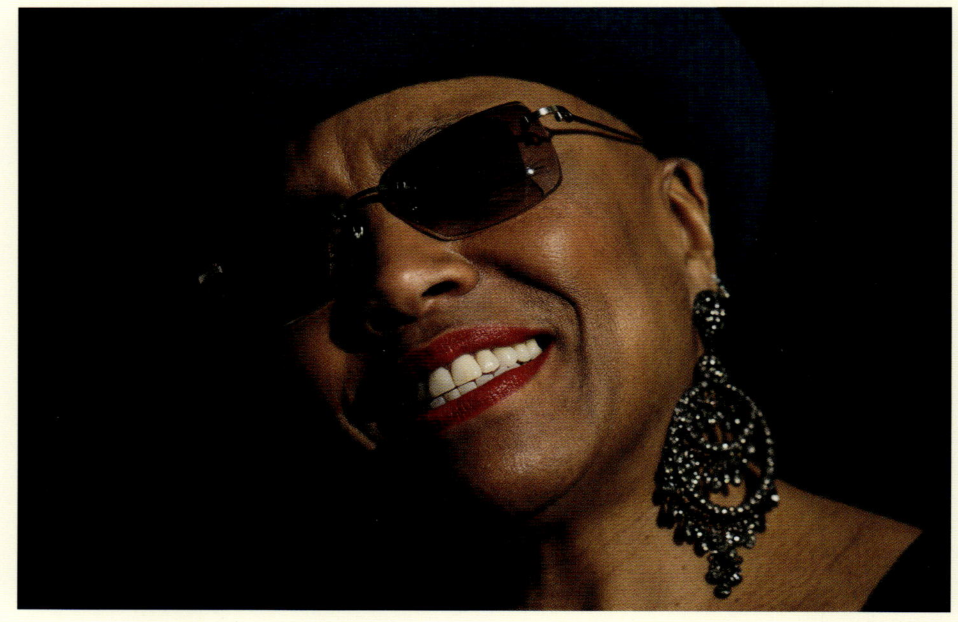

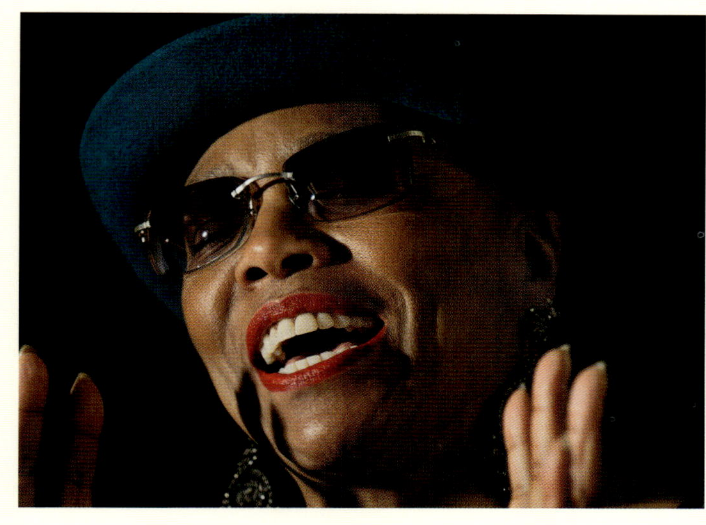

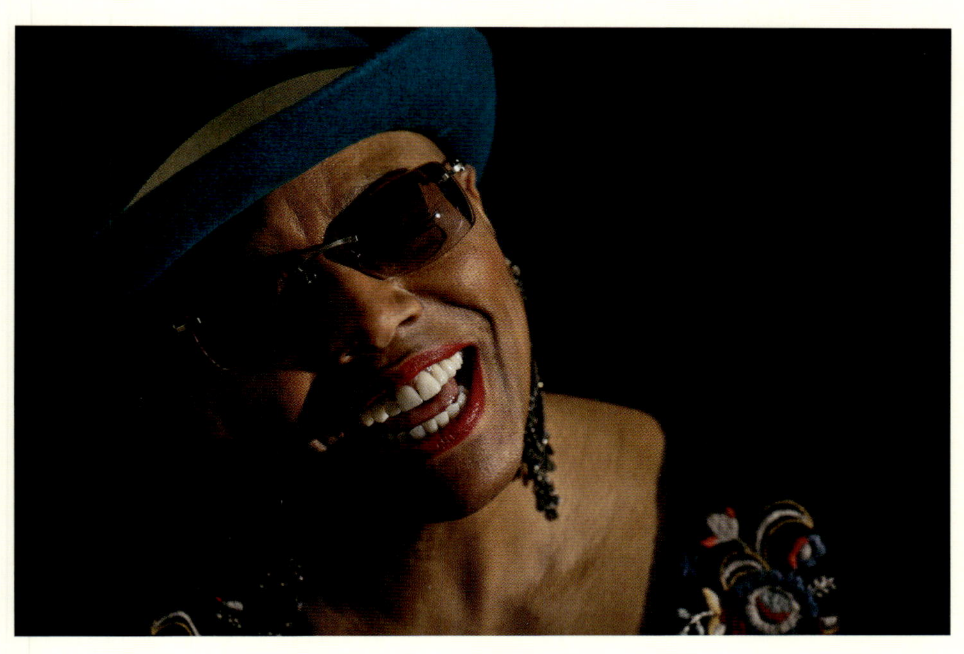

DAVE BRUBECK at home, Sharon, Connecticut, September 15, 2011

Darius Brubeck & Afro Cool Concept – *Tugela Rail*
Brubeck Brothers Quartet – *Vignettes for Nonet, Mvt. III*
David Braid & Matt Brubeck – *Improvisation 17.04.2006*

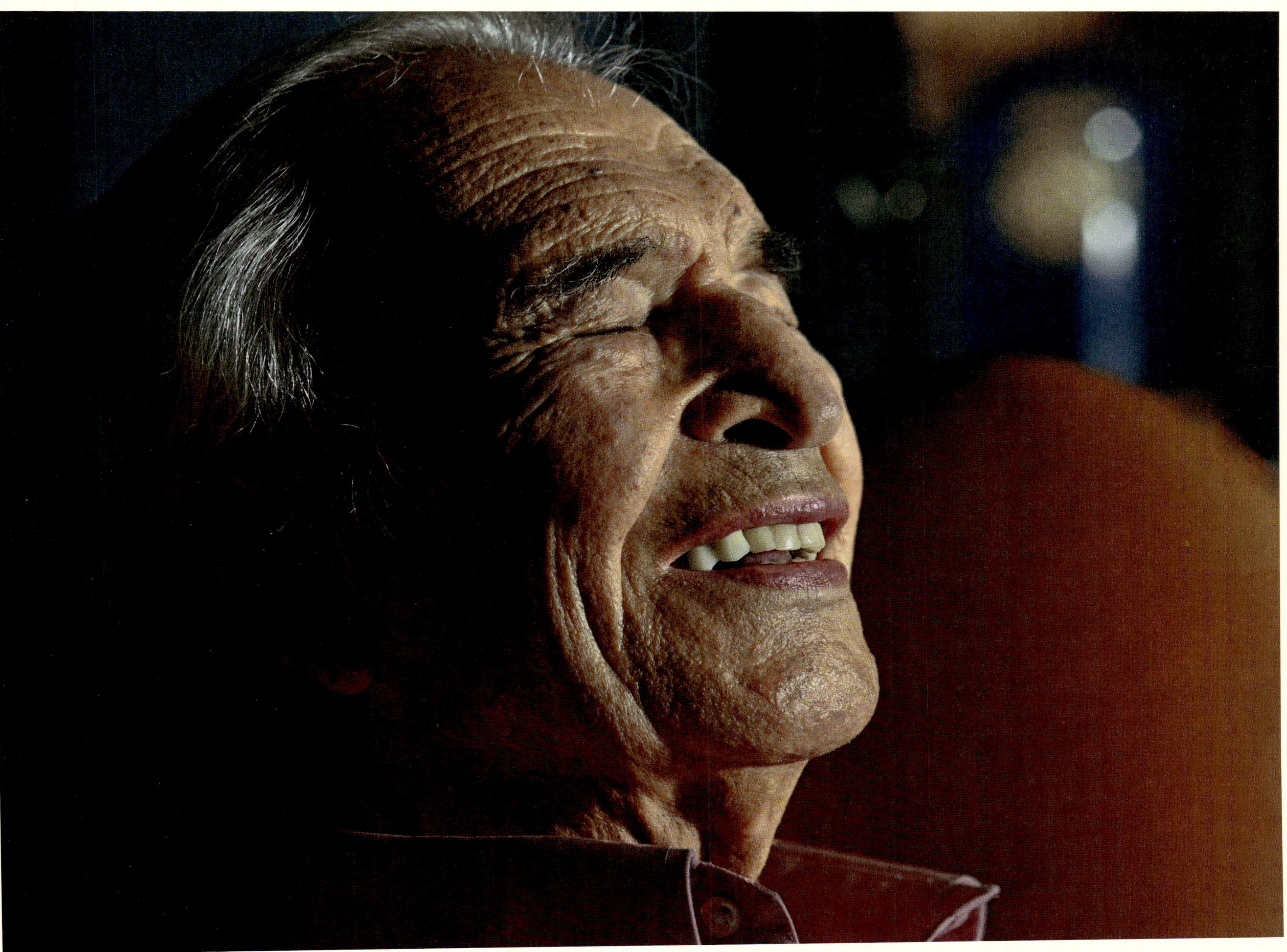

The man who put jazz music on the cover of *Time* magazine, Dave Brubeck, made cool jazz in the 50s that came to define the era. His 1959 masterpiece album *Time Out* in its fascinating 9/8 and 5/4 time signatures became the first jazz album to sell over one million copies and remains one of the landmark albums in the history of music. *Take Five* from that album became the biggest selling jazz single of all time. Brubeck, who died in 2012, one day short of his 92nd birthday, was one of the world's most celebrated jazz musicians of his lifetime. Although the immensely prolific jazz composer and performer had his own massive body of work to contemplate, he chose instead to listen to music by his sons, all formidable musicians on their own. He may have been one of the best known musicians in the world at one point, but he was a proud and loving father first. The sons began their careers playing together (and touring with their father), but eventually branched off into different rewarding and provocative directions. Chris Brubeck followed a more mainstream jazz direction, touring and recording extensively, although some of his more recent classical compositions have been performed by the Czech National Symphony Orchestra. He and his brother Dan record and perform with the Brubeck Brothers Quartet. Matt Brubeck is one of the great jazz cello players, and Darius Brubeck moved to South Africa in the early 80s and first recorded this piece of original township jive, "Tugela Rail," shortly after he arrived.

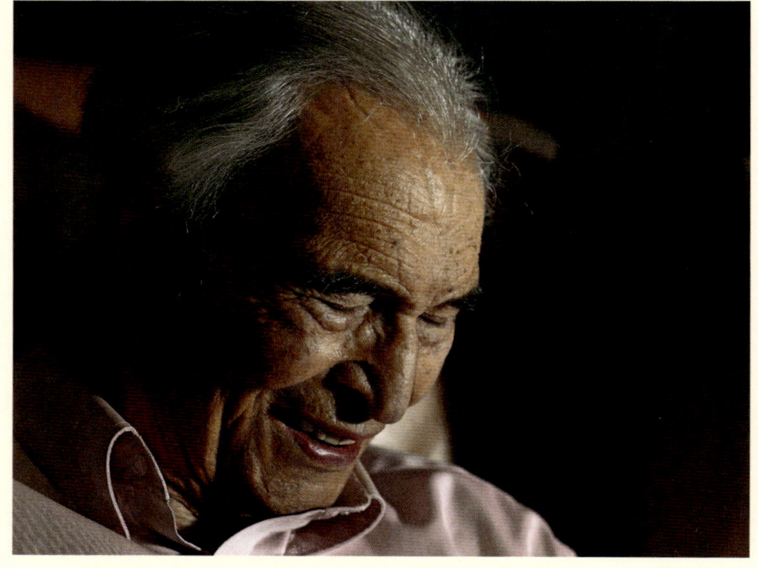

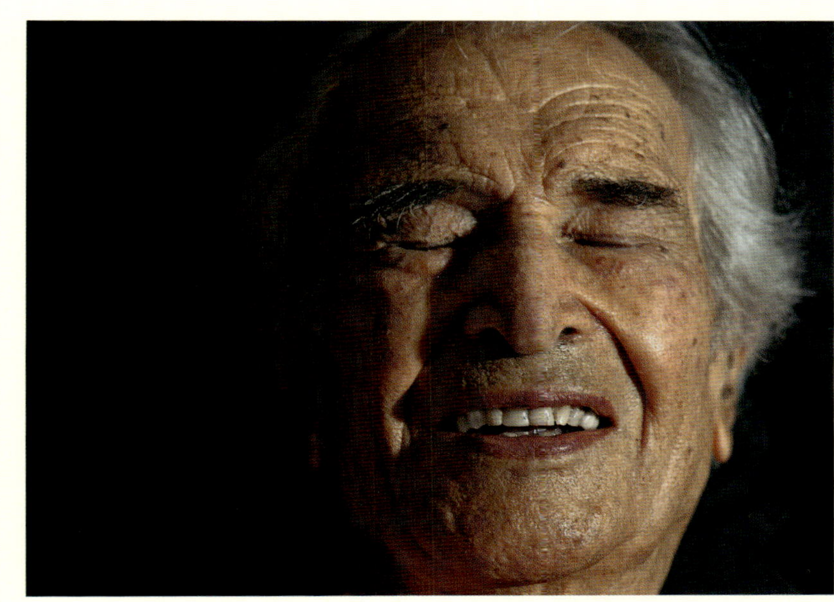

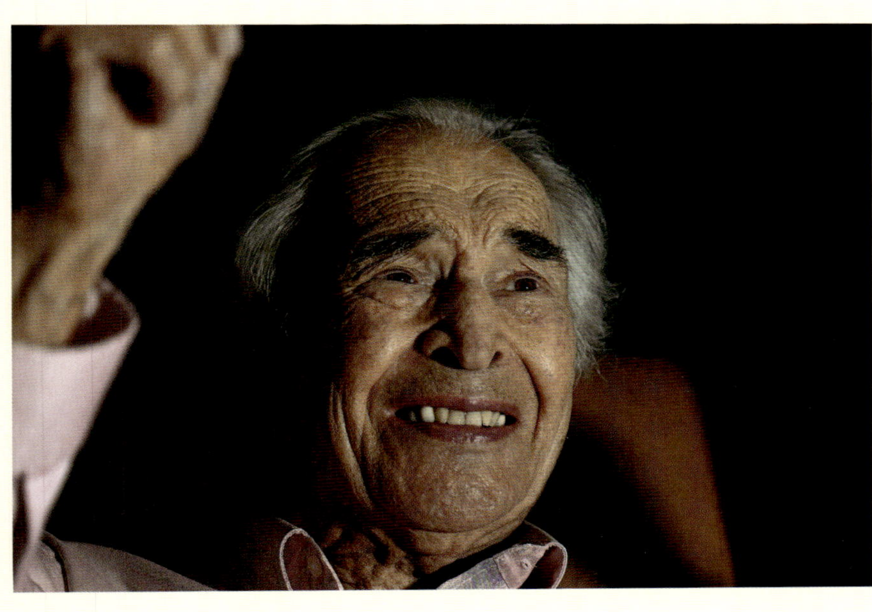

MICHAEL BUBLÉ at Humberto Gatica Studio, Los Angeles, July 26, 2011

Donny Hathaway – *A Song for You*
Louis Prima – *Buona Sera*
Jackson 5 – *I Want You Back*

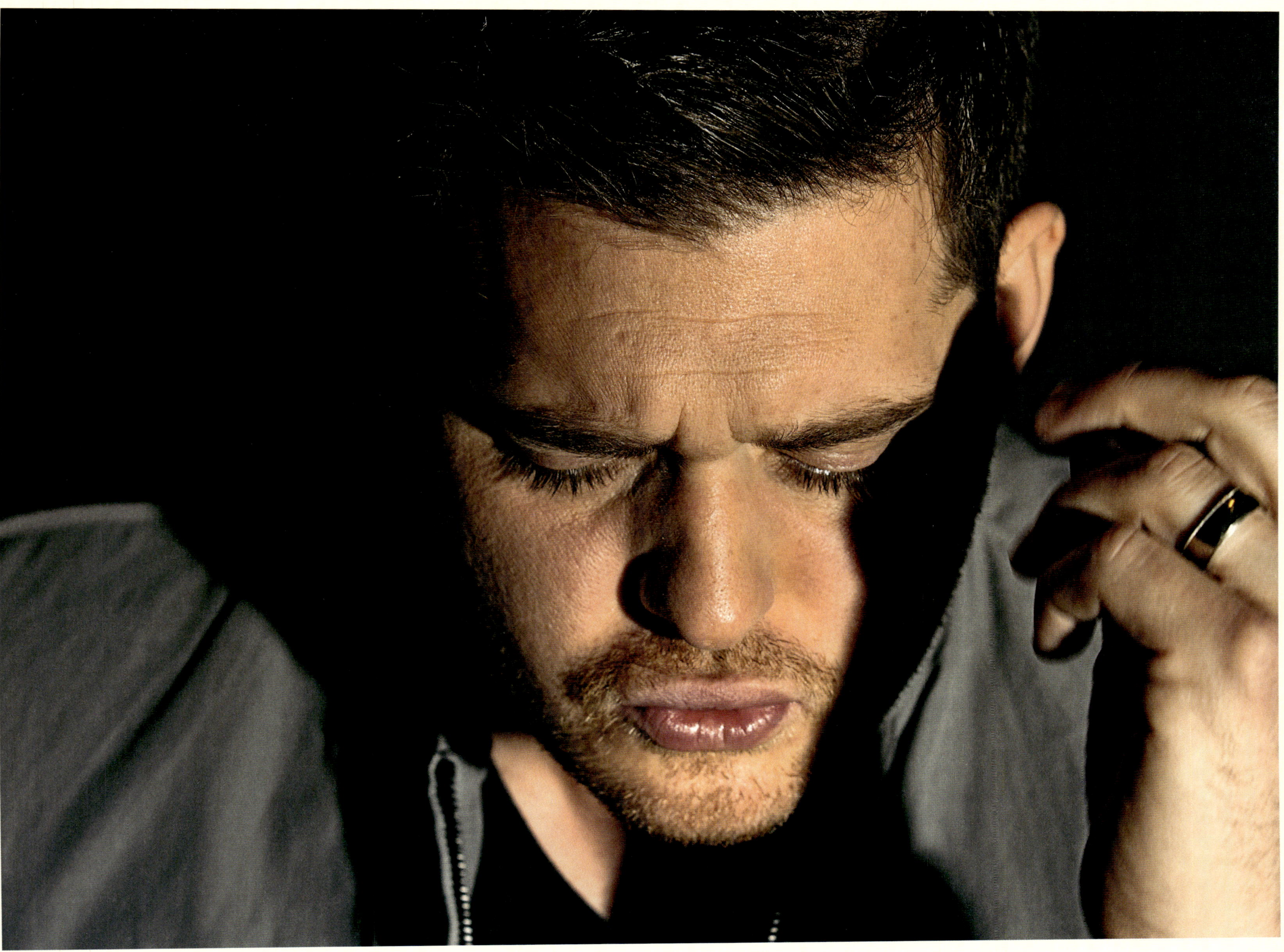

This bright, shiny young Canadian throwback brought big band pop vocals back to the top of the charts for the first time since Bobby Darin with his 2007 breakthrough third album, *Call Me Irresponsible*. He is the anti-Bieber—sophisticated, swinging, unapologetically wholesome—and the hit album, first of four consecutive number one smashes, vaulted him into the forefront of American pop vocalists: Grammy awards, sold-out concerts, TV appearances, even his own Christmas specials. The son of a British Columbia salmon fisherman, young Bublé was encouraged in music by his Italian grandfather, who paid for singing lessons and played him jazz records. He was discovered performing at the wedding of Canadian Prime Minister Brian Mulroney's daughter by Hollywood record producer David Foster in 2000, who subsequently steered Bublé's career in the recording studio. His first album was released in 2003, after he relocated to Los Angeles. Bublé is both a Canadian citizen and a naturalized Italian. He picked three disparate selections—the classic Leon Russell ballad as performed by the little-known but extraordinarily gifted vocalist Donny Hathaway, the raucous Italianate 50s pop of Louis Prima and Keely Smith, and the spunky, irresistible slab of soul that introduced the world to the remarkable Michael Jackson.

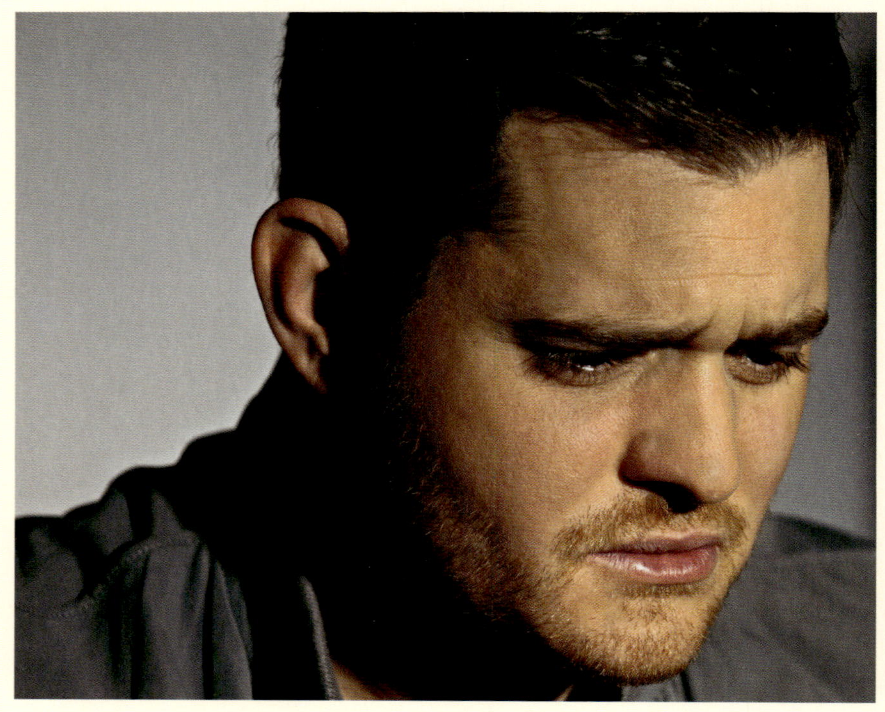

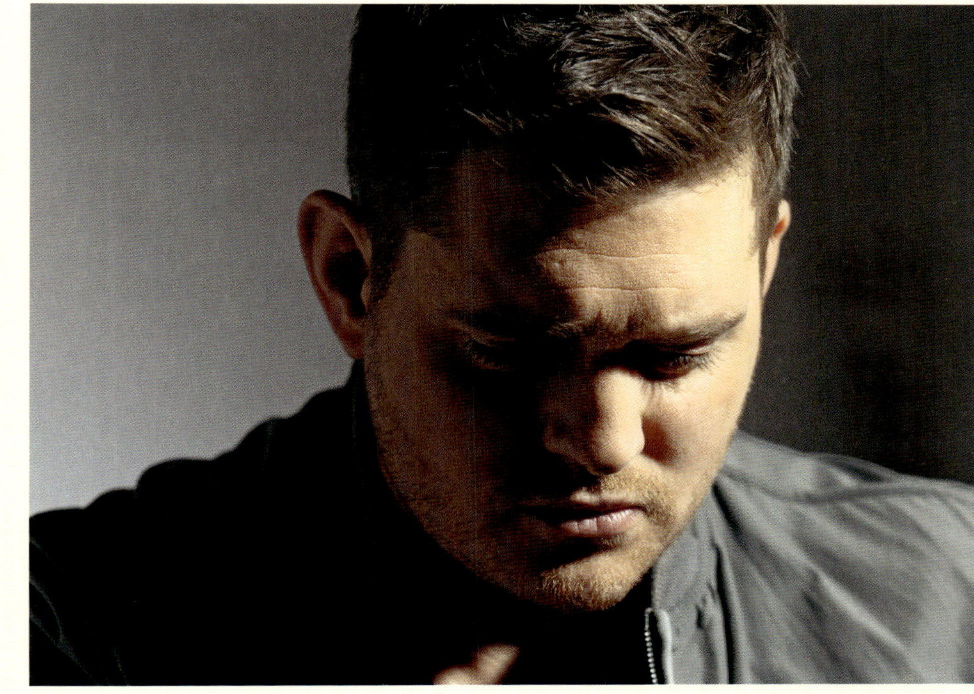

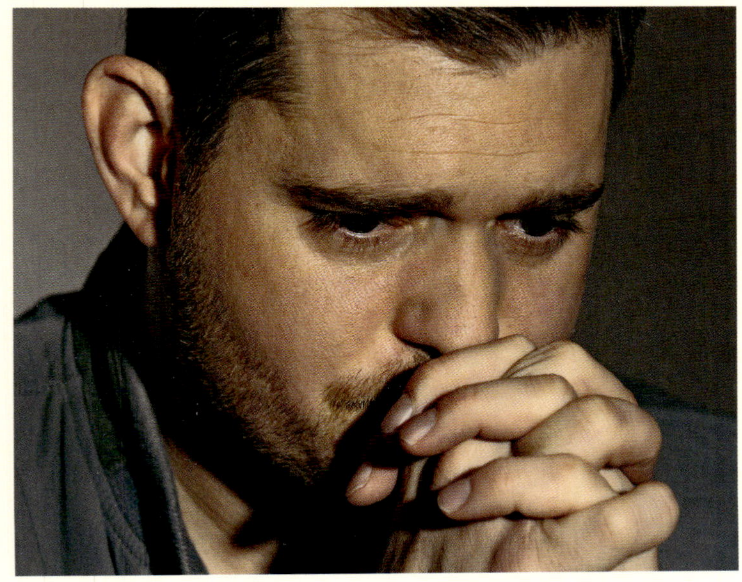

KENNY BURRELL at the UCLA Herb Alpert School of Music, Los Angeles, February 24, 2012

Charlie Parker with Strings – *Just Friends*
Duke Ellington – *A Tone Parallel to Harlem*
Tony Bennett – *The Shadow of Your Smile*

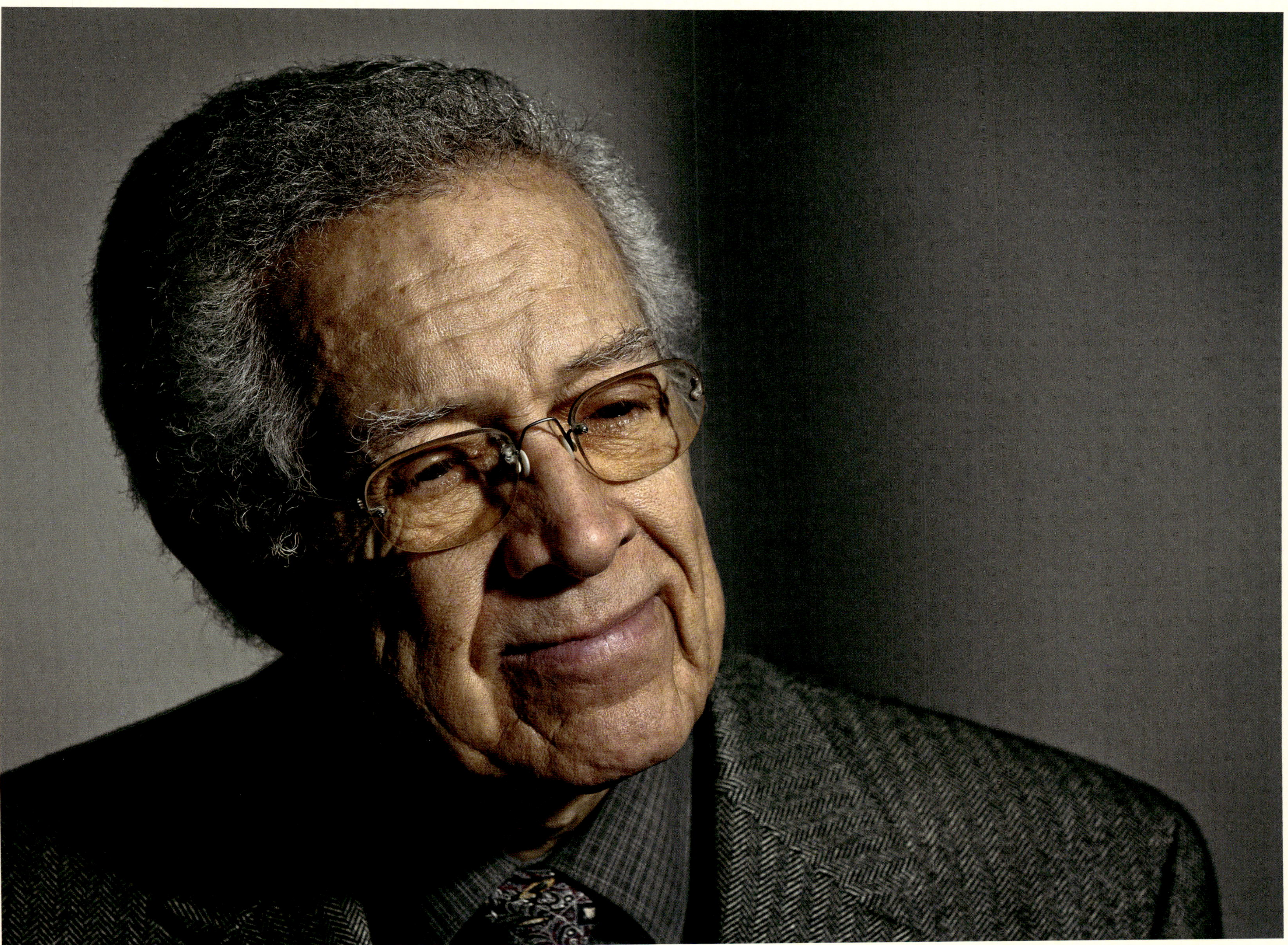

The shadow of Kenny Burrell's guitar falls across a good portion of jazz history. No other guitarist in the music can match the depth and breadth of his enormous body of work. His solo recordings for the Blue Note label in the 50s brought the instrument into the world of hard bop—the album *Blue Lights* is an enduring classic. Burrell famously recorded with John Coltrane, dueted effectively with saxophonist Stanley Turrentine on his 1962 album *Midnight Blue,* joined trumpeter Donald Byrd on the groundbreaking 1964 album *A New Perspective,* recorded *Guitar Forms* with arranger Gil Evans in 1965, and accompanied organist Jimmy Smith on a memorable series of recordings. He held the Charlie Christian chair in the Benny Goodman band in 1957 and recorded as sideman on more than four hundred jazz records—from Billie Holiday to James Brown. He made his recording debut as a twenty-year-old student at Wayne State University on important small combo dates with Dizzy Gillespie in 1951. After graduating in music, he moved to New York and first worked for six months with pianist Oscar Peterson, launching his career. He is Director of Jazz Studies at UCLA and famous as an expert on the music of Duke Ellington (his 1975 album *Ellington Is Forever* was an important tribute). Burrell played with Ellington on the TV show *Love You Madly* in 1973, and Ellington claimed Burrell to be his favorite guitar player.

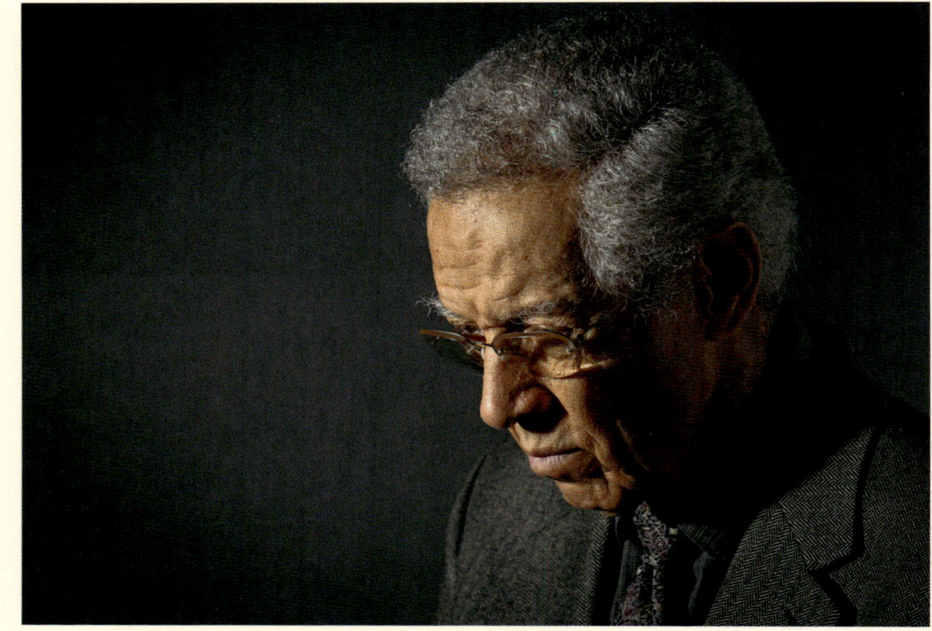

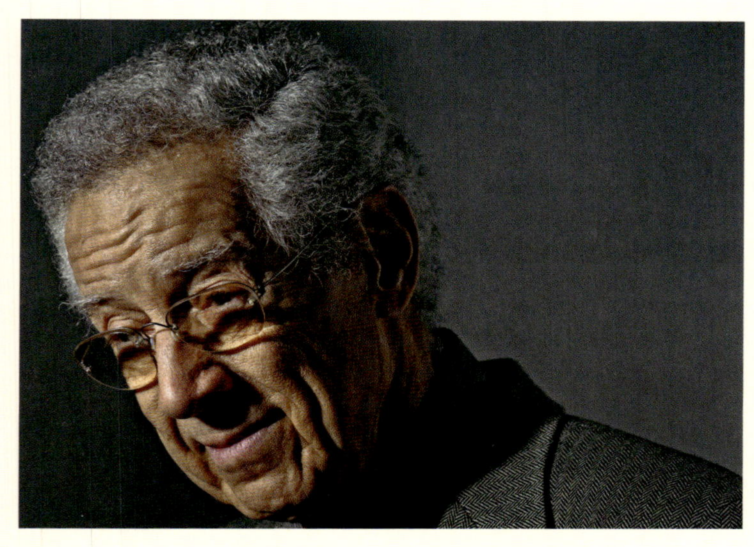

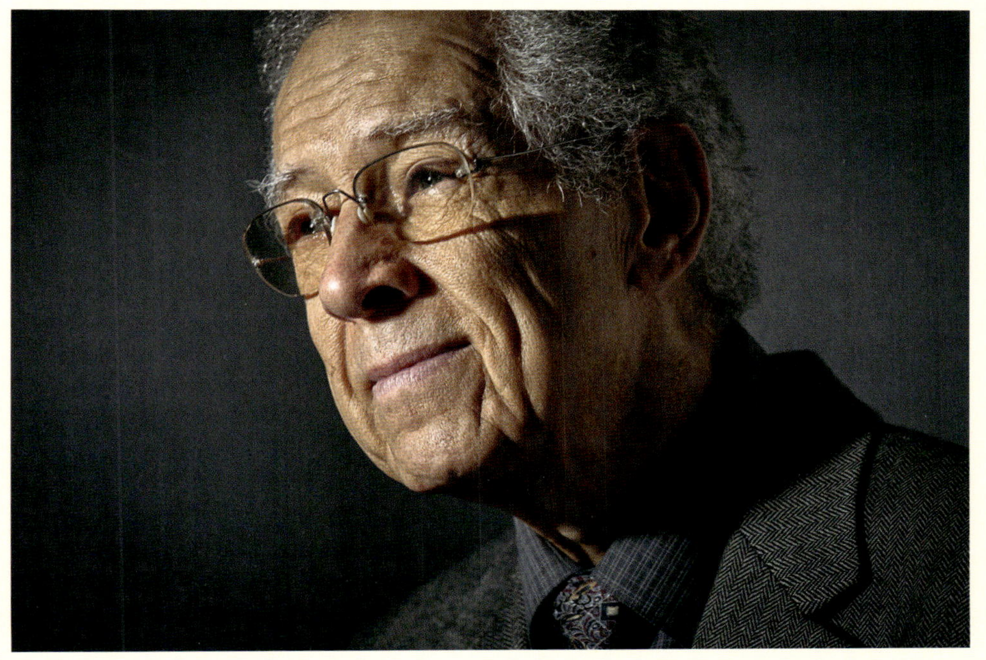

ROSANNE CASH at home, New York City, August 10, 2014

The Beatles – *You've Got to Hide Your Love Away*
Arvo Pärt – *Spiegel im Spiegel*
The Decemberists – *This Is Why We Fight*

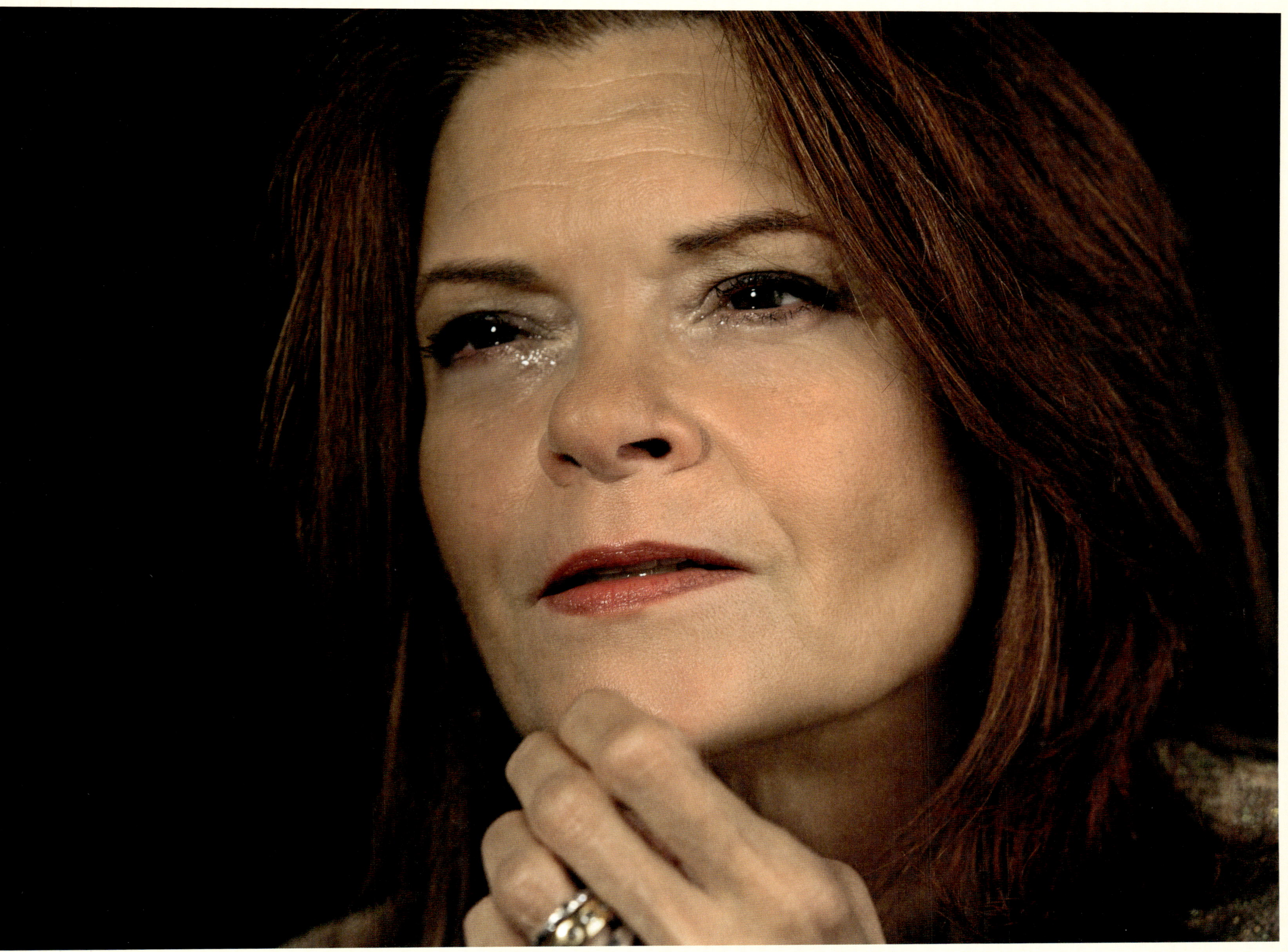

Johnny Cash's oldest daughter long ago established an artistic life of her own, leaving behind the constricting politics of the Nashville country music world for life as a singer-songwriter in downtown Manhattan. Her brilliant 1990 album *Interiors* effectively ended her highly successful career in the conventional country field in favor of the stark, emotionally vivid and dark songs she wrote in the wake of the dissolution of her marriage to country musician Rodney Crowell. She has been married to her second husband, record producer John Leventhal, for more than twenty years and has pursued an array of creative projects. She has written a number of books and her short stories and journalism have been published widely. Her recordings since leaving Nashville have been bold strokes such as her 1996 album *10 Song Demo* that featured entirely undecorated songwriting demos; *Black Cadillac*, her 2006 contemplations on the death of her father and stepmother June Carter Cash; or *The List*, a 2009 set of country music classics drawn from a list compiled by her father for her when she was starting out. Her selections mirror her genre-proof artistic life—from the soft, acoustic Beatles ballad to the almost severely minimalist piece by the famed Estonian composer Arvo Pärt to the jangly 2011 alt-rock of The Decemberists.

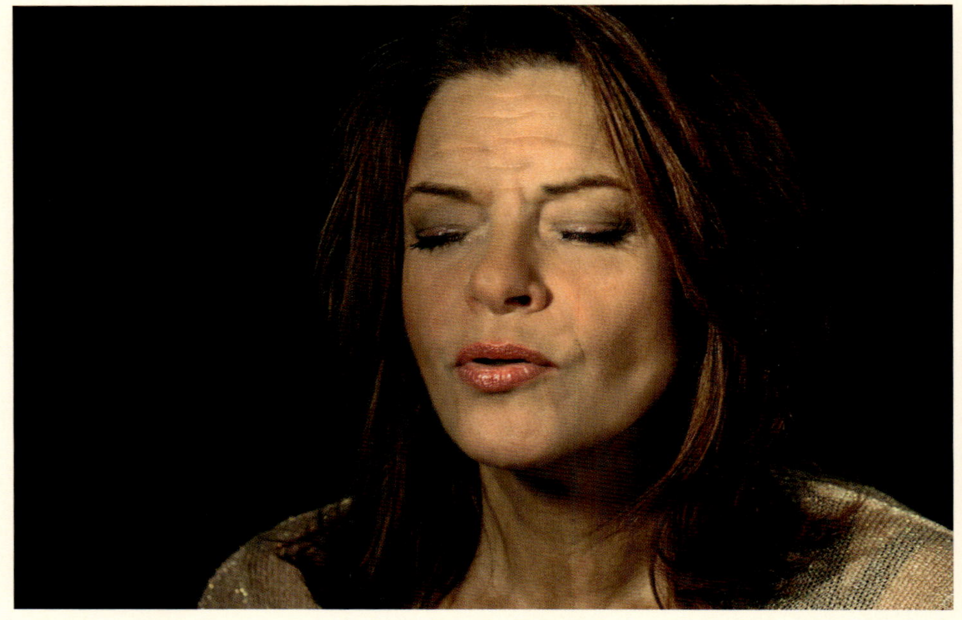

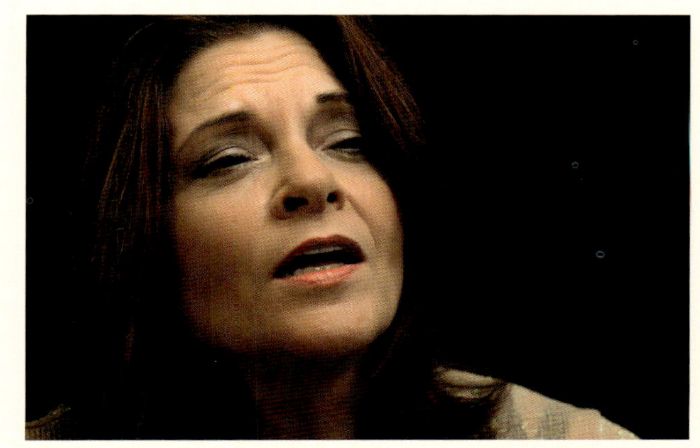

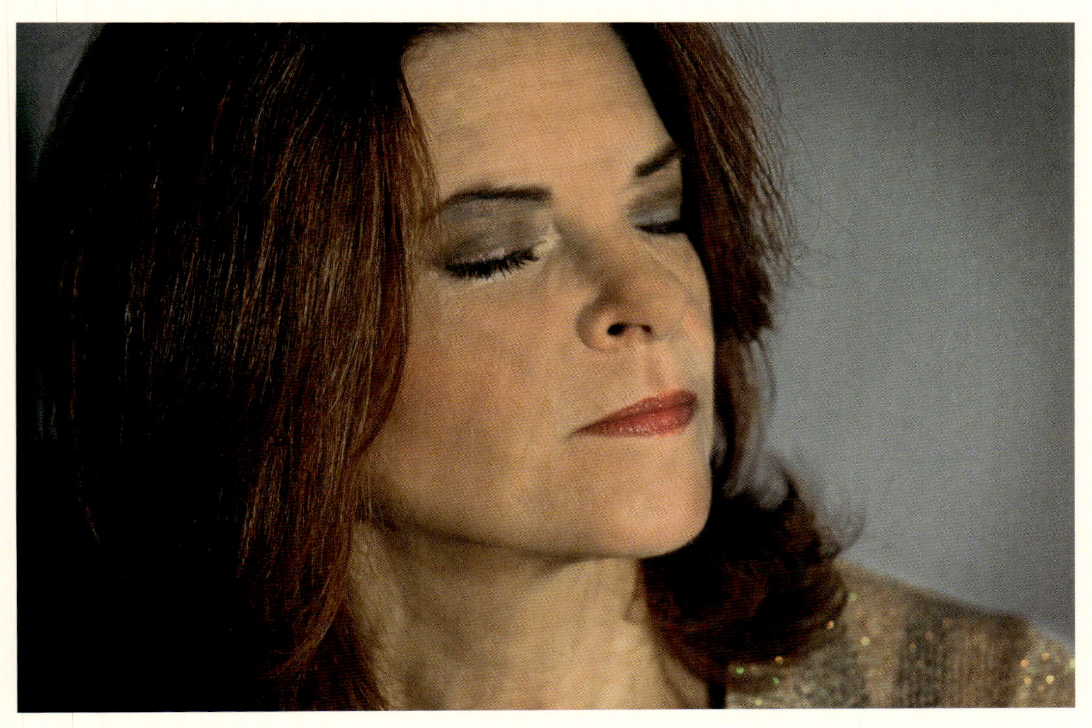

SHERYL CROW at Milk Studio, Los Angeles, California, May 14, 2014

Stevie Wonder – *Love's in Need of Love Today*
Fleetwood Mac – *Landslide*

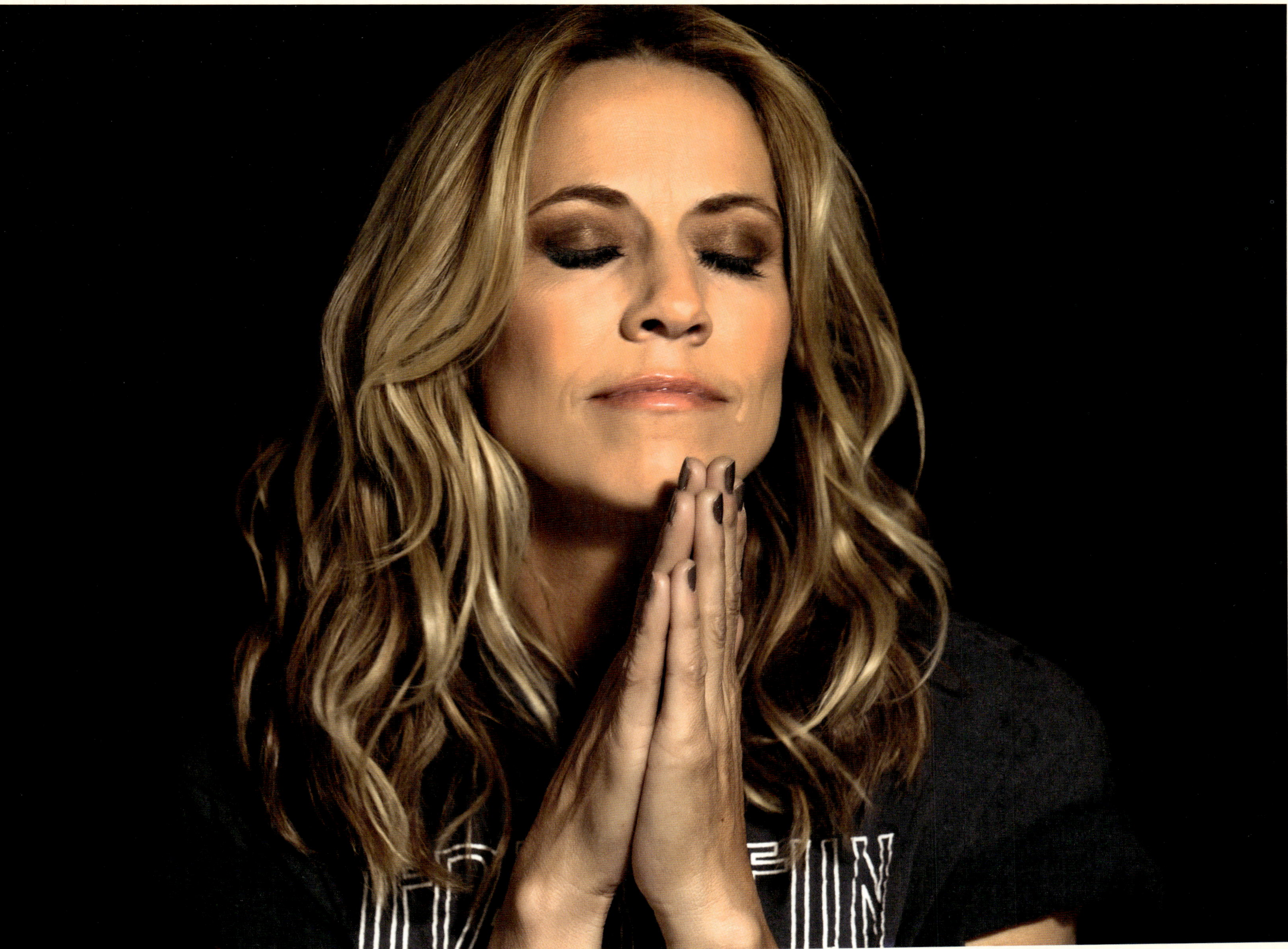

Emerging from the anonymity of the background chorus on Michael Jackson's "Bad" tour to full-blown Grammy-anointed rock goddess with her 1993 solo debut *Tuesday Music Club*, Sheryl Crow was the wicked combination of good looks, great singing and solid musical ability. The one-time elementary school music teacher in St. Louis came to Los Angeles to make music. Her then-boyfriend Kevin Gilbert brought her to the informal sessions by music business professionals who gathered weekly at producer Bill Bottrell's Pasadena studio, where she sang the song "Leaving Las Vegas" that would launch her career. The number one hit "All I Wanna Do"—the lyrics were discovered in an old poetry book lying around the studio—won the Grammy Award for Record of the Year. She has proven to be a most protean lady rock star, equally at home as a gussied-up glamour gal or one of the guys in blue jeans, comfortable under the hood with her music as a writer and player. She supplied the theme to the James Bond film *Tomorrow Never Dies* and dueted memorably with Sting on her song "Always on Your Side." A Soul survivor who has outlasted many other female singers, Crow has gravitated toward country music on recent recordings from Nashville, where she lives on a farm with her two adopted sons.

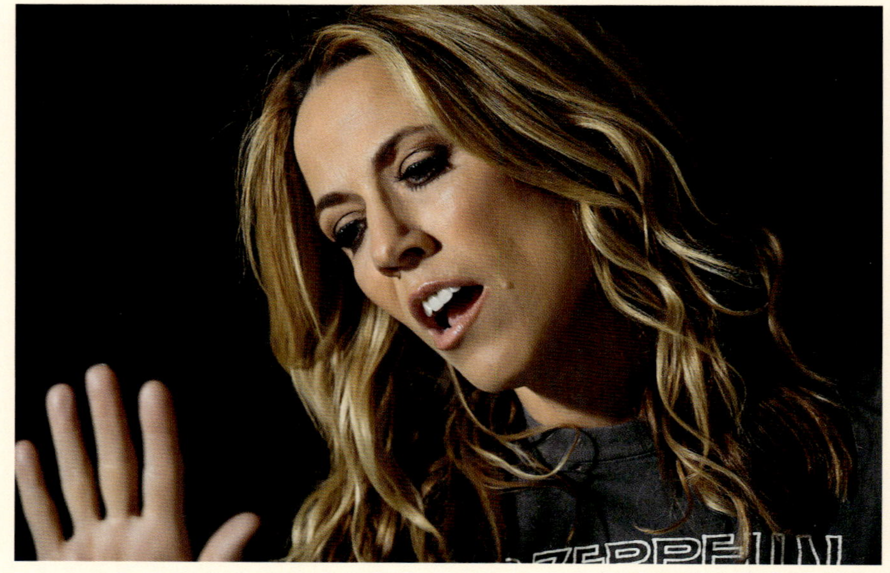

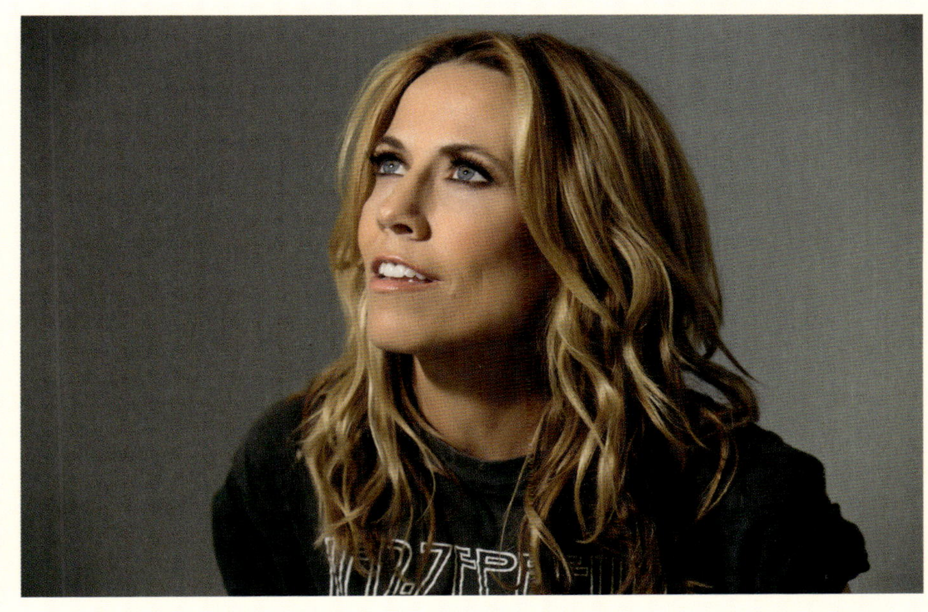

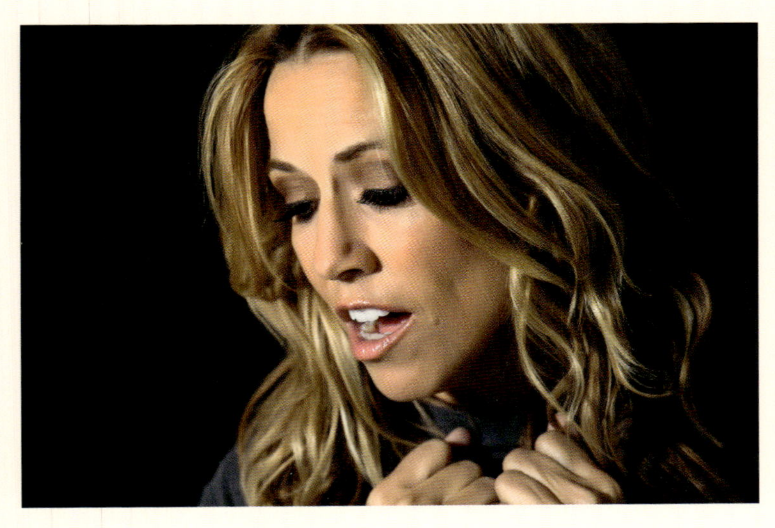

ROGER DALTREY at CenterStaging, Burbank, California, August 9, 2013

Edith Piaf — *Non, Je Ne Regrette Rien*

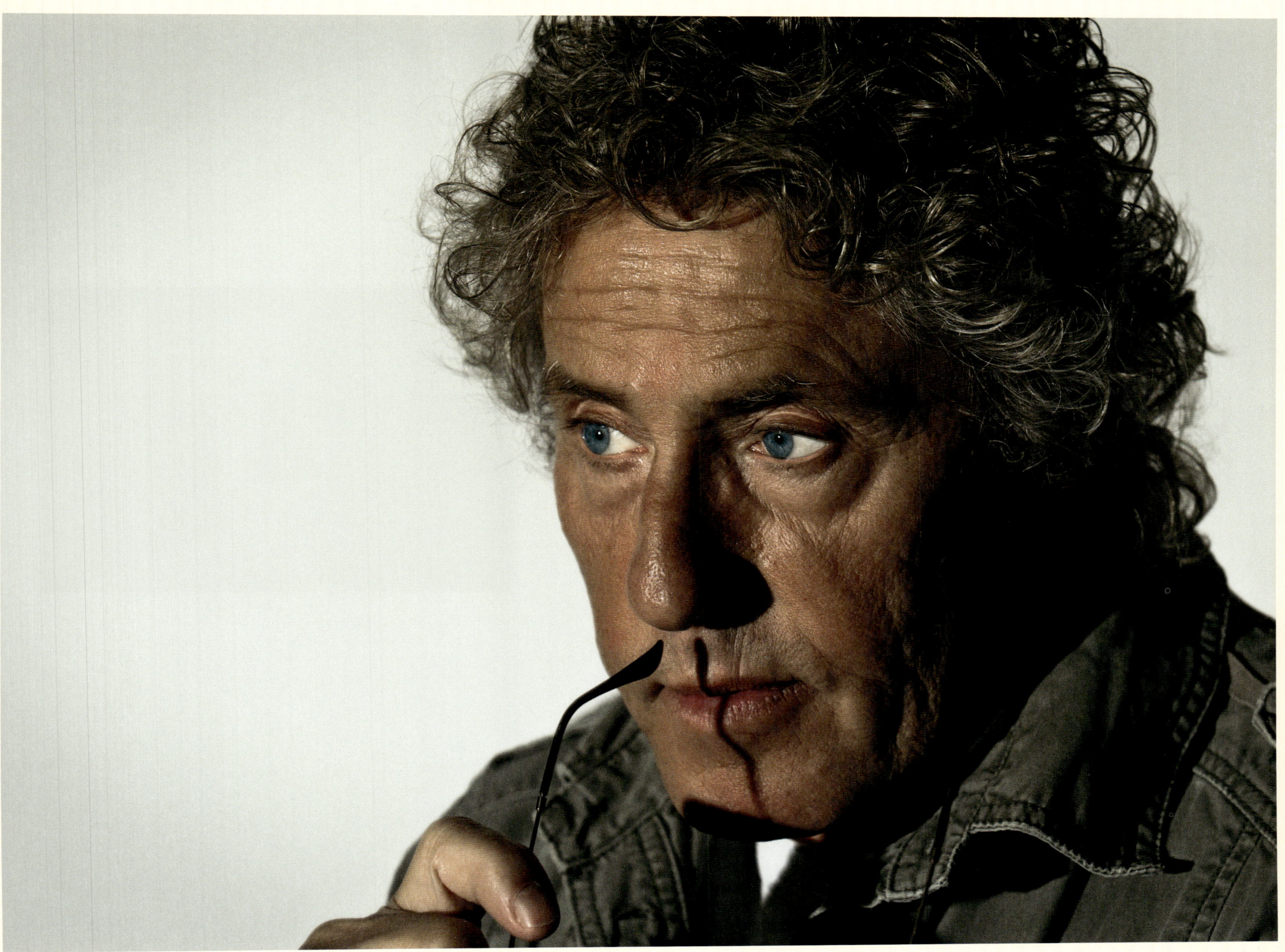

The dashing, charismatic lead vocalist of The Who, one of rock's greatest groups, is a strutting bantam rooster who stands five foot five, but who ruled the band in the early days with his fists. A sheet metal worker from a working-class neighborhood in London who had been expelled from school for smoking (he had been a good student otherwise), Daltrey invited John Entwistle to play bass in his band and Entwistle introduced him to Pete Townshend, who also joined the group on guitar. With the addition of wild man drummer Keith Moon, The Who became one of the leading bands of the new rock movement in Great Britain and developed one of the most exciting and powerful live shows of any rock band ever. Bare-chested Daltrey in that fringed vest he wore at Woodstock was the epitome of a rock star vocalist, a Greek god with a microphone cord lasso and tambourine he beat to tatters. Although he has also recorded solo albums, acted in movies and television, his legacy has always been anchored to The Who. In 1994, twelve years after Townshend retired the band, he presented "Daltrey Sings Townshend" at Carnegie Hall and slowly coaxed Townshend back into a full-scale Who reunion in 1997. The band celebrated its fiftieth anniversary in 2015.

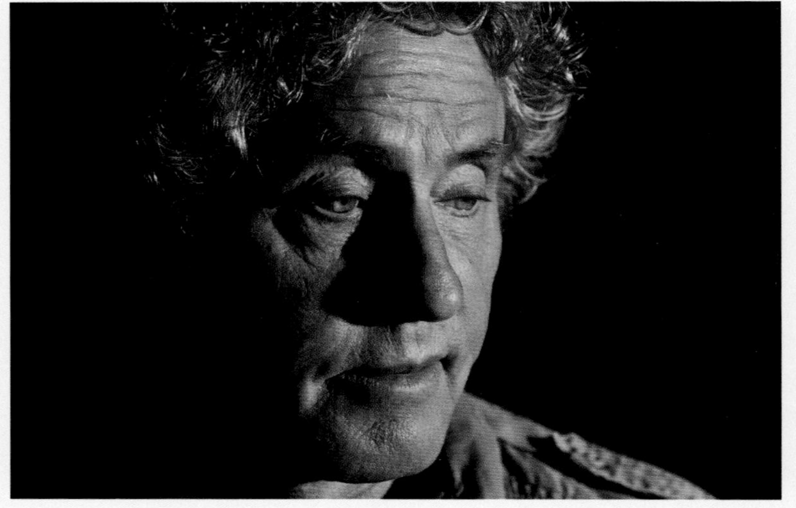

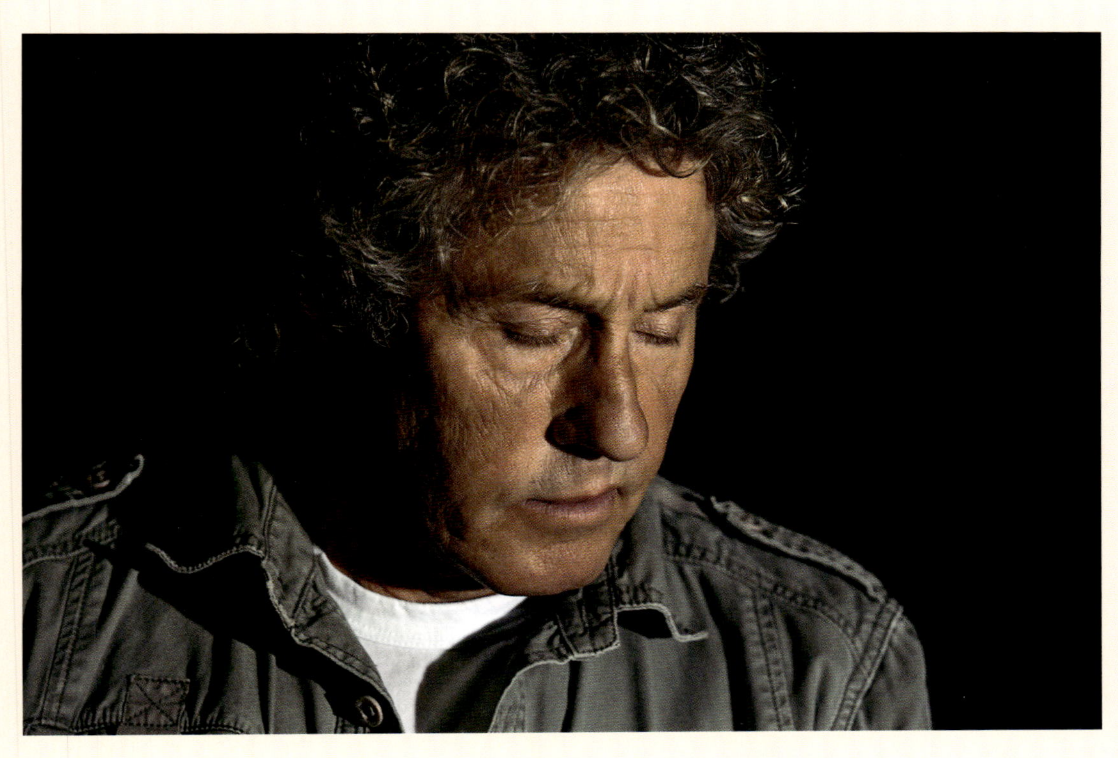

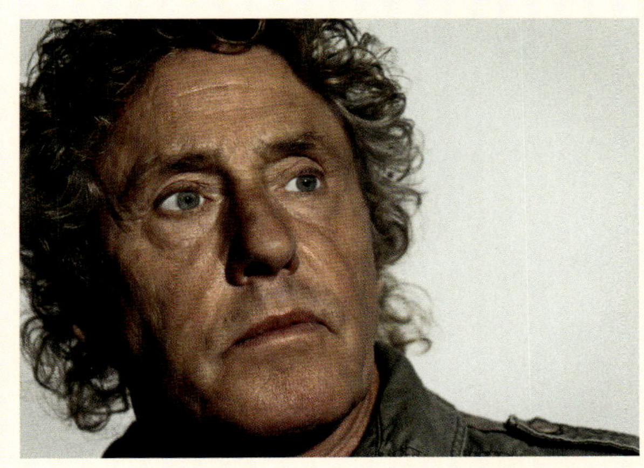

JOHN DENSMORE at home, Los Angeles, California, February 15, 2012

Modest Mussorgsky – *Pictures at an Exhibition, N° 10: The Great Gate of Kiev* (played by the Chicago Symphony Orchestra, Seiji Ozawa)
Ravi Shankar – *Improvisations and Theme from Pather Panchali*
John Coltrane Quartet – *Out of this World*

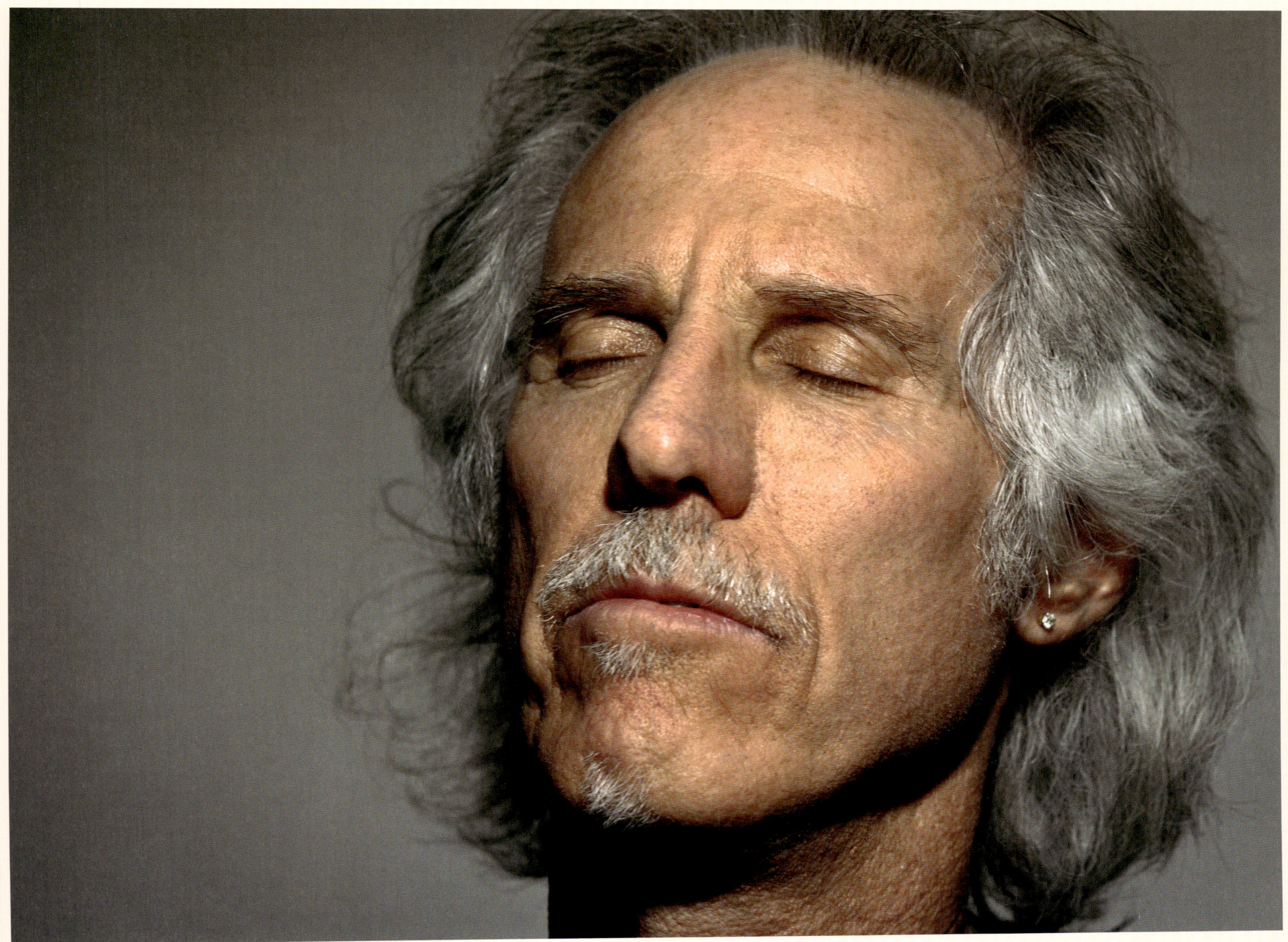

John Densmore was attending San Fernando Valley State College in spring 1966 when he drove down to Manhattan Beach to play drums at a jam session with a keyboard player he had met some months before. In the corner of the garage, twenty-year-old film school dropout Jim Morrison showed Densmore lyrics he had written to a song called "Break on Through." For the next five years, holding down the drummer's chair for The Doors, Los Angeles' untamed psychedelic rock band, Densmore took the ride of his life. After Morrison's death in 1971, the drummer participated in some post-Doors musical ventures with his erstwhile bandmates, but he left music in the early 80s. He has pursued a restless creative life, working as playwright, actor and producer. He wrote a 1990 bestselling account of his life with The Doors and was the one member of the group who stopped the band from licensing Doors songs for commercials. He picked three out-there classics—the climax to Mussorgsky's majestic, turbulent symphonic masterpiece, a Ravi Shankar sitar piece that was prototypical hippie pad soundtrack material, and jazz great Coltrane's epic instrumental take on the Harold Arlen standard.

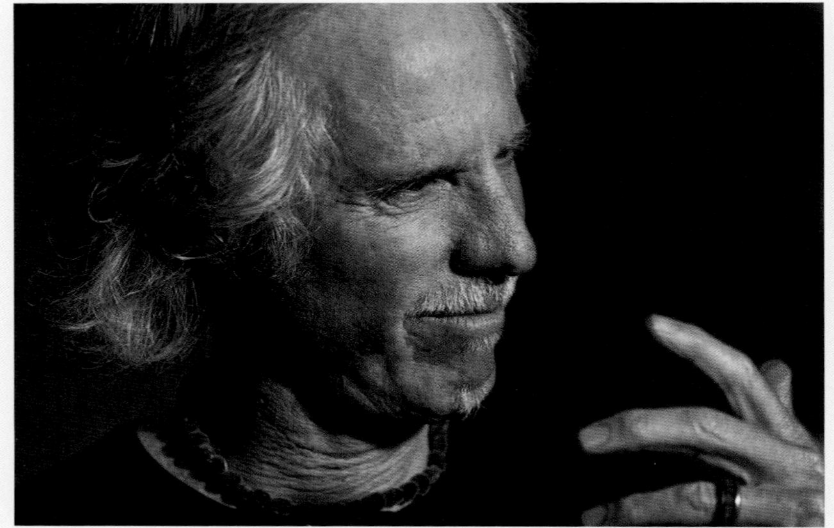

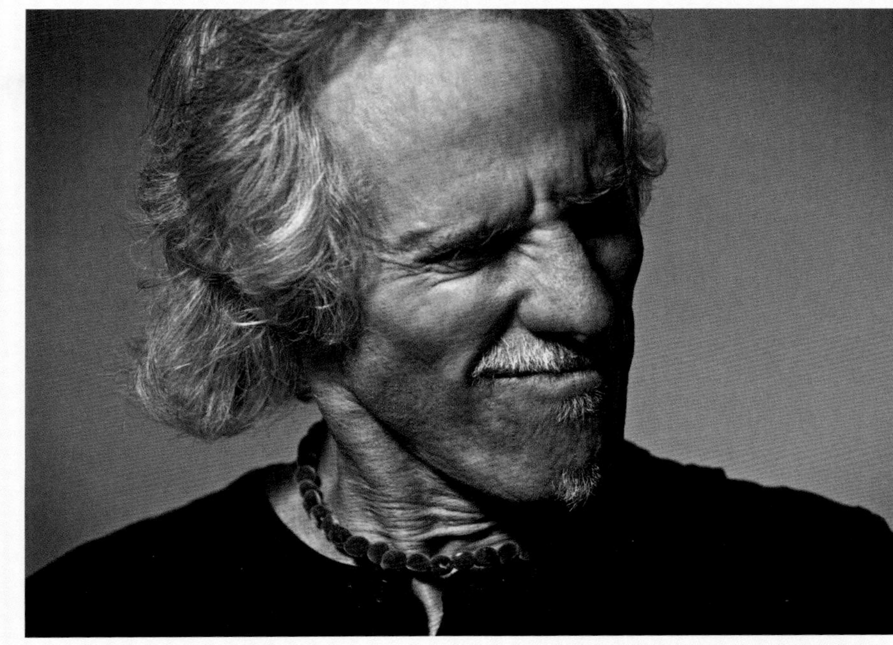

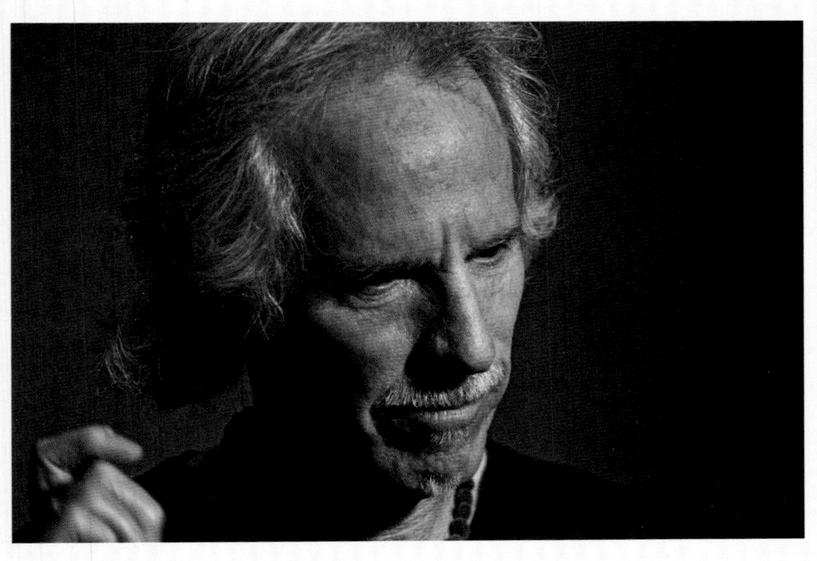

GUSTAVO DUDAMEL at Walt Disney Concert Hall, Los Angeles, California, March 5, 2015

Simón Díaz – *Arbolito Sabanero*
Simón Díaz – *Tonada de Luna Llena*

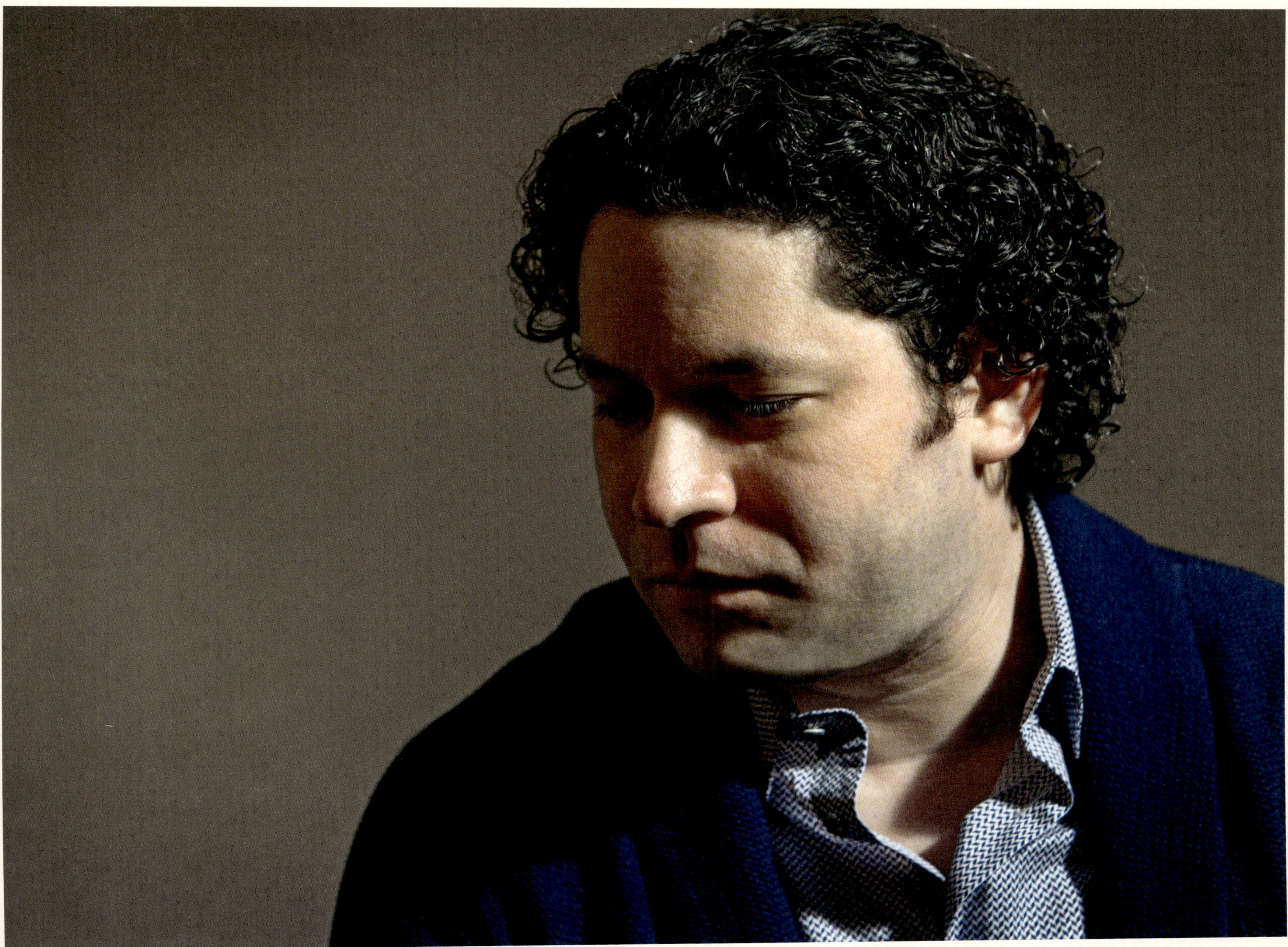

This bright, young superstar conductor burst like fireworks over the classical music world after making his debut at age twenty-four conducting the Los Angeles Philharmonic Orchestra in 2005. Shortly thereafter he was named principal conductor, a position which, following two subsequent contract extensions, he will hold through at least 2022. Son of a school teacher and trombonist for local salsa bands, raised in modest circumstances in provincial Venezuela, Dudamel was schooled under the ambitious El Sistema, a nationwide program providing musical training to children starting at an early age. Dudamel began his studies on violin at age ten. When he assumed the baton of the Orquestra Sinfónica Simón Bolívar, the national youth orchestra, in 1999, he came under the close supervision of José Antonio Abreu, founder of El Sistema. He won the Gustav Mahler conducting competition in Germany in 2004 and made his debut the following year leading the Gothenburg Symphony Orchestra at Royal Albert Hall in London. His youth and charismatic good looks have brought Dudamel the kind of media attention usually reserved for pop stars. He has been dubbed "The Dude," but he also retains the utmost respect from the classical music world. "He is the most astonishingly gifted young conductor I have come across," said venerable Sir Simon Rattle. For his photo session backstage before conducting a full program, he listened to the music of Simón Díaz, the great folklorist of Venezuela.

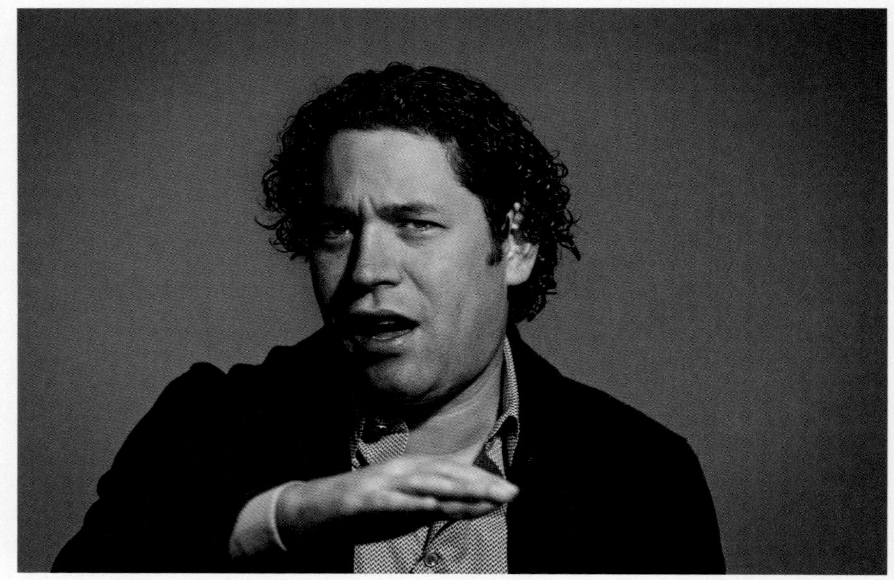

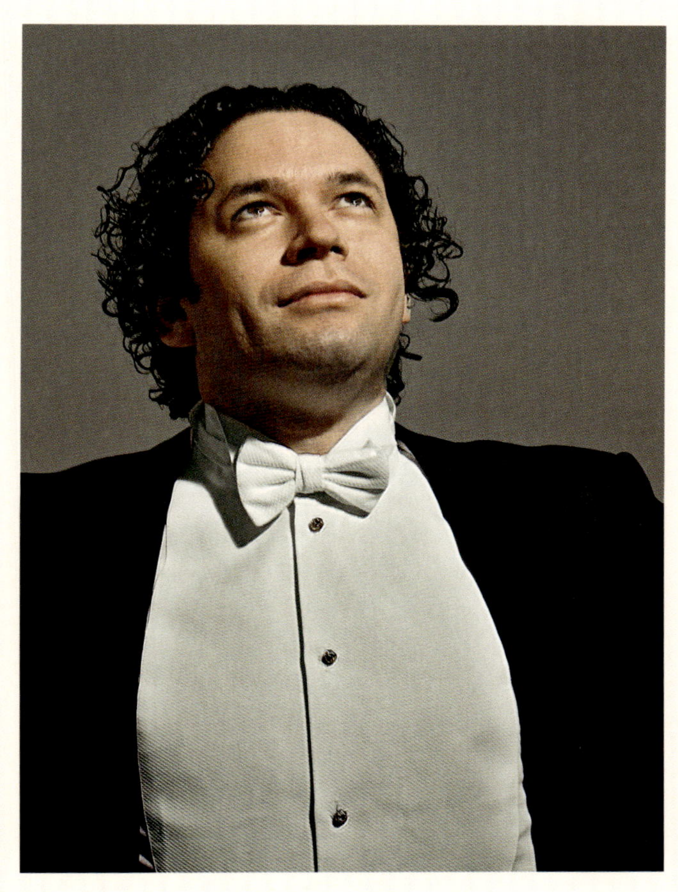

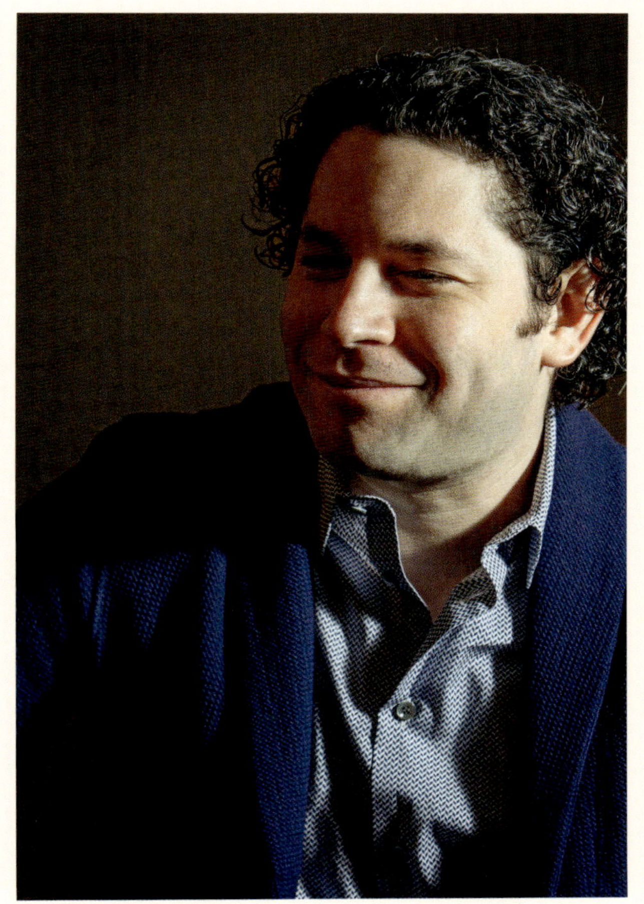

RENÉE FLEMING at Irving Penn's former studio, New York City, January 22, 2015

Herbie Hancock & Wayne Shorter — *Joanna's Theme*
Robert Schumann — *Frauenliebe und -leben, Op. 42* (sung by Janet Baker)
Giacomo Puccini — *Vissi d'arte* (from *Tosca*, sung by Leontyne Price)

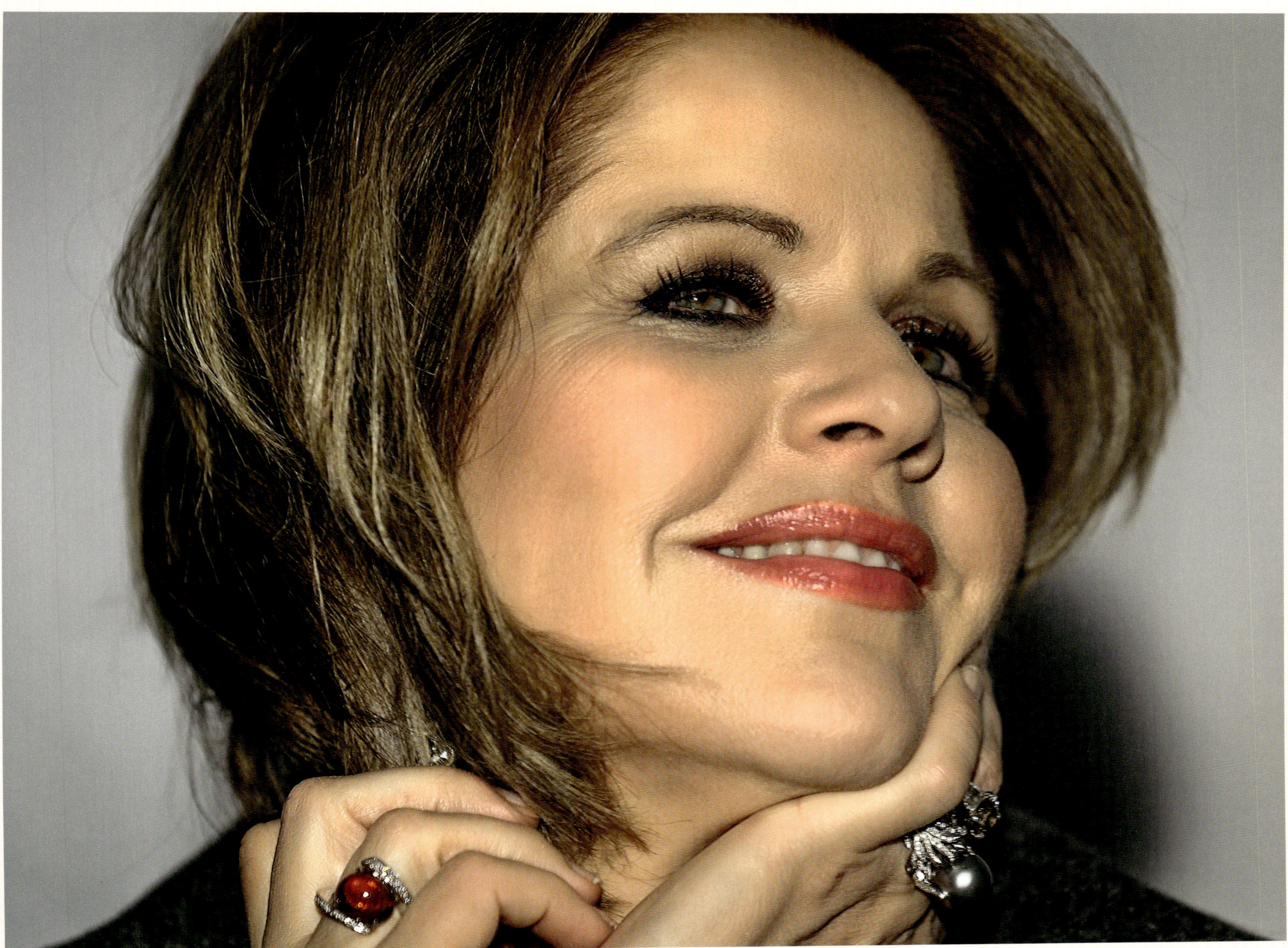

American opera's greatest superstar is known for her sense of humor and willingness to subvert the conventional notion of divas. She has taught children to count on *Sesame Street*, sung Christmas music on *The View*, performed on *The Lord of the Rings* soundtrack, made a number of appearances on radio's *A Prairie Home Companion*, named Joni Mitchell's song "River" as her top pick on BBC's *Desert Island Discs*, covered alt-rockers Muse on *Good Morning America*, played at Buckingham Palace for the Diamond Jubilee Concert and sang "The Star-Spangled Banner" at Super Bowl XLVIII before the largest TV audience in history. Her appearance with the YouTube Symphony Orchestra attracted thirty-three million online views. The daughter of two music teachers from Rochester, New York, has truly become America's diva. She sang jazz in nightclubs to support her graduate studies at the Juilliard School and made her debut at the Metropolitan Opera Company in New York in 1991 at age thirty-one. Having learned more than fifty opera scores over her career, Fleming has gravitated toward concert performances rather than appearing in full opera productions in the recent past, but her stature in the opera world goes without question.

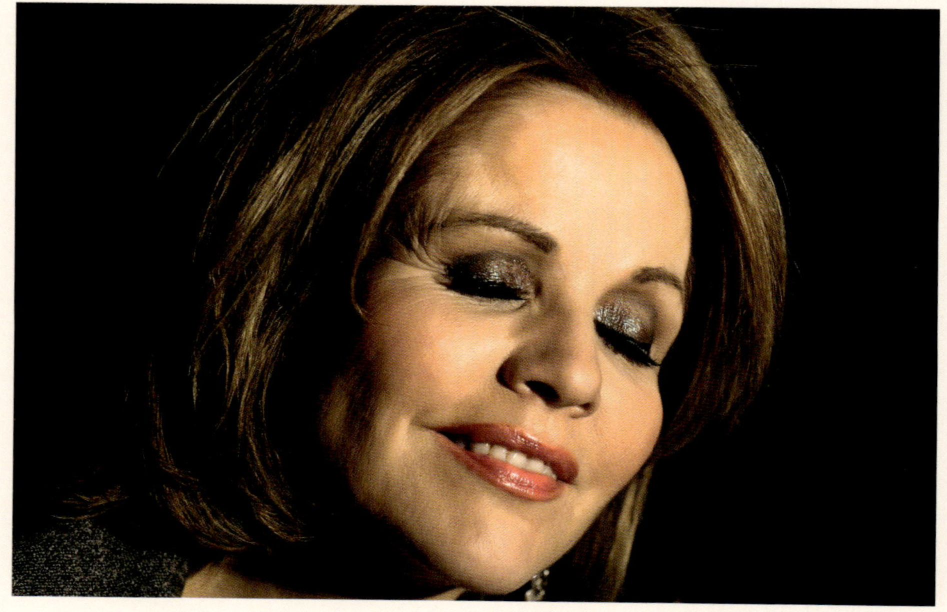

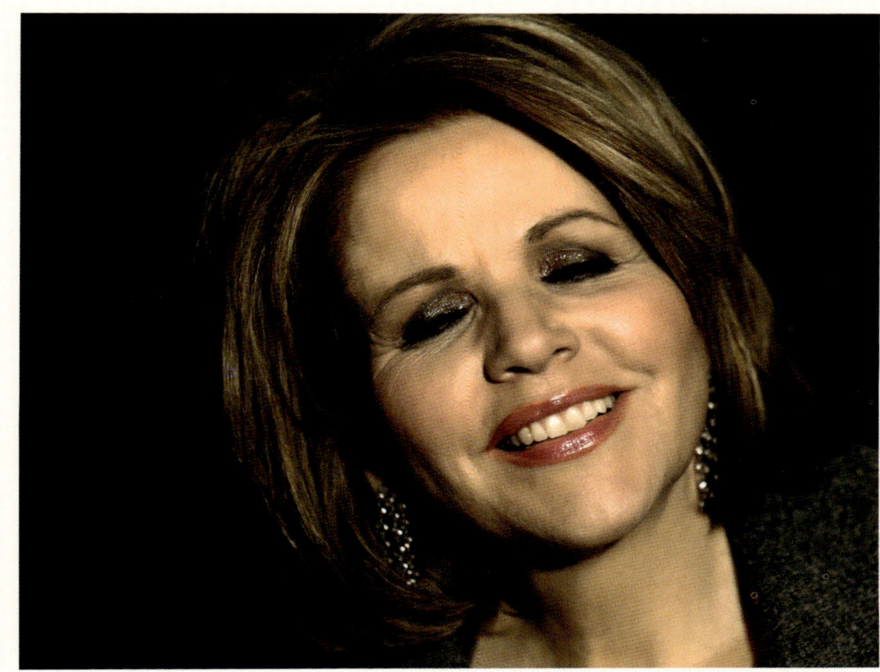

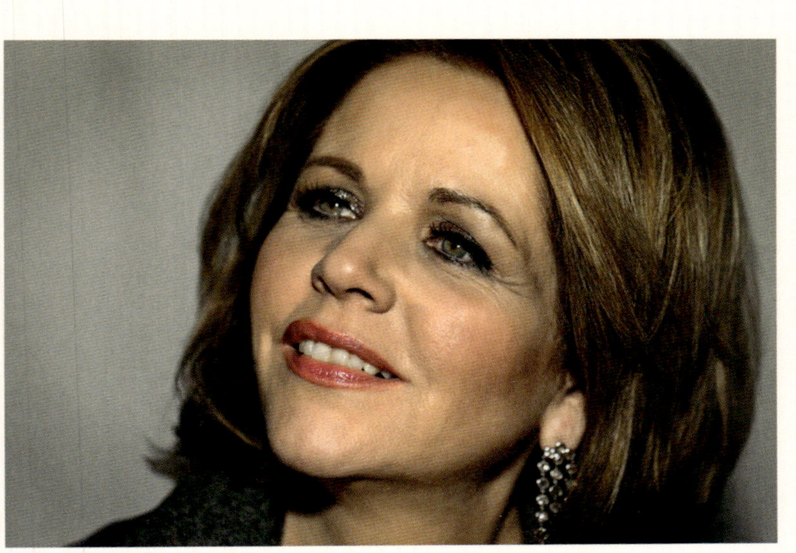

PHILIP GLASS at Royce Hall, UCLA, Los Angeles, California, May 4, 2014

Philip Glass – *String Quartet N° 2*
Philip Glass – *Piano Etudes*

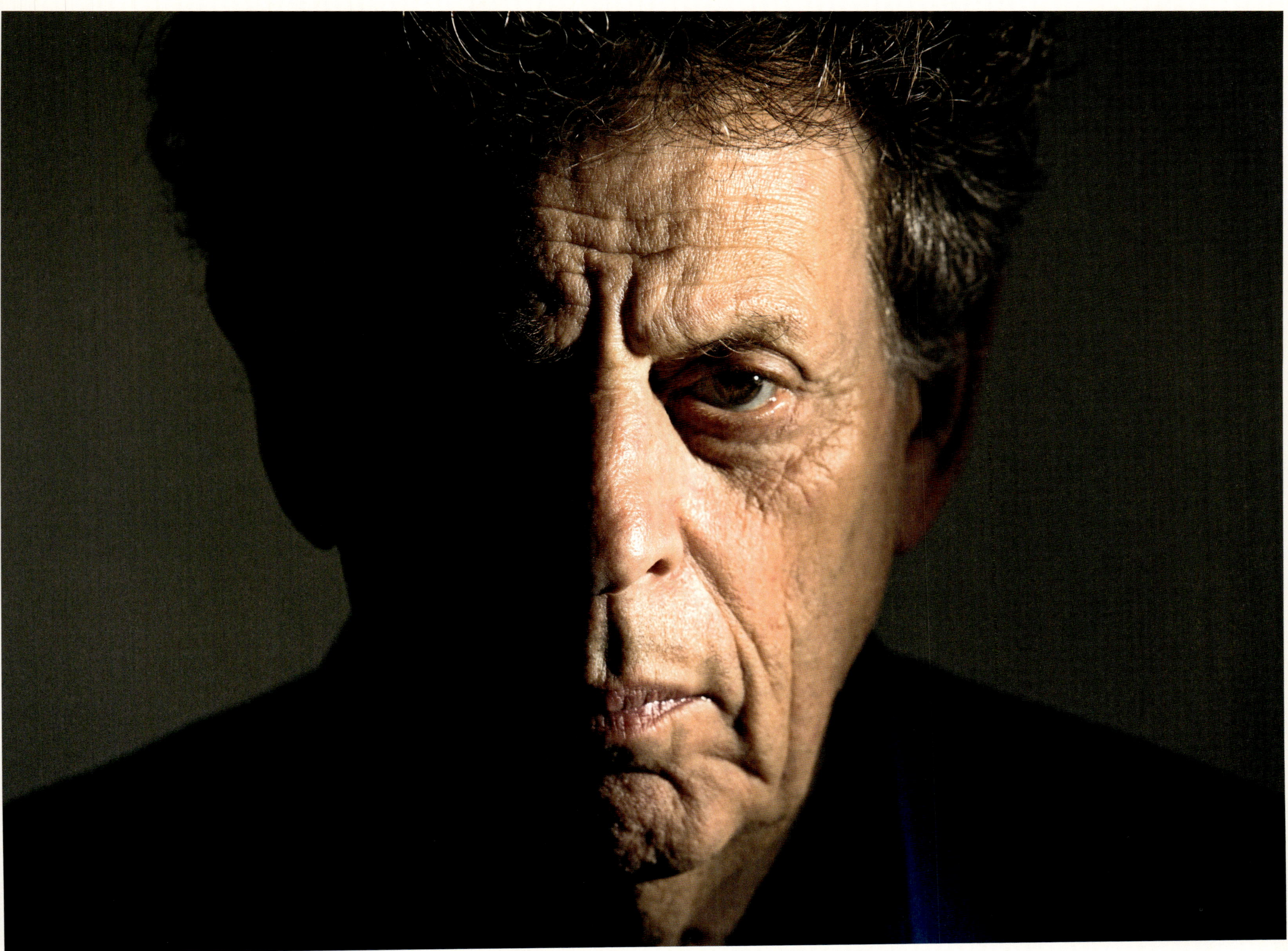

The world's best-known contemporary composer drove a cab in New York City right up until the premiere of his groundbreaking opera with playwright Robert Wilson in 1976, *Einstein on the Beach*. The father of modern minimalist music—he would prefer the description "music with repetitive structures"—had long been world-famous for his avant-garde music before he could fully make his living as a composer. His father was a Jewish immigrant who ran a record store in Baltimore and Glass grew up listening to the unsold merchandise, which included a lot of modern music. As a teenager, while enrolled in the accelerated college program at University of Chicago, he was already composing twelve-tone trio works. He has written operas, symphonies, chamber music, piano concertos, string quartets, Oscar-nominated motion picture soundtracks. He has collaborated on recordings with Paul Simon, Suzanne Vega, David Byrne, Leonard Cohen, Mick Jagger, among others. His 1988 reciter-piano performance with Allen Ginsberg came after a chance meeting with the poet in an East Village bookstore, which in turn led to the full-length theater piece *Hydrogen Jukebox*. A dedicated follower of Tibetan Buddhism, Glass is today a thoughtful, revered tribal elder, no longer the *enfant terrible* who music critics railed against, but a living monument to the triumph of modern music. His 2015 autobiography, *Words Without Music: A Memoir*, was a *New York Times* bestseller.

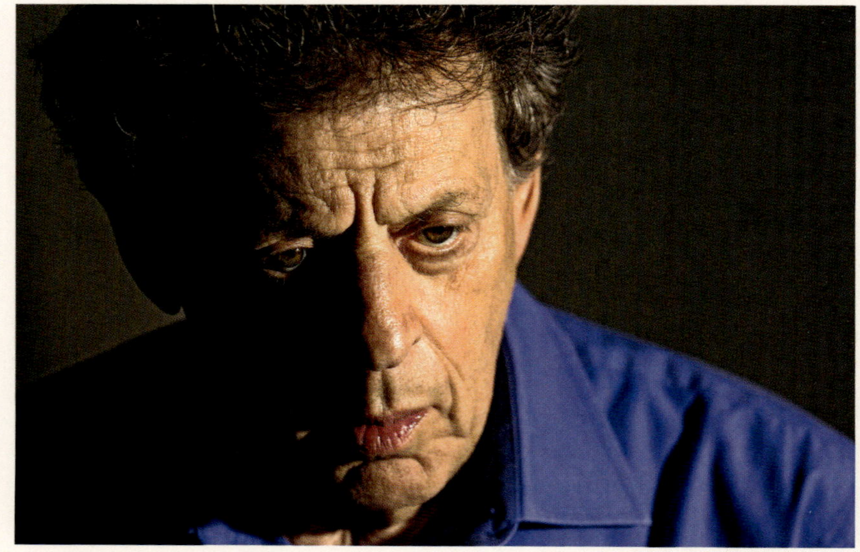

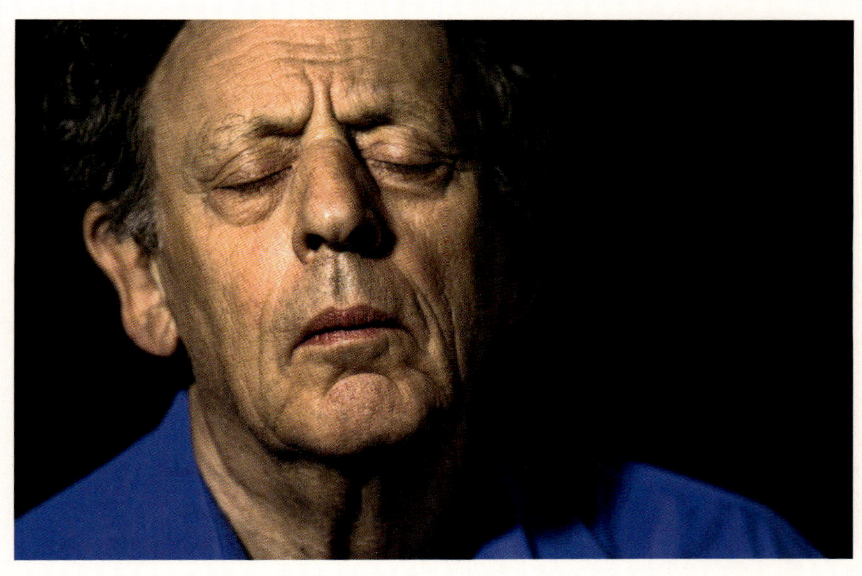

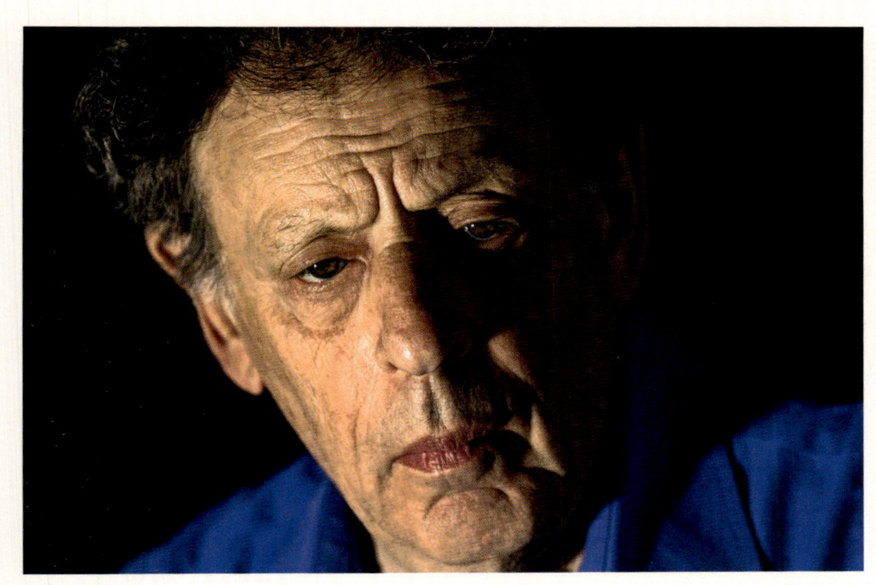

JOEL GREY at home, New York City, June 15, 2011

The Beatles – *And I Love Her*

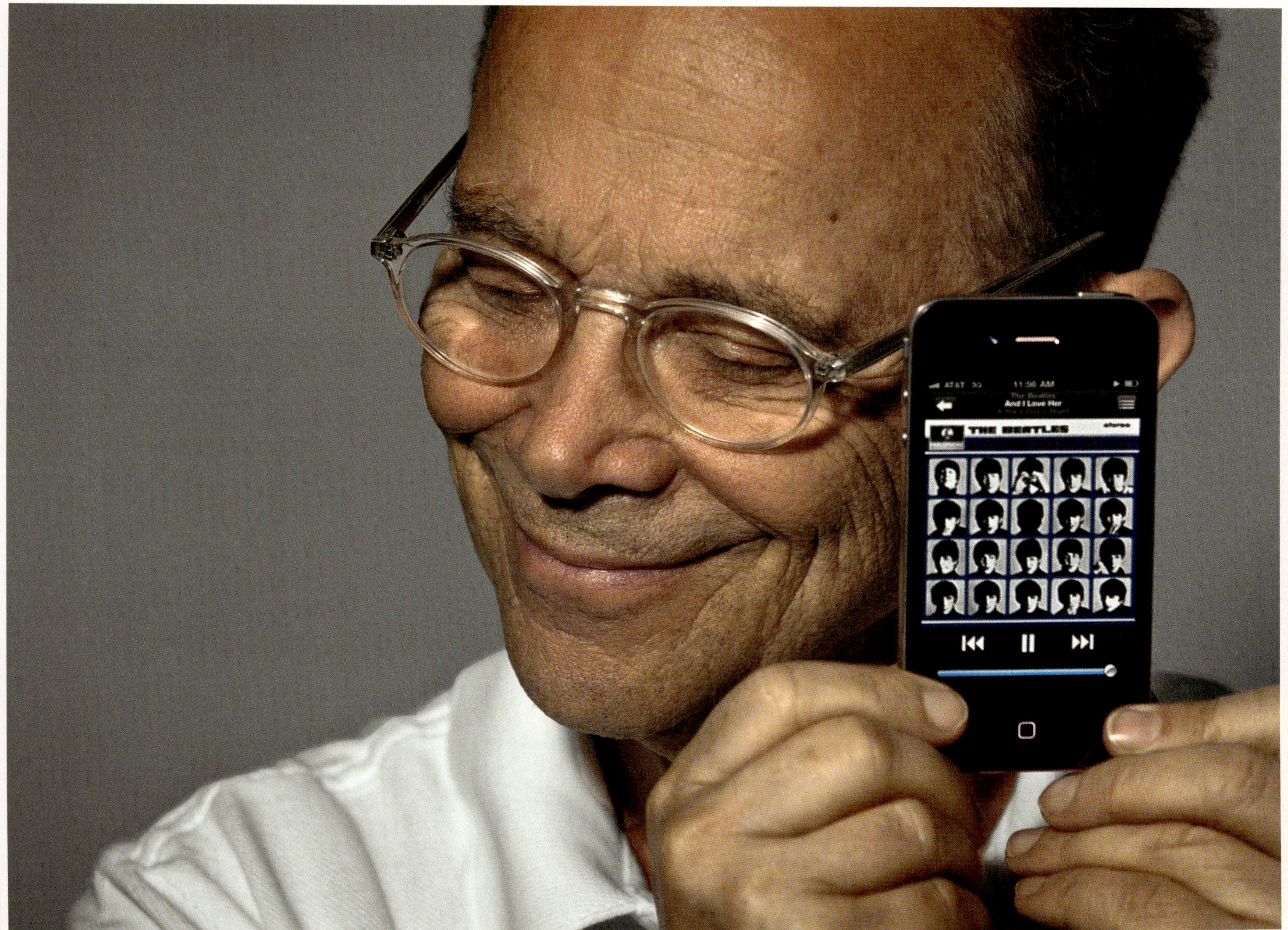
11:56 AM
And I Love Her
THE BEATLES

Few actors have been as completely identified in their careers with one role as Joel Grey, a multi-talented singer/actor/dancer who will forever be remembered as the Master of Ceremonies in both the stage version and movie musical *Cabaret*. He won the Tony for the role he originated on Broadway and the Oscar for repeating the part in the 1972 motion picture version. Since that professional epiphany, Grey has continued to do high-grade work in films and television—drama, comedy, musicals—and perform in nightclubs and concert halls, an act that has earned him acclaim as a consummate entertainer. He started in show business billed as Mickey Katz Jr. His father Mickey Katz was the country's best-known Yiddish singer, well known for popular parodies such as "Schleppin' My Baby Back Home," and Grey's daughter, Jennifer Grey, is a third generation in show business, star of the film *Dirty Dancing* and others. Grey's accompanist was another young fellow, also just starting out in show business: pianist Burt Bacharach. Grey would later record with Bacharach, including the original version of "What's New Pussycat?" He chose The Beatles' "And I Love Her," an early Paul McCartney ballad from the group's third album, *A Hard Day's Night*—a delicate melodic piece frequently recorded by other artists and often cited as a precursor to McCartney's "Yesterday."

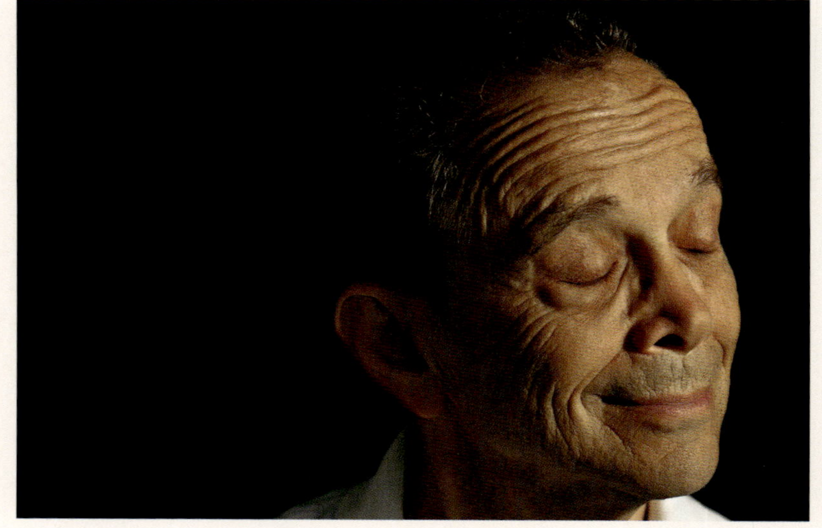

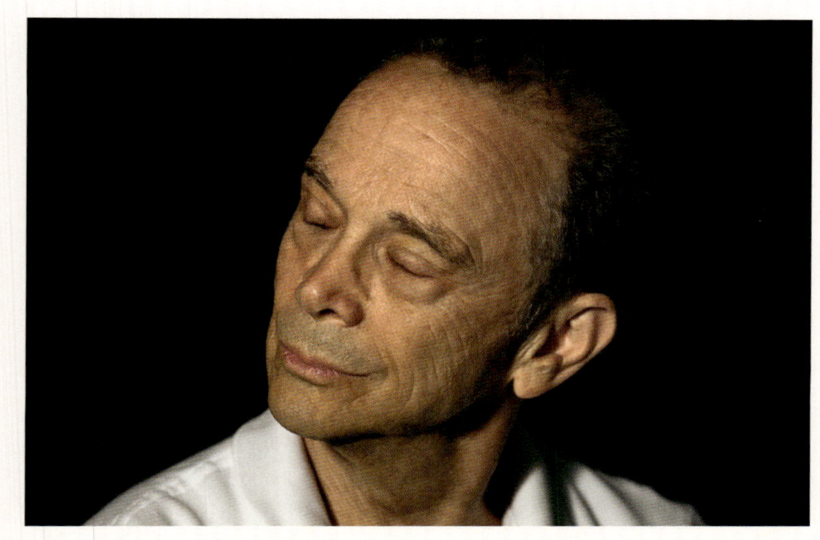

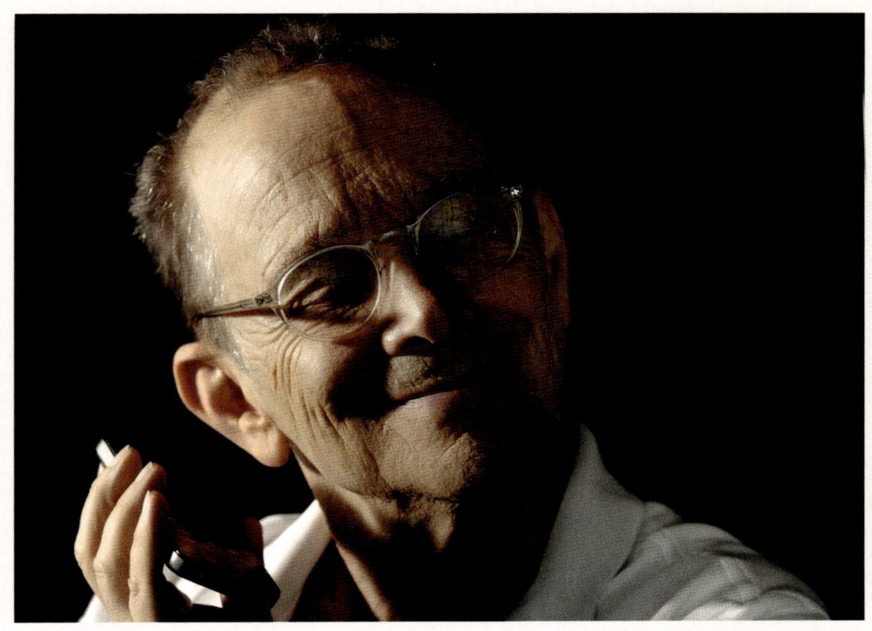

SAMMY HAGAR at Red Rocker Studios, San Rafael, California, November 18, 2013

The Band – *Up on Cripple Creek*
Otis Redding – *Cigarettes and Coffee*
Rolling Stones – *Honky Tonk Women*

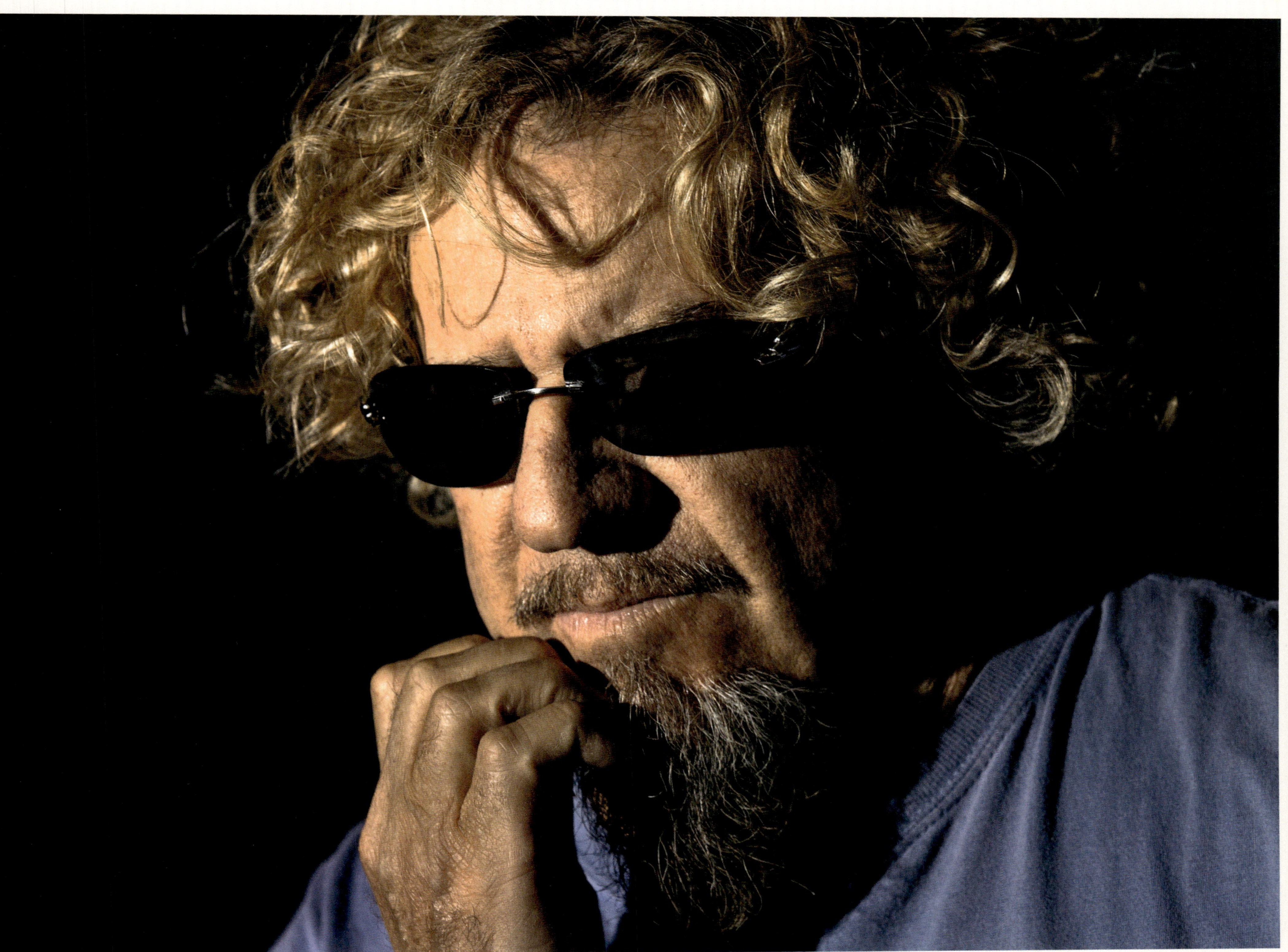

The Red Rocker loves 60s rock. The one-time vocalist for hard rock heroes Van Halen has made mighty music across four decades of hits—from his early days with Montrose ("Rock Candy") to his stellar solo albums. When he joined Van Halen in 1986, he led the group on a high-octane run of three consecutive number one albums before the Van Halen brothers fired him and watched their band disappear from the charts. He returned to the fold for a triumphant 2005 reunion tour, by which time he had firmly established his Cabo Wabo nightclub in Mexico and bestselling brand of tequila. With genius guitarist Joe Satriani, bassist Michael Anthony of Van Halen and drummer Chad Smith from Red Hot Chili Peppers, Hagar embarked on his fourth platinum career with his new band Chickenfoot in 2010. Photographed at the Marin County rehearsal hall and recording studio he keeps on the same block as studios by James Hetfield of Metallica and Bob Weir of Grateful Dead, Hagar wanted to listen to the classic Levon Helm vocal on "Up on Cripple Creek," the 1968 Rolling Stones hit that might arguably be the band's greatest single, and a ballad by the late, great Otis Redding, who teenager Hagar saw perform at the 1967 Monterey Pop Festival.

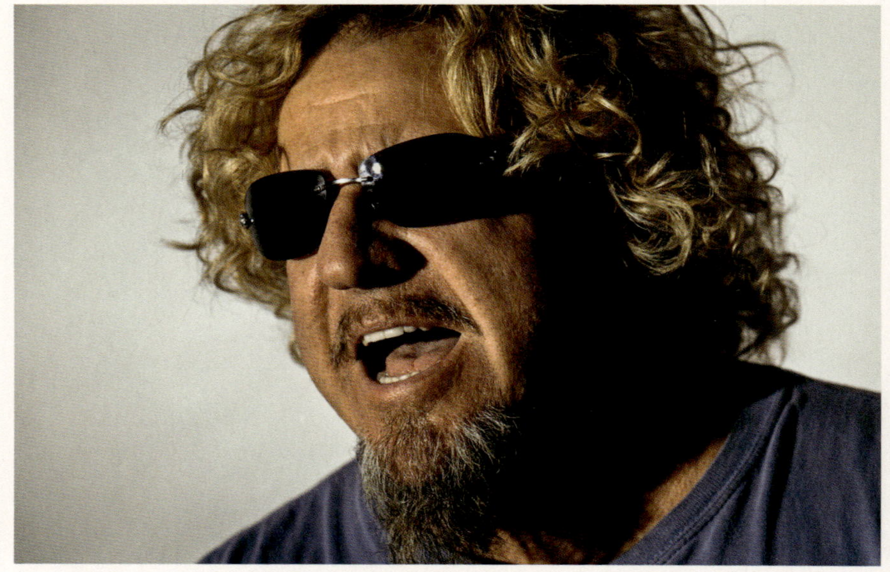

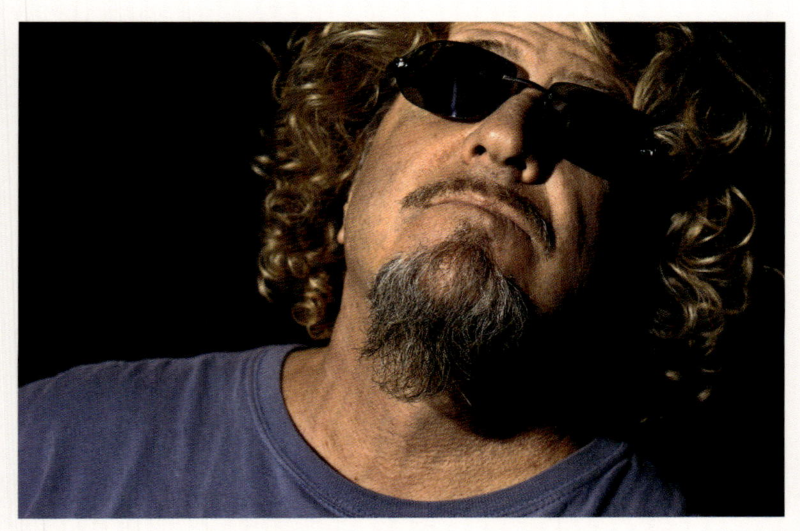

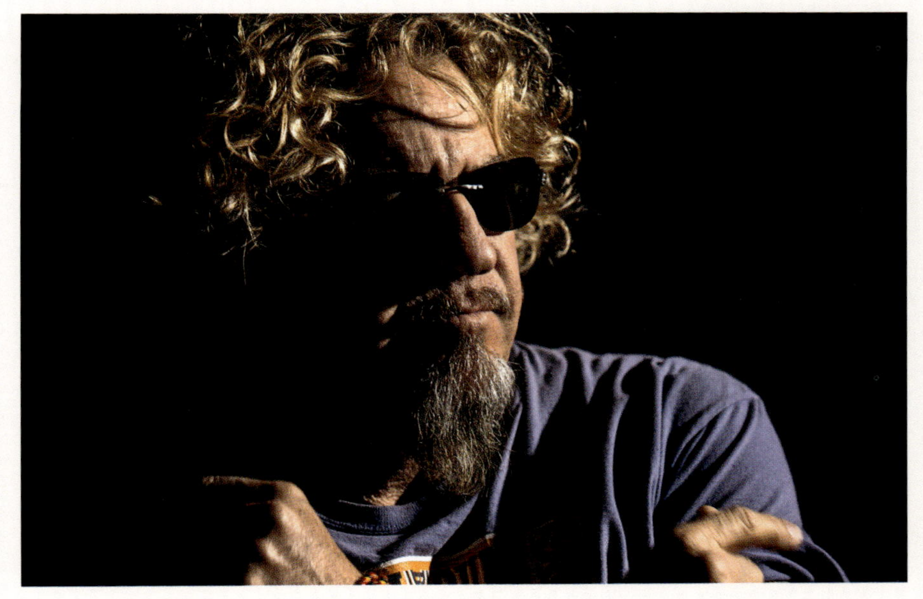

LANI HALL at home, Malibu, California, May 31, 2011

Bill Evans Trio with Symphony Orchestra (conducted by Claus Ogerman) – *Granadas*
Bill Evans Trio with Symphony Orchestra (conducted by Claus Ogerman) – *Prelude*

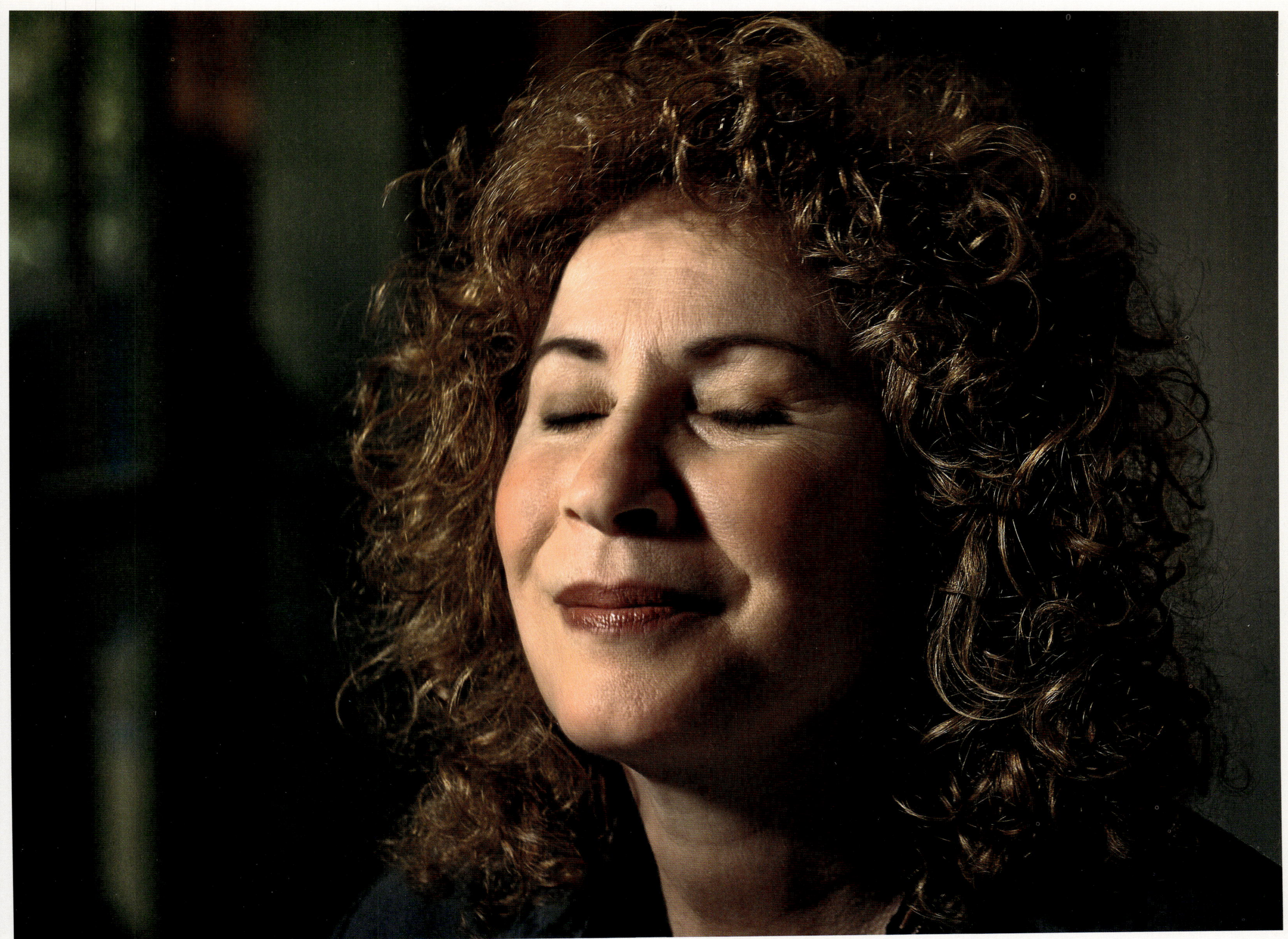

The sweet-faced young beauty with the fresh, attractive voice lit up the hit sound of Sérgio Mendes and Brasil '66, whose album, produced by trumpeter Herb Alpert, instantly established the Latin-flavored pop group with the so-called middle-of-the-road or easy-listening crowd at the height of the rock era. Lani Hall sang like a bell on the group's big hits, "Mas Que Nada" and "Fool on the Hill," and left to begin her solo recording career in 1971. Having picked up a bit of a Latin following in her years with Brasil '66, Hall started recording in Spanish in 1981, made four successful Latin albums, culminating with the Grammy-winning *Es Fácil Amar* in 1986. Laid low by medical problems, it would be thirteen years before Hall would return, singing in Portuguese, with her 1998 album *Brasil Nativo*. Ironically, this famous Latin pop vocalist, who Mendes discovered singing in nightclubs in her native Chicago, does not speak either Spanish or Portuguese. Another eleven years passed before Hall returned to the scene, this time with her husband Herb Alpert with their album *Anything Goes* in 2009. The couple put together a band, recorded a series of albums (including the Grammy-winning *Steppin' Out*) and, when they aren't staying home in Malibu watching their three grandchildren grow, continue to tour, packing out New York's tony Café Carlyle at their annual engagements, lines out the door.

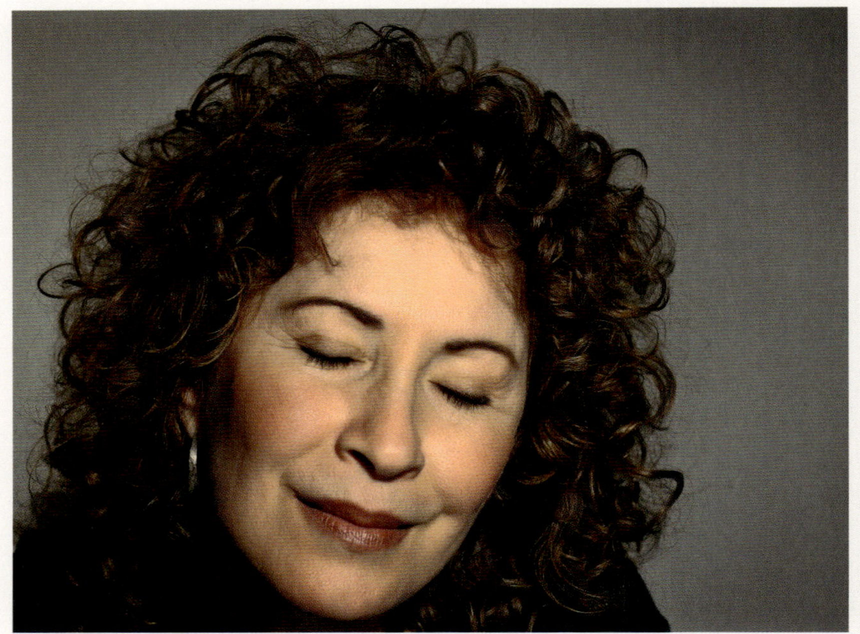

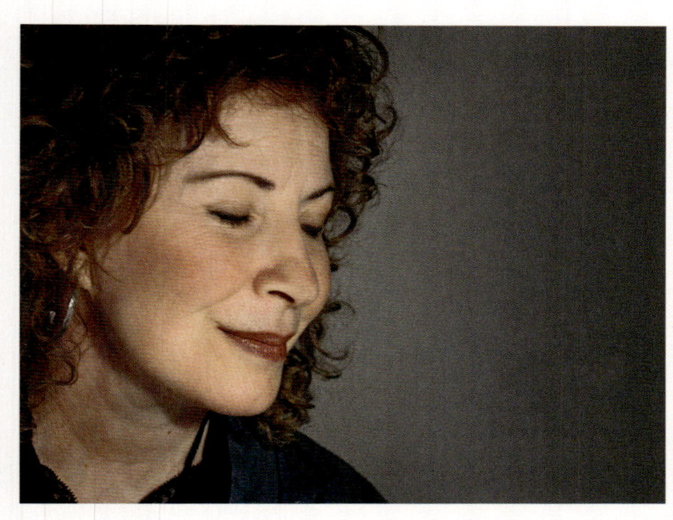

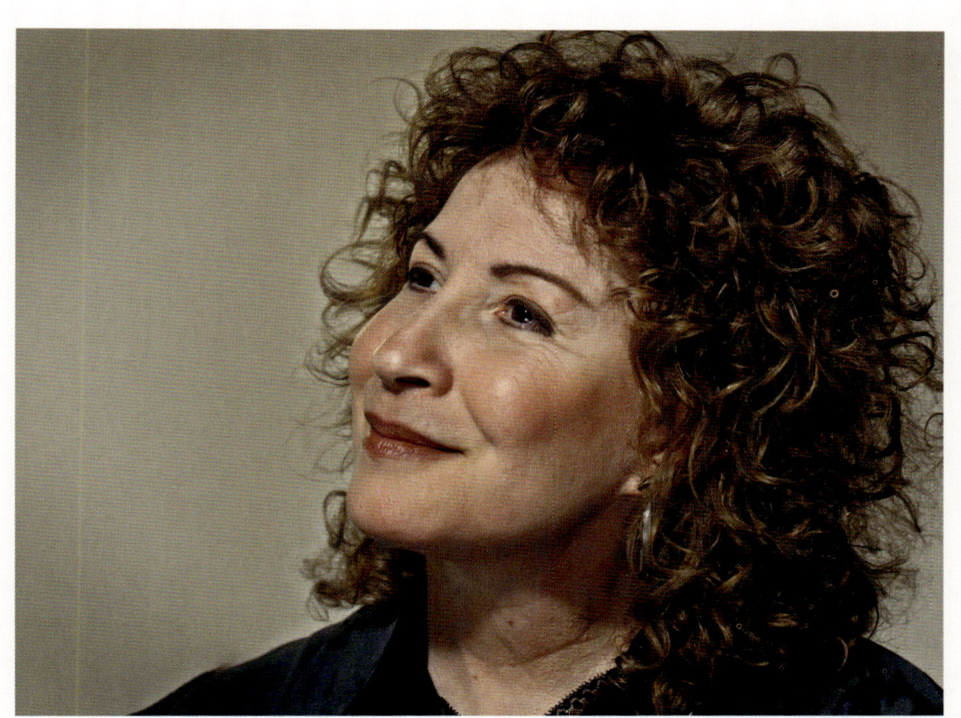

HERBIE HANCOCK at home, Los Angeles, California, October 17, 2011

Miles Davis – *The Meaning of the Blues*
Miles Davis – *Lament*
Miles Davis – *Springsville*

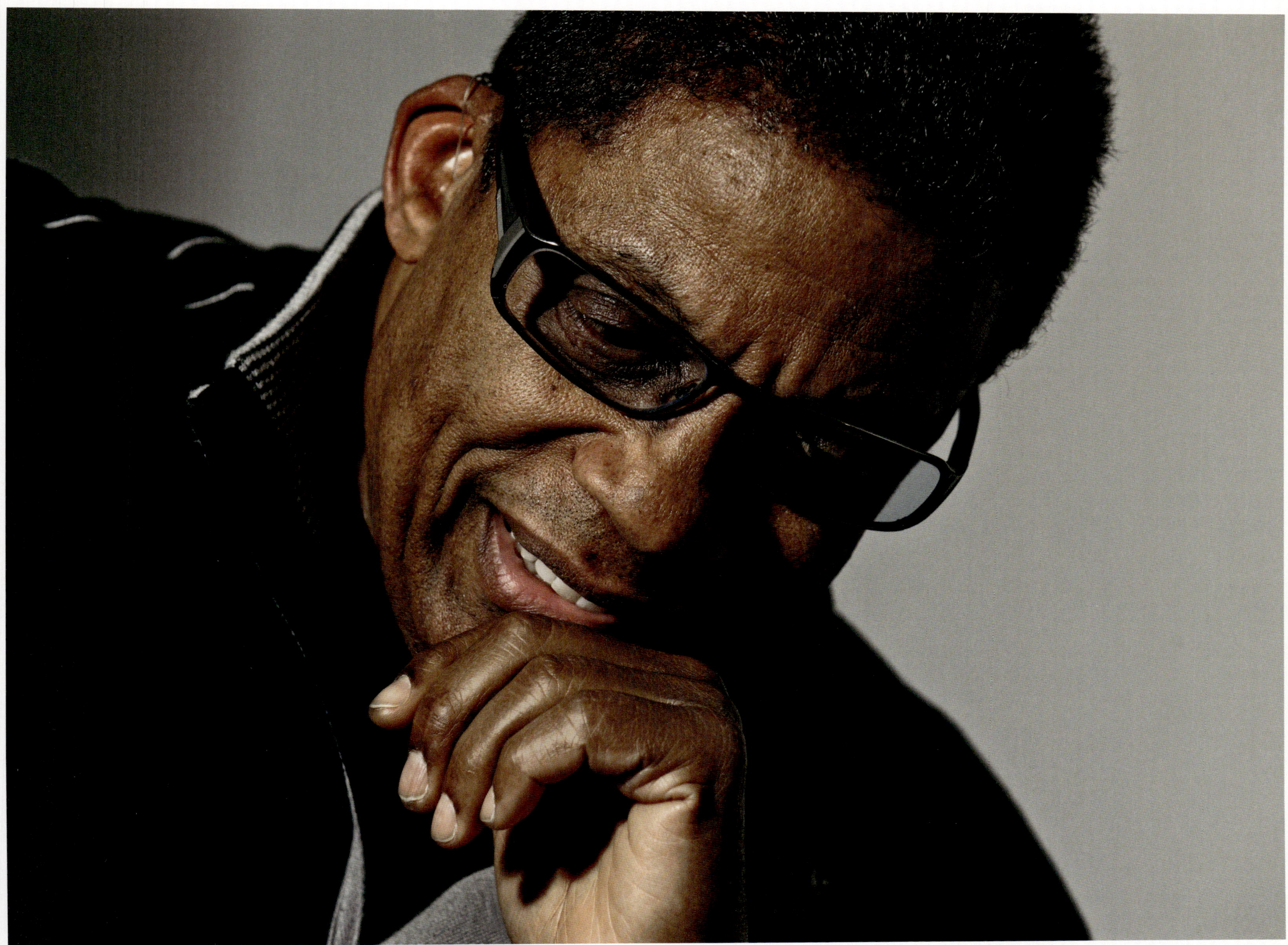

Herbie Hancock both expanded the musical possibilities of jazz and found an audience for his music far beyond the confines of that limited universe. Not only did he bring the celestial chordings of Debussy to modern jazz with his landmark work with Miles Davis, but his funk-influenced synthesizer album, *Head Hunters*, remains the bestselling album in jazz history. A musical prodigy in his home town of St. Louis, pianist Hancock performed Mozart with the city's symphony orchestra when he was eleven years old. His 1962 debut album featured his composition "Watermelon Man," a huge hit for Latin bandleader Mongo Santamaría. His impressive solo work brought him to the attention of trumpeter Davis, and Hancock joined his band in 1963 for five of the most productive, creative years of Davis' historic career, not insubstantially inspired and elevated by Hancock's contributions. Hancock has always pushed the boundaries of jazz, often to spectacular effect. His 1983 collaboration with producer Bill Laswell, "Rockit," stormed MTV with a smash music video. His 2007 Joni Mitchell tribute album, *River: The Joni Letters,* won the Grammy as Album of the Year, only the second jazz record to do so. Given their musical association, it is not surprising to have Hancock listen to three tracks from the 1957 Miles Davis masterpiece album, *Miles Ahead,* an important early collaboration with the brilliant arranger Gil Evans and a record on which the only soloist is Davis.

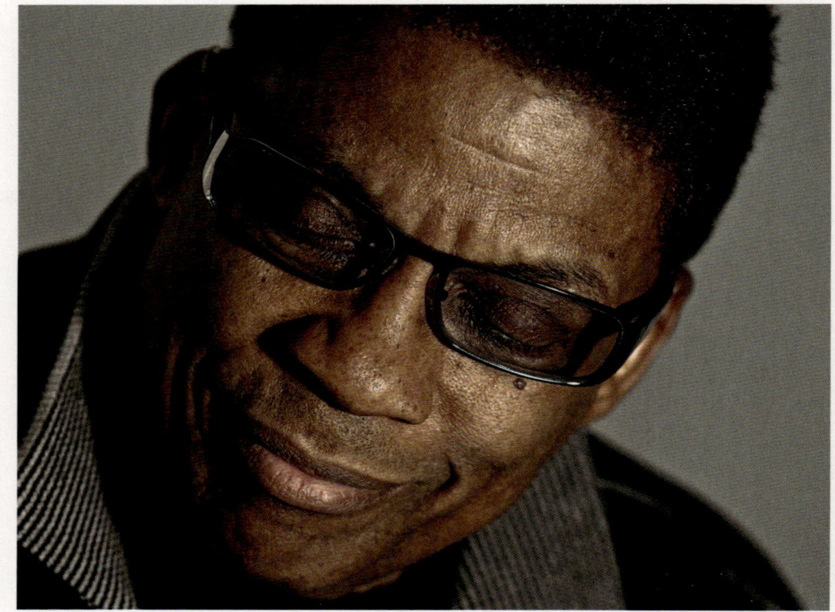

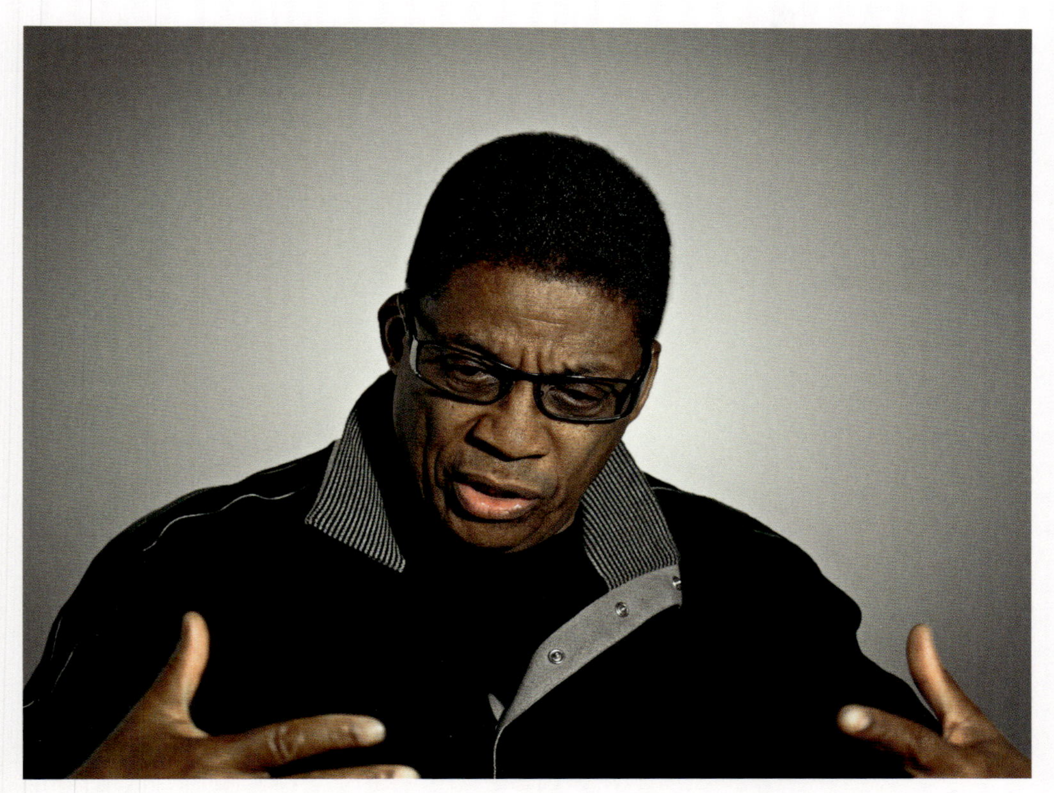

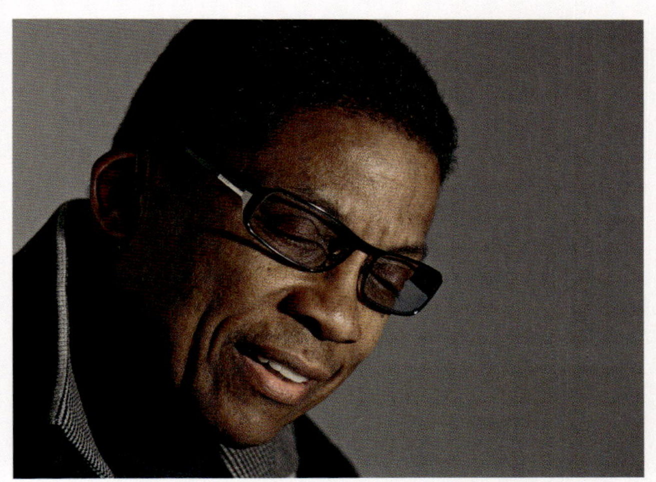

EMMYLOU HARRIS at Wiltern Theater, Los Angeles, California, April 10, 2014

Sinéad O'Connor – *In This Heart*

Kate and Anna McGarrigle – *Matapédia*

Sweet Honey in the Rock – *We Are Climbing Jacob's Ladder*

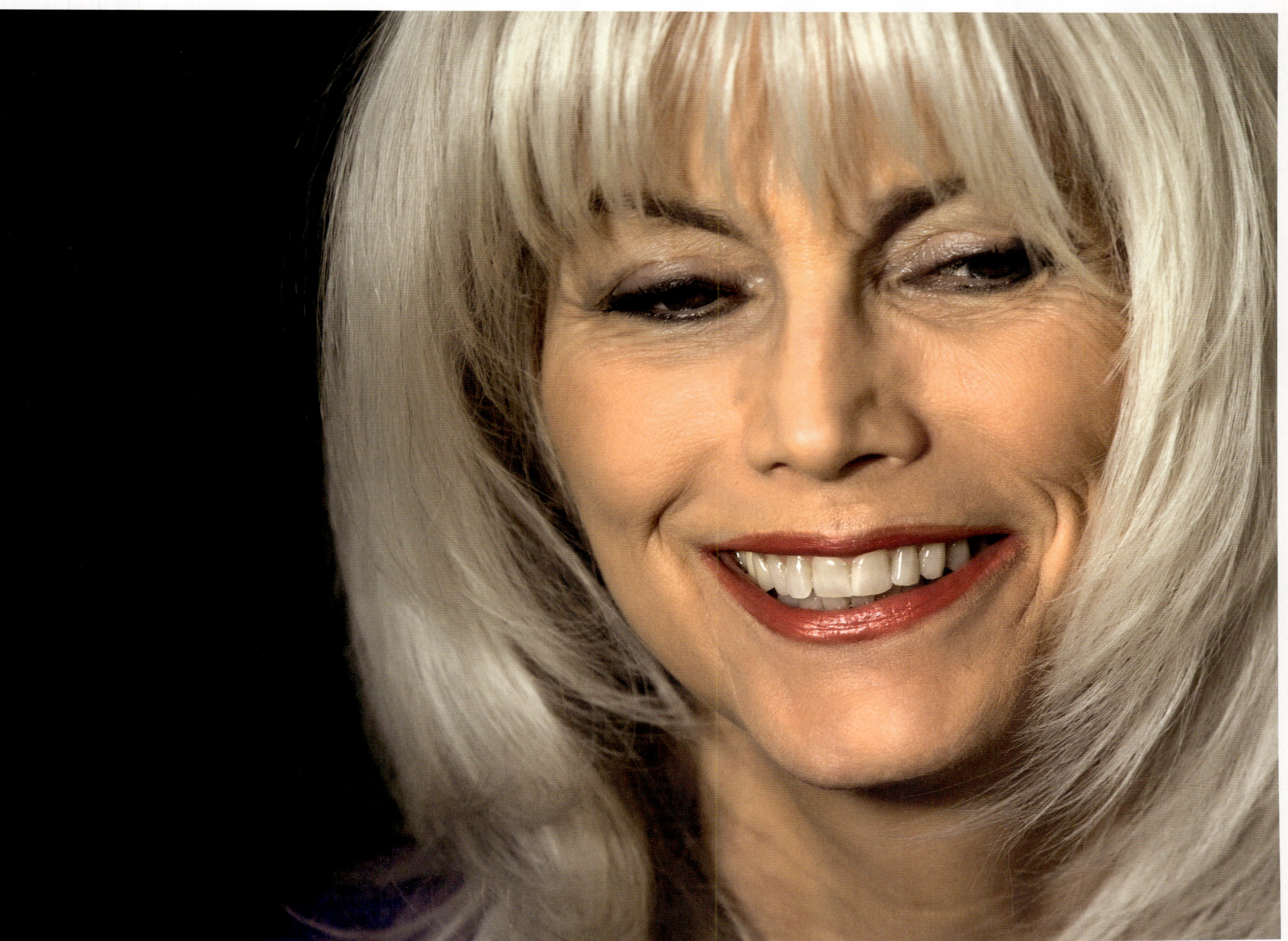

An artist so pure and uncompromising in her vision, the entire genre of modern Americana music developed largely around her. In addition, she is the greatest harmony vocalist in the business who has made a vast array of other singers sound great: Dolly Parton, Mark Knopfler, Bob Dylan, Neil Young, Linda Ronstadt, Roy Orbison, among others. She was discovered by country-rock aristocrat Gram Parsons, who groomed her to accompany his solo debut, but died before it could be released. A series of country albums established her during the 80s, and she was named Female Vocalist of the Year from the Country Music Association in 1980. In 1995 she released her *sui generis* masterpiece, *Wrecking Ball,* produced by Daniel Lanois. Producer "T Bone" Burnett tapped her as keystone artist on his 2000 soundtrack to the Coen brothers' film *O Brother Where Art Thou?,* an album that served as national comfort food after the twin towers assault. A thirteen-time Grammy winner and member of the Country Music Hall of Fame, Harris was awarded Sweden's 2015 Polar Music Prize, often described as the Nobel Peace Prize of music.

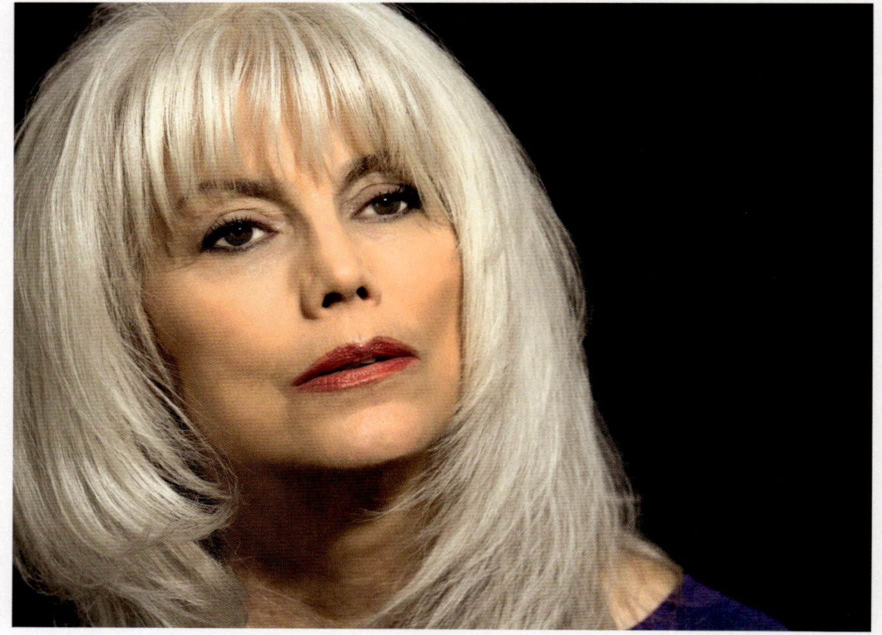

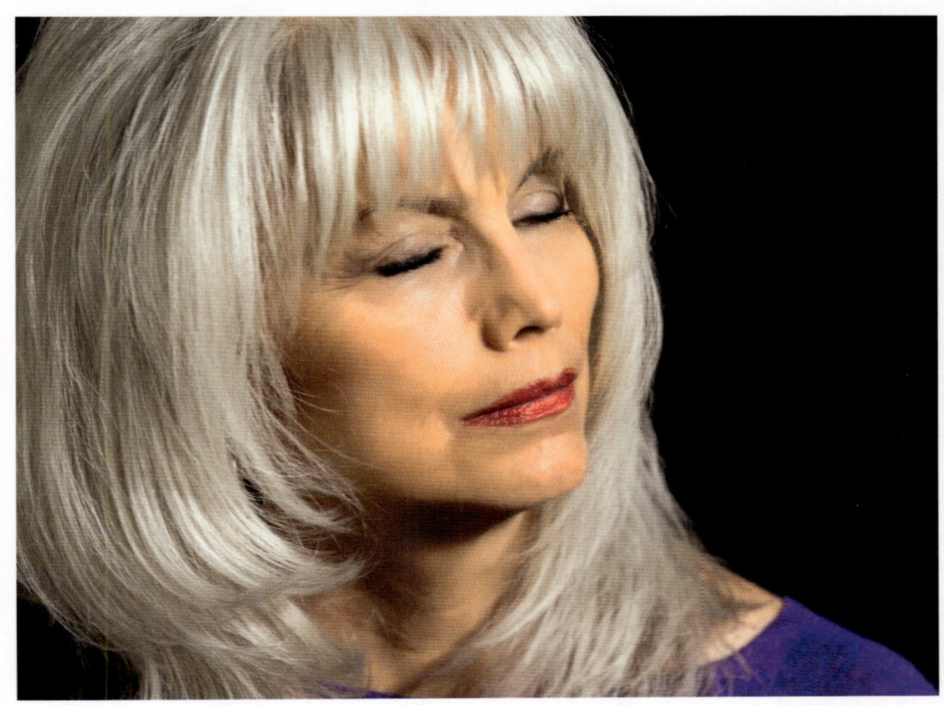

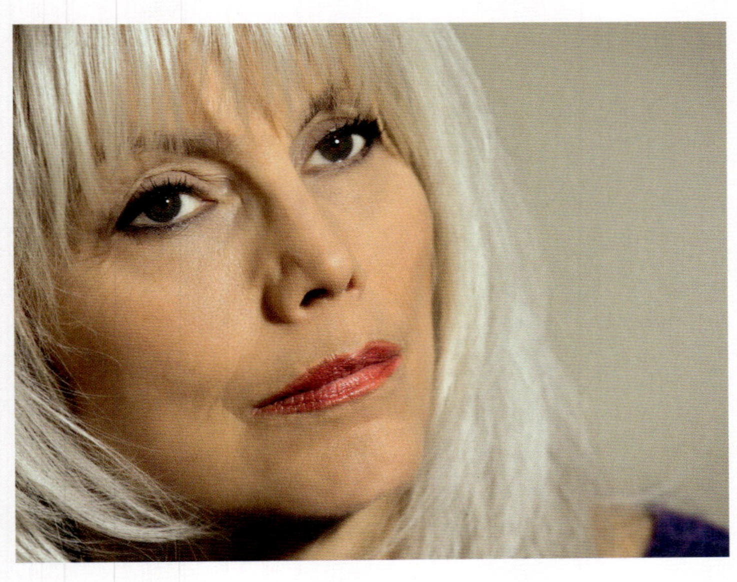

MICKEY HART at Yolo Ranch, Sebastopol, California, November 17, 2013

Gyuto Monks – *Yamantaka*
Ustad Sultan Khan – *Raga: Bageshree*
Doudou N'Diaye Rose – *Lingueyou Ndeye*

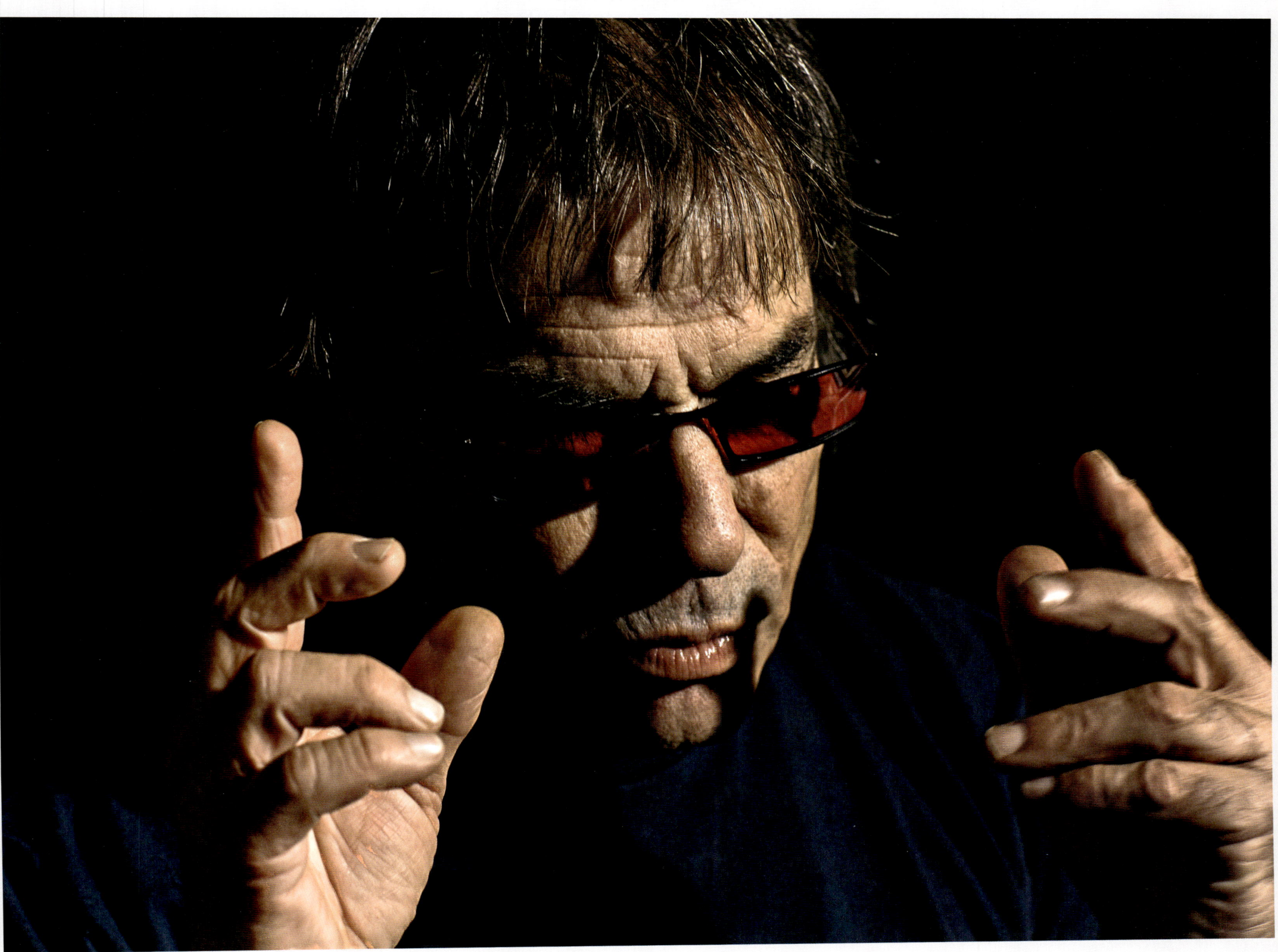

So much more than the drummer for the Grateful Dead, Mickey Hart is a force of nature, a whirlwind of percussion, a global rhythm master and a serious musicologist who has recorded everything from pygmies in the rainforest to Latvian women's choirs. Both his father and mother were rudimentary drummers and Hart served in the Marine Drum and Bugle Corps at the White House in his youth. When he joined the band in 1967, he brought the world of polyrhythms and raga time signatures to the Grateful Dead. His service with the Dead took him around the globe—from the hills of Woodstock to the valley of the Nile. He is the author of three books on percussion, and his collection of exotic drums has been exhibited in the San Francisco airport. He has done recording experiments with astrophysicists and neuroscientists and is a member of the Board of Directors of the Library of Congress. He came to know and be friends with Joseph Campbell and Walter Cronkite in their later years, tribal elders fascinated by Hart's intense, restless energy. His own ambitious solo recording projects have ranged from multicultural, all-percussion supergroup Planet Drum to the smooth, almost European pop of his *Mystery Box*. He chose to listen to tracks from world music recordings he has produced, including an Indian sarangi master, a Senegalese master drummer, and the extraordinary Gyuto Monks (famously sampled by Van Halen, a major contribution by itself). The four surviving members of Grateful Dead performed historic final concerts—*Fare Thee Well*—in Chicago over the Fourth of July weekend 2015.

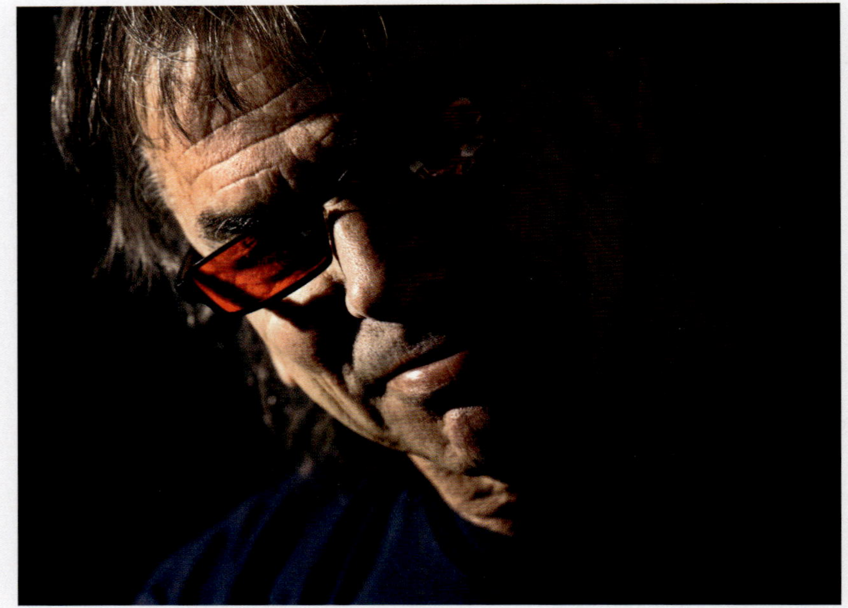

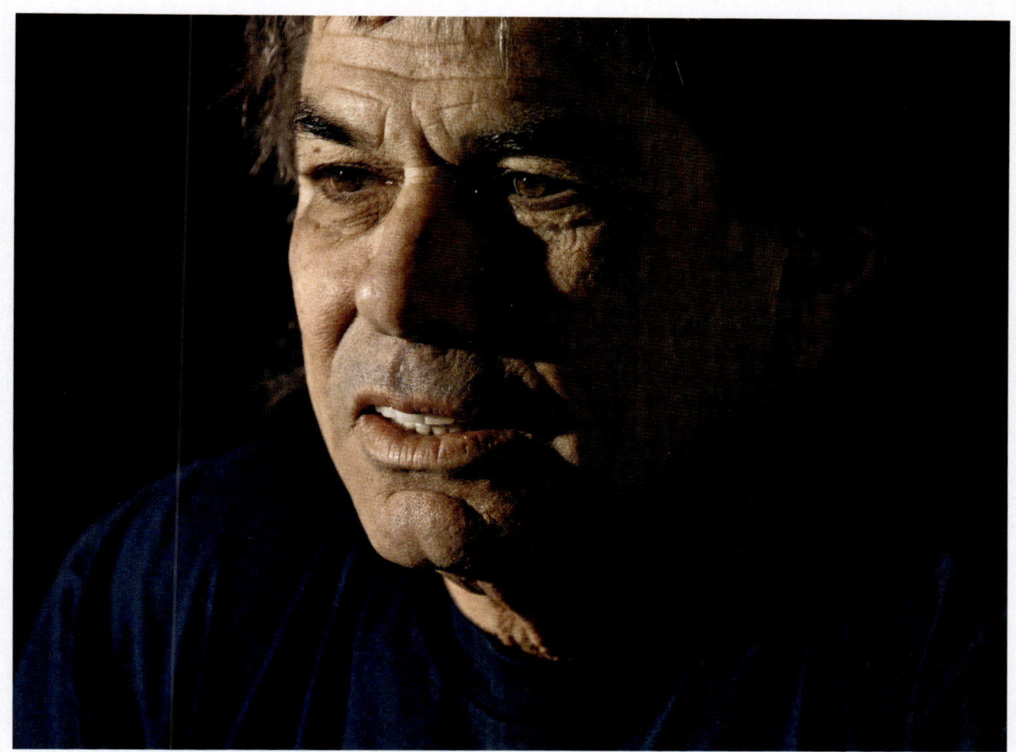

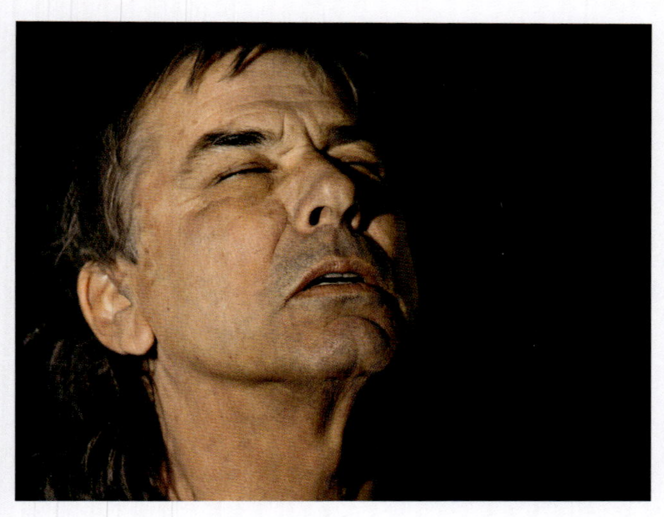

QUINCY JONES at home, Los Angeles, California, August 30, 2012

James Ingram and Patti Austin – *How Do You Keep the Music Playing*

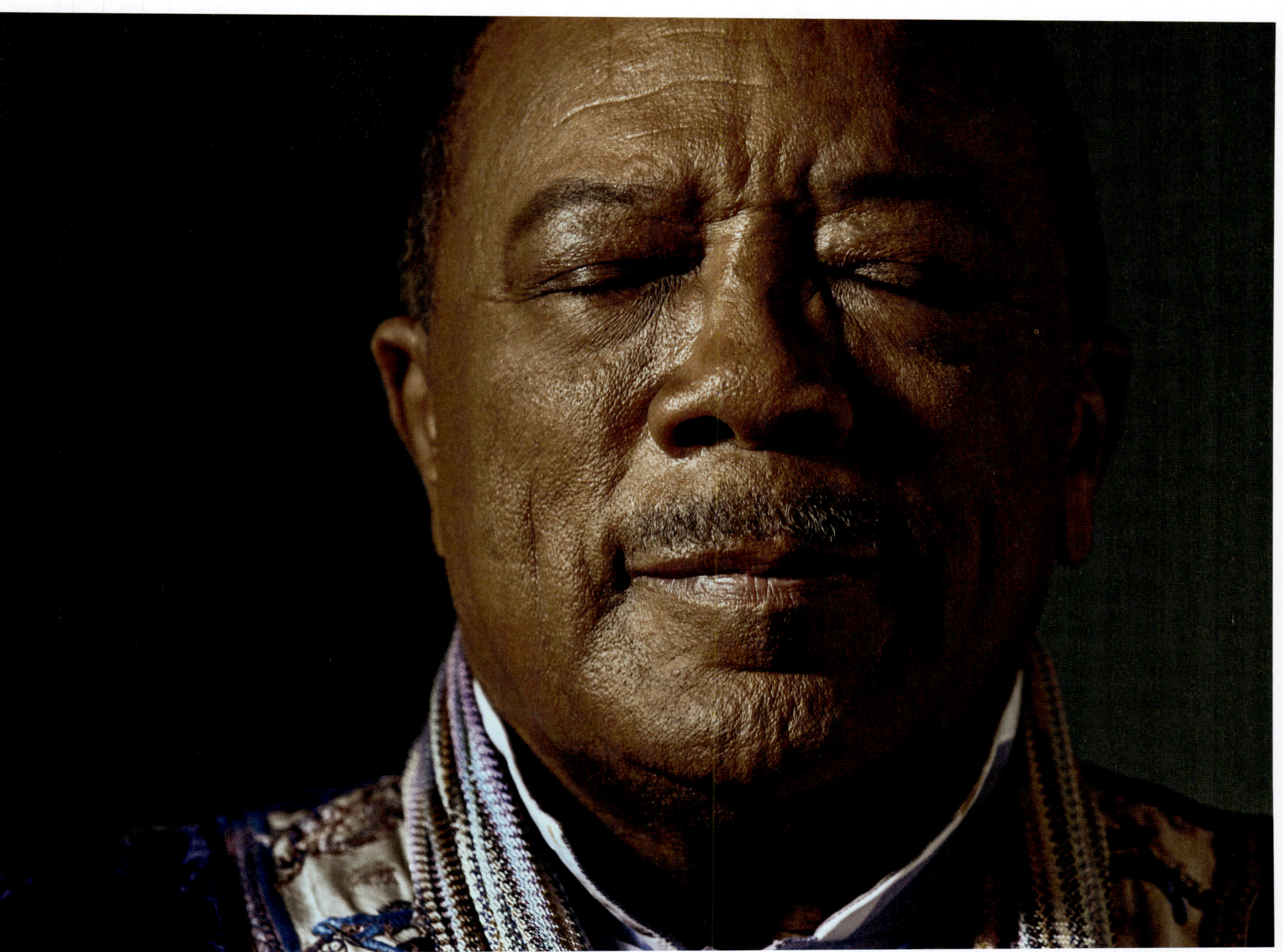

What hasn't Quincy Jones done? He produced the biggest-selling album of all time, Michael Jackson's *Thriller*. He wrote the arrangements for the timeless Frank Sinatra album with the Count Basie Orchestra, *Sinatra at the Sands*. He supervised the all-star recording session that produced the worldwide anthem "We Are the World." He has won an astonishing twenty-seven Grammys and has written seven Oscar-nominated motion picture scores. He was given an honorary Academy Award for his humanitarian work. *Time* magazine named him one of the most influential jazz musicians of the 20th century. His solo albums have sold millions and featured some of the greatest talents in music. He took a private audience with the Pope alongside Bono of U2. Ray Charles taught teenaged Jones how to write music in their early days in Seattle. His big band song "Soul Bossa Nova" was memorably reprised in the *Austin Powers* films. When he was running the artists and repertoire department of Mercury Records in the 60s, he produced the Lesley Gore hit "It's My Party." He talked Miles Davis into making his last album. No career in American music can match his contributions and accomplishments. With all the music in his career, Jones picked the love theme from the 1982 film *Best Friends* which he produced (with Johnny Mandel), written by Michel Legrand with Alan and Marilyn Bergman, arranged by David Foster, with vocalists James Ingram and Patti Austin (who also happens to be his goddaughter).

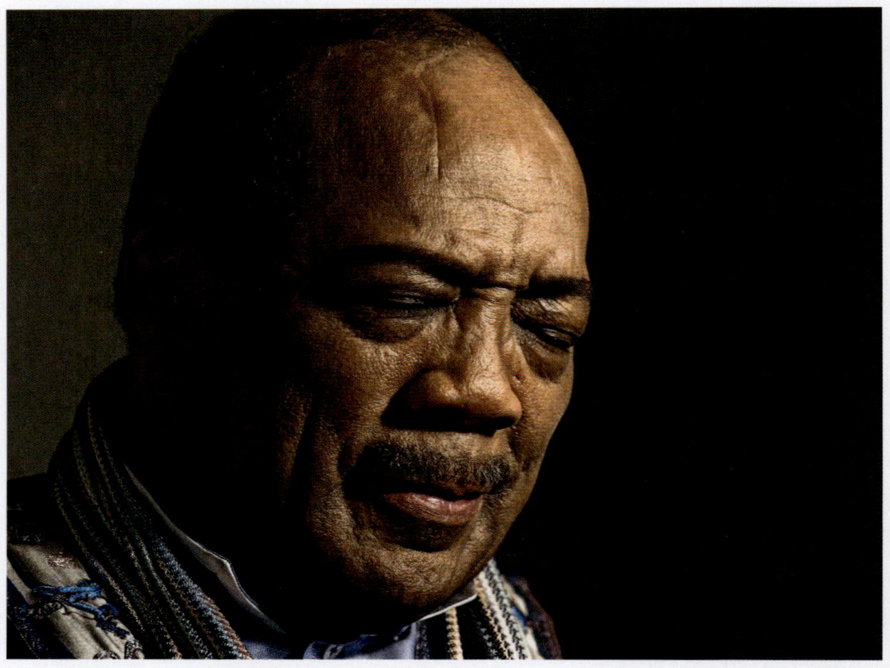

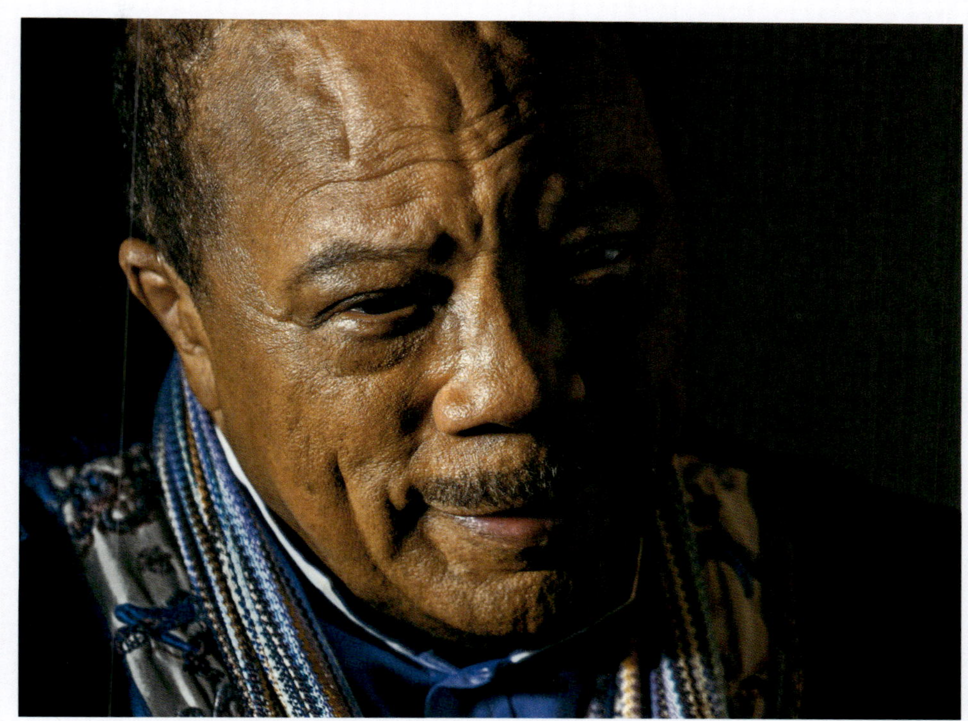

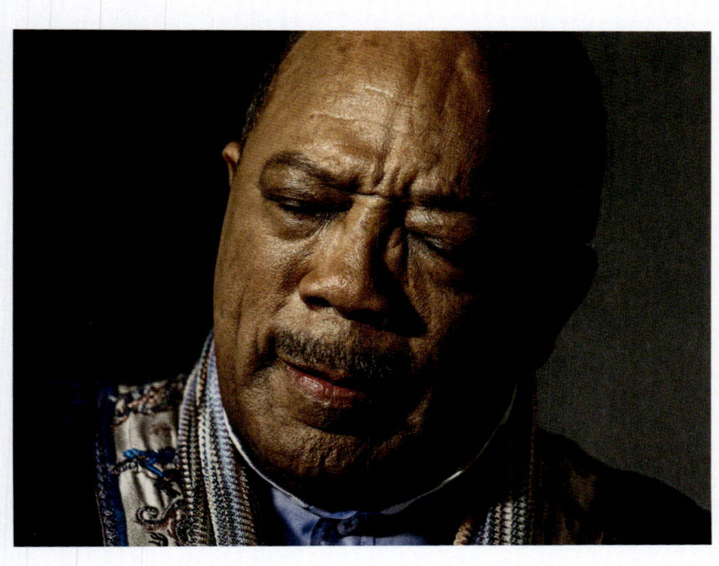

ROBBY KRIEGER at Horse Latitudes Studio, Glendale, California, November 11, 2014

Janis Joplin – *Summertime*
Frank Ifield – *I Remember You*
Cream – *Crossroads*
Bob Dylan – *Mr. Tambourine Man*

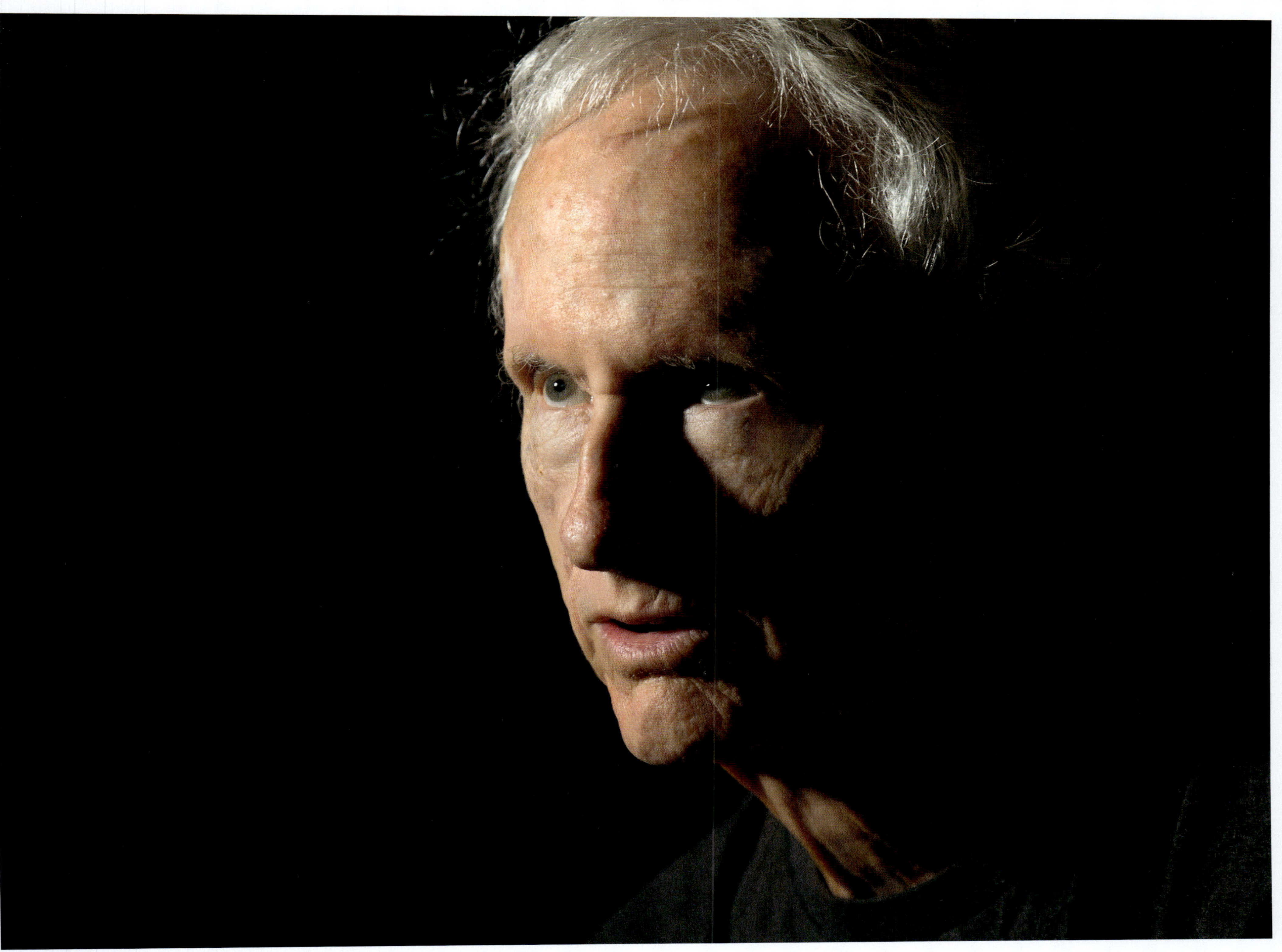

The first time the four musicians who would become The Doors played together, guitarist Robby Krieger pulled out a bottleneck slide for the song "Moonlight Drive." Vocalist Jim Morrison went wild for the sound, initially insisting that Krieger play bottleneck on every song. A few weeks later, Krieger turned up at rehearsal with a song he had written called "Light My Fire" that would become the number one hit across the country during the Summer of Love and establish The Doors as one of the leading rock groups of the day. Sent away to military school after getting caught smoking pot in high school, Krieger taught himself flamenco guitar and considered himself more a jazz guitarist when he started fooling around in an electric blues band called the Psychedelic Rangers with drummer John Densmore. John introduced him to the other two members of The Doors, Morrison and keyboardist Ray Manzarek. In the years since The Doors, he has collaborated with jam band Particle, Blue Öyster Cult, Alice Cooper and Eric Burdon, performed on the "Experience Hendrix" tours and revisited The Doors songbook with bandmate Manzarek as Doors of the 21st Century. Krieger and drummer Densmore have resolved longstanding differences in the wake of Manzarek's death in 2013 and Krieger continues to work with his own band, Jam Kitchen, as well as develop his Horse Latitudes recording studio.

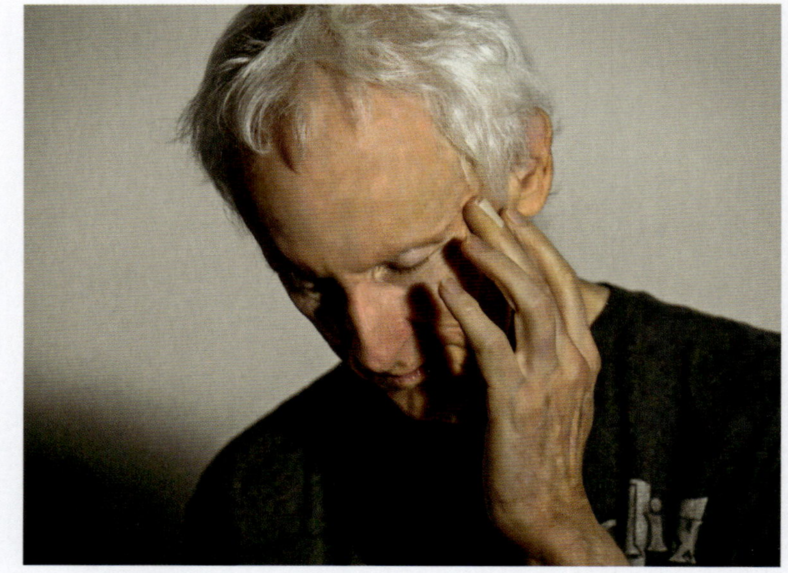

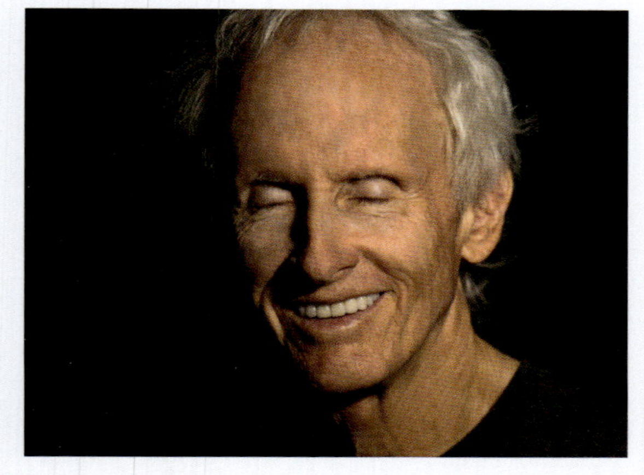

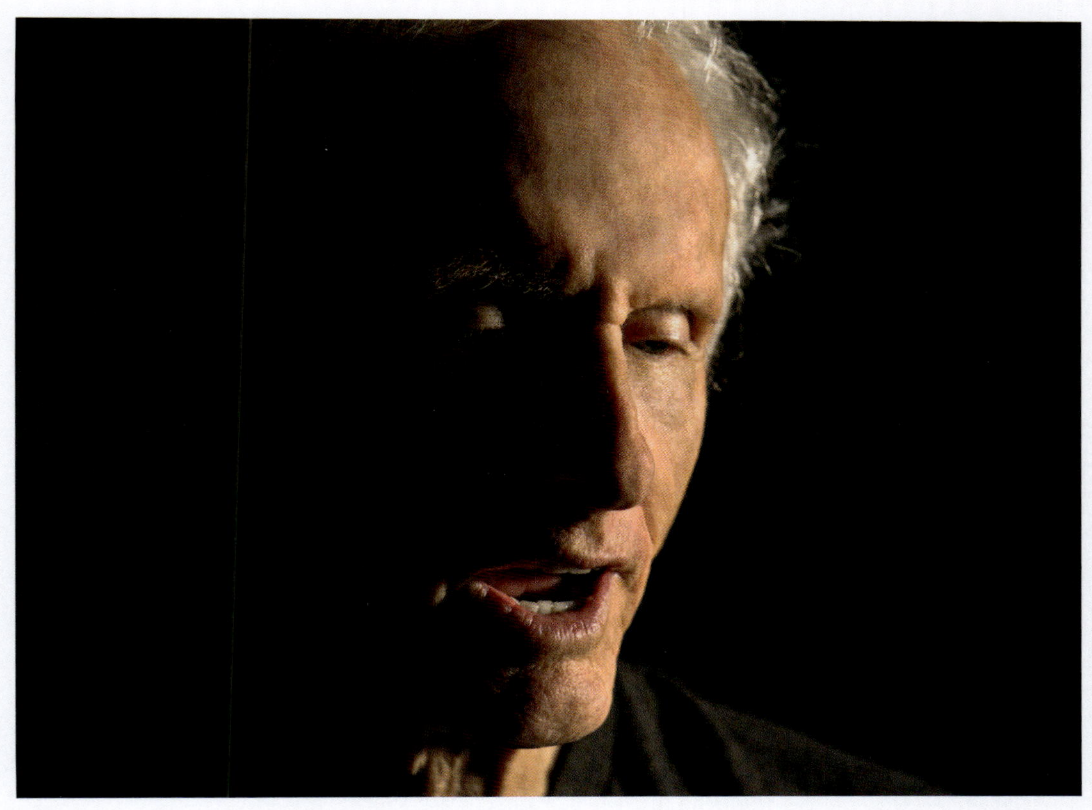

HUEY LEWIS at Huey Lewis and the News office/rehearsal hall, San Rafael, California, November 18, 2013

Johnnie Taylor – *Just the One I've Been Looking for*
Rance Allen Group – *Ain't No Need of Crying*
Frank Sinatra – *Summer Wind, Time After Time*

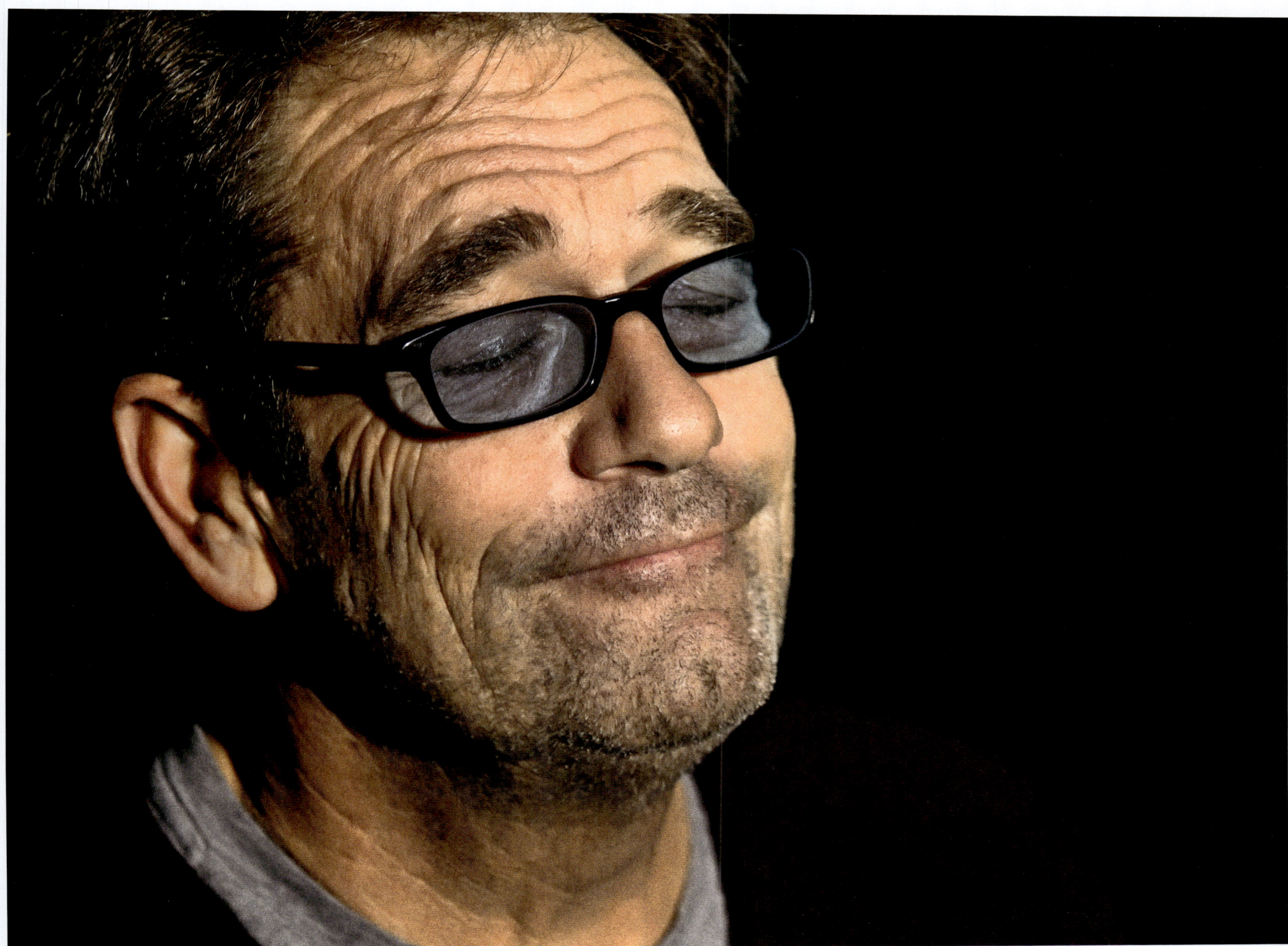

Huey Lewis' choices almost perfectly triangulate his own unique musical character. Memphis soul man Johnnie Taylor's raucous romp and gospel singer Rance Allen's heavenly cries mirror the R&B underpinnings of all his music and the smooth sophistication of Sinatra reflects the genial, easygoing style that has always been his trademark. Lewis took a brave turn on Broadway in the 2006 revival of "Chicago" and his longstanding band, Huey Lewis and the News, have moved in their latter years from skinny-tie new wave rock to more Memphis R&B with a three-piece horn section. He grew up in Marin County with hippie parents (his mother painted the Day-Glo peacock at the Fillmore Auditorium) and belonged to a quintessential Marin hippie country-rock band called Clover, who moved to England in time to back Elvis Costello on his first album. Huey Lewis and the News, another bunch of Marin musicians Lewis put together after Clover dissolved on returning from England, were darlings of the MTV set and one of the most popular American rock bands of the day with a string of hits that included "Power of Love" from the motion picture "Back to the Future." Lewis, who lives in remote Montana when he isn't on tour, couldn't keep still during his photo shoot, on his feet, finger-snapping, singing along.

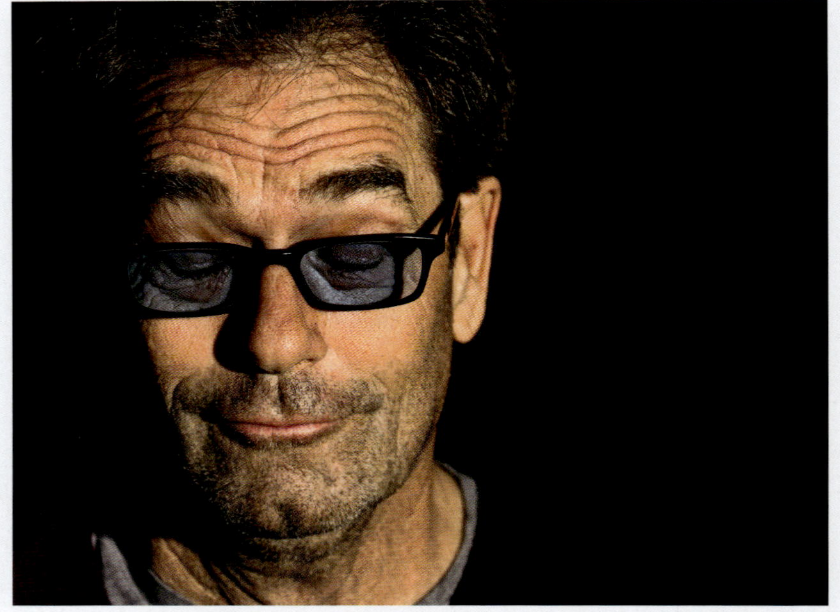

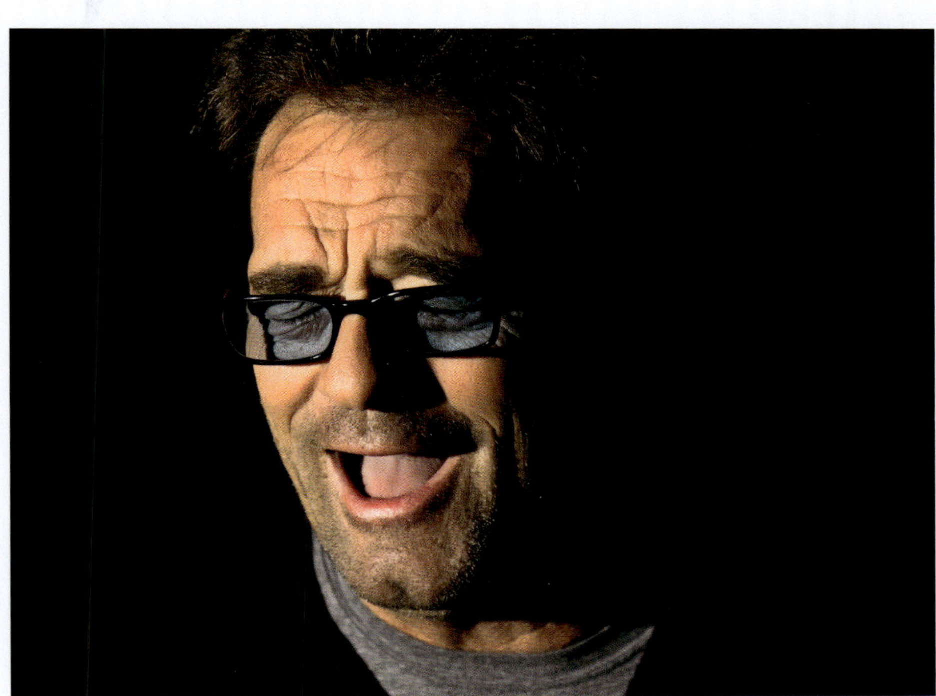

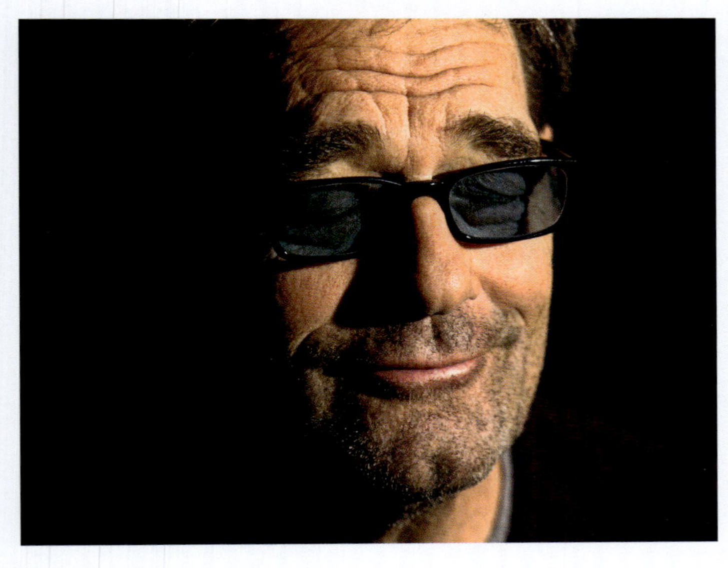

JOHN LYDON (JOHNNY ROTTEN) at home, Malibu, California, May 17, 2013

The Congos – from *Heart of the Congos*
Captain Beefheart and His Magic Band – from *Trout Mask Replica*
Kate Bush – *This Woman's Work*
Led Zeppelin – *Physical Graffiti*
Public Image Ltd – *This is PiL*

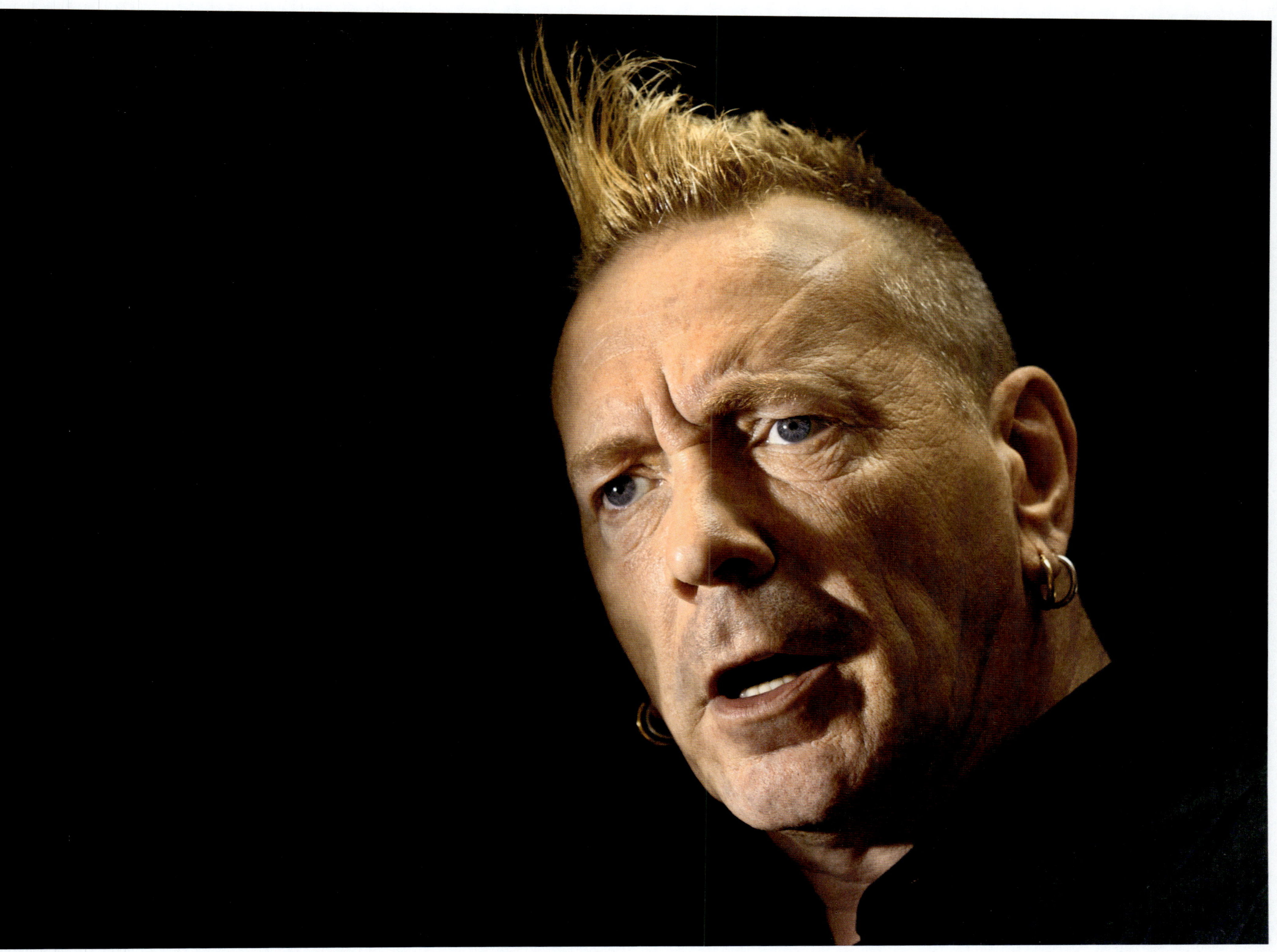

Irascible, petulant John Lydon used the proceeds of a cheeky 2008 British TV commercial for British Country Life Butter to fund the reunion of his post-Sex Pistols experimental rock group Public Image Ltd, better known as PiL. Seventeen years after the band first dissolved, Lydon and company returned to the stage and eventually recorded a new, ninth album, *This Is PiL*, in 2012. As Johnny Rotten, captain of the pirate crew called the Sex Pistols, the spiky-haired, foul-mouthed provocateur was the face of punk rock. Raised in North London by working class Irish immigrants, Lydon was hospitalized for an entire year during childhood with spinal meningitis and the treatments left him with a permanent curvature of the spine. He was a young, aimless, club-going malcontent with orange hair squatting in an empty Hampstead mansion with a bunch of older hippies when he passed an impromptu audition at the fetish clothing store run by impresario Malcolm McLaren, who was putting together the band that would become the Sex Pistols. The band's glorious reign was a brief but unforgettable meteor flash across the rock sky. His selections hark back to his pre-punk fascination with roots reggae (The Congos, produced by the great Lee Perry) and the Dada rock of Captain Beefheart at his strangest, along with a bit of Zep, a latter-era Kate Bush hit and selections from his latest record with PiL. He recently published a new book, *Anger is an Energy: My Life Uncensored*.

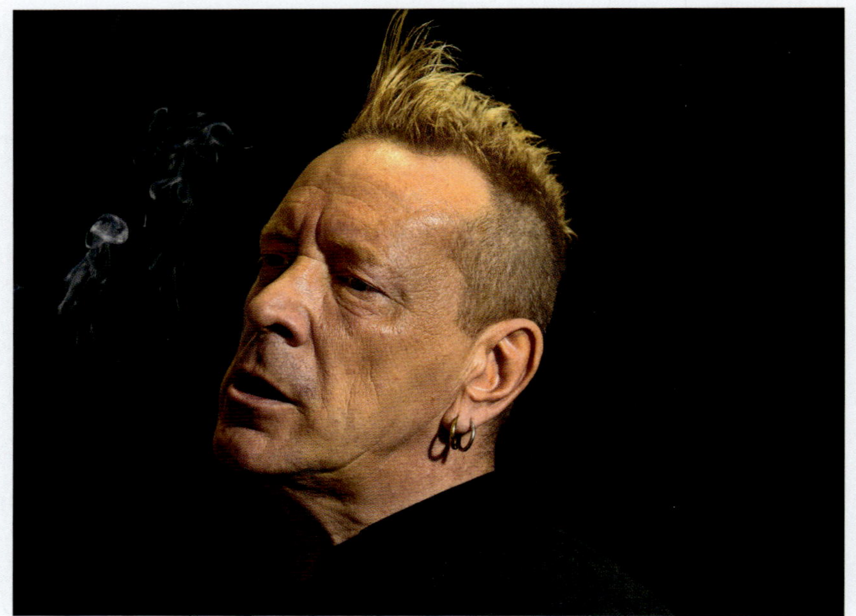

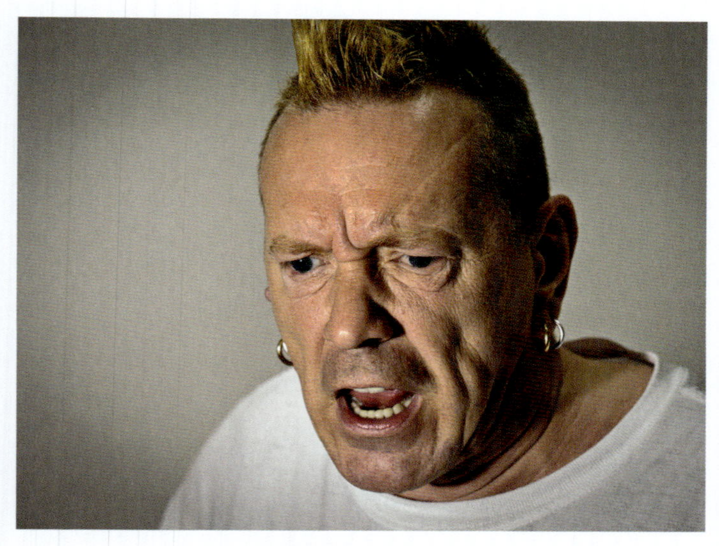

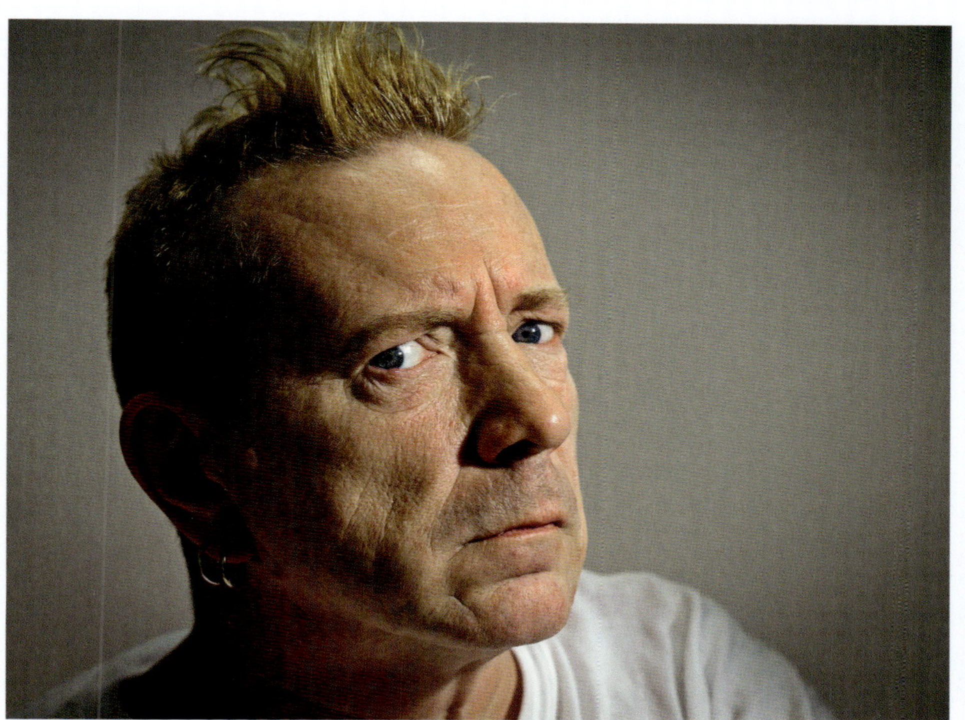

SÉRGIO MENDES at home, Encino, California, January 29, 2012

Antônio Carlos Jobim – *Passarim*

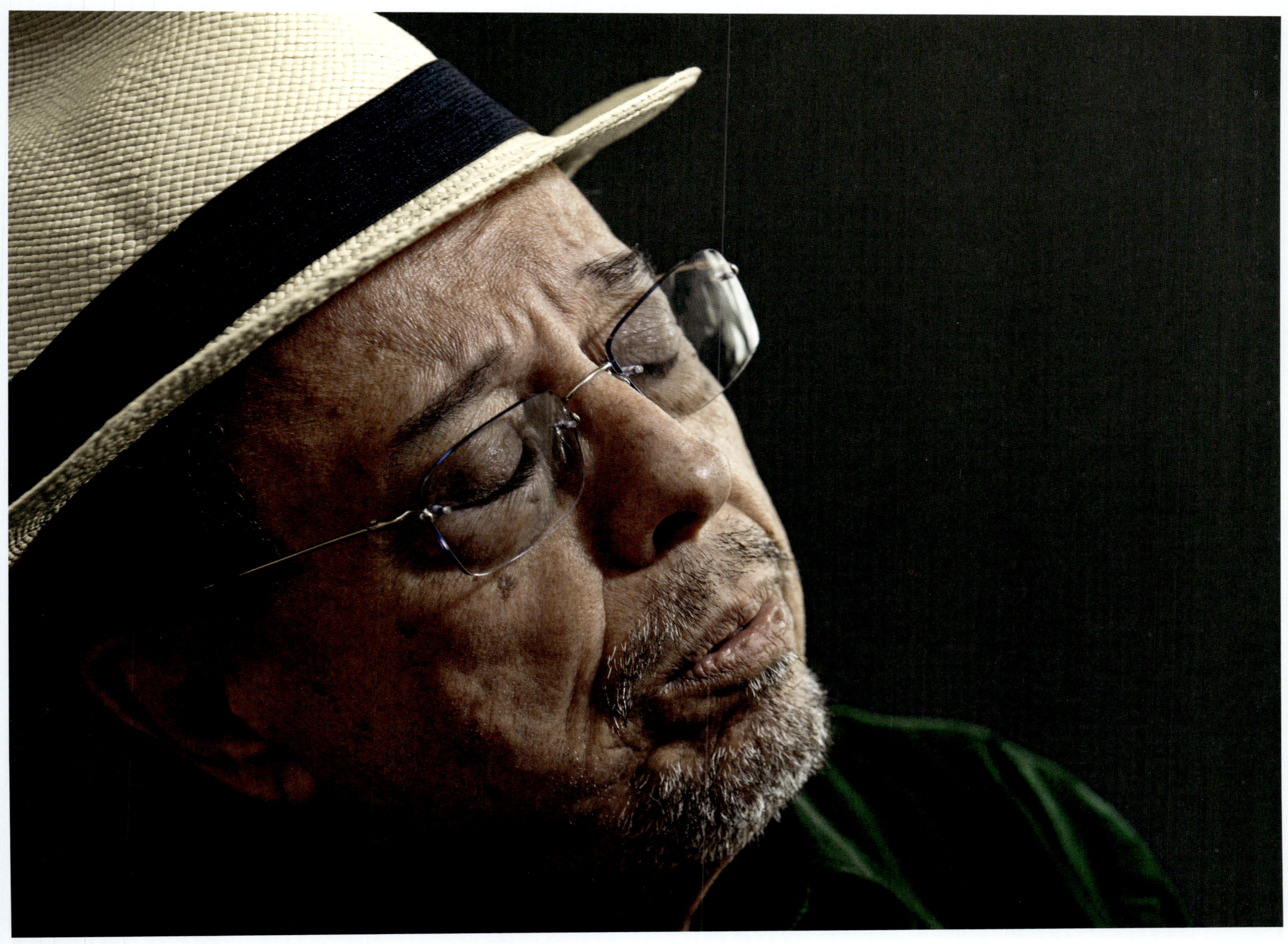

One of the great ambassadors of Brazilian pop, Sérgio Mendes was a classically-trained pianist who began playing in night-clubs as bossa nova first emerged on the scene in Brazil in the late 50s, working with, among others, the father of bossa nova, Antônio Carlos Jobim. He moved to New York in 1964, where he recorded a couple of highly regarded jazz albums with Portuguese language vocals. But when he started his new group, Sérgio Mendes and Brasil '66, with bilingual vocalists, and came under the influence of producer Herb Alpert, Mendes broke through with the smash hit "Mas Que Nada." He enjoyed immense popularity, performed at the White House, before fading away from American bestselling charts, although he maintained enthusiastic followings in Latin America and Japan. He found his way back on the charts in the early 80s and, by the time he released his 1993 Grammy-winning masterpiece album, *Brasileiro*, Mendes was widely recognized as the leading exponent of jazz-flavored Brazilian pop. His 2006 re-recording of "Mas Que Nada" with The Black Eyed Peas was a worldwide hit. For his photo session, Mendes picked the title track to the 1987 album by his mentor Jobim, the final studio album by the great master, which finds Jobim's rough voice awash in swooning female background vocals, swathed in rich, almost florid orchestrations from a large band filled with family members.

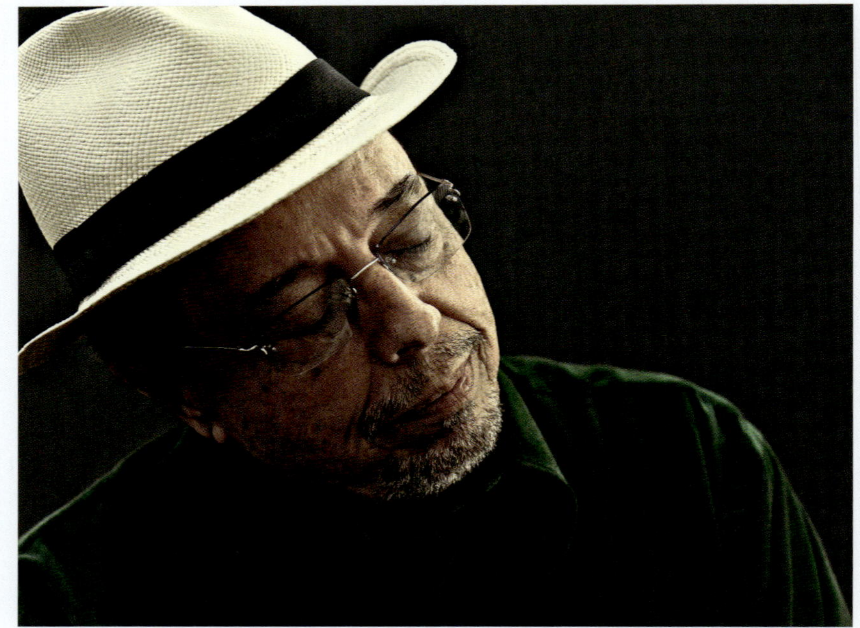

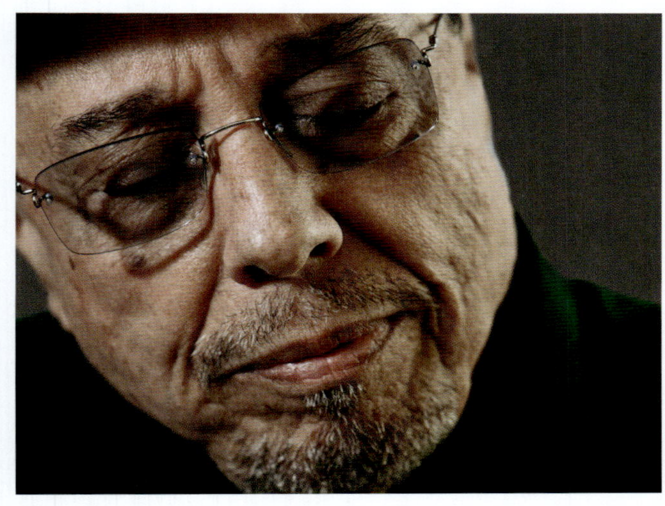

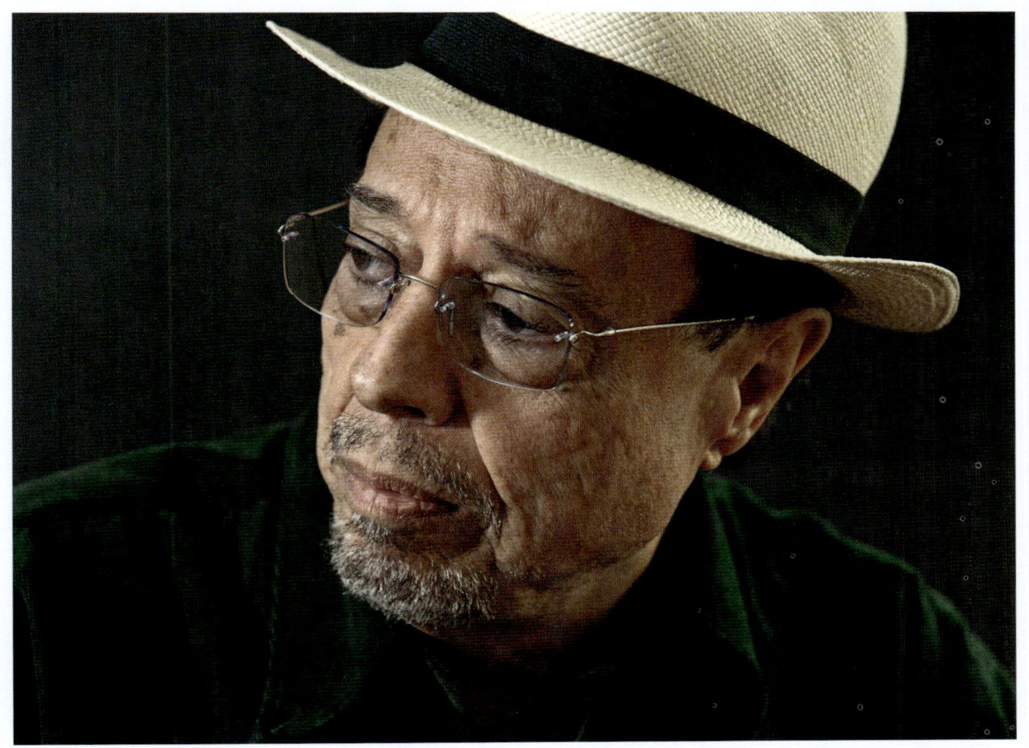

ALLISON MOORER at home, New York City, August 11, 2014

Shelby Lynne – *Miss You Sissy*
Bruno Mars – *Locked Out of Heaven*
Leon Russell – *A Song for You*

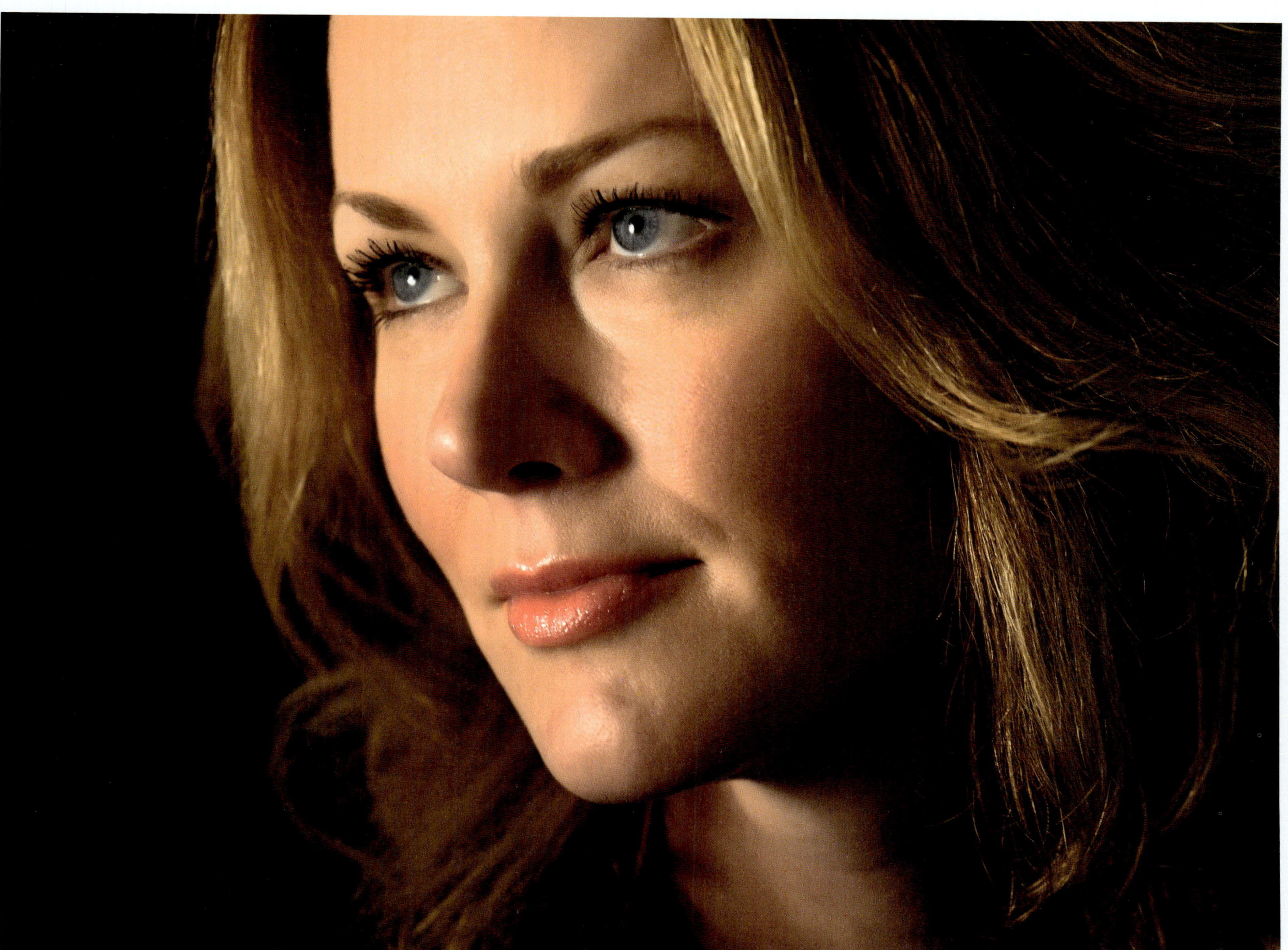

Behind the selection of "Miss You Sissy," one of country singer Allison Moorer's song choices, lies a poignant, painful story. Her older sister Shelby Lynne struggled over the course of six albums to establish herself as a country singer in Nashville before winning the Grammy Award for Best New Artist in 2000 with the breakthrough pop album *I Am Shelby Lynne*. On "Miss You Sissy," a song Lynne wrote and originally recorded for that album that went unreleased for fifteen years because it was simply too personal, Lynne reached out to her then-estranged sister to repair a lifetime of damage. The two sisters were teenagers living in Alabama when their abusive father shot and killed their mother before turning the gun on himself. For years, the girls—who grew up singing three-part harmony with their mother in the car on the way to school to songs on the radio—didn't speak. Moorer, who has recorded eight albums of her heartfelt, introspective songs, watched her song "A Soft Place to Fall" from her 1998 debut, *Alabama Song*, wind up on the film soundtrack for *The Horse Whisperer*, get nominated for an Academy Award and she sang the song herself on the Oscar telecast. Moorer—who now has a young son of her own with her ex-husband, alt-country songwriter Steve Earle—and her sister finally did reunite. They have performed together, recorded together and restored their family ties, thanks to "Miss You Sissy."

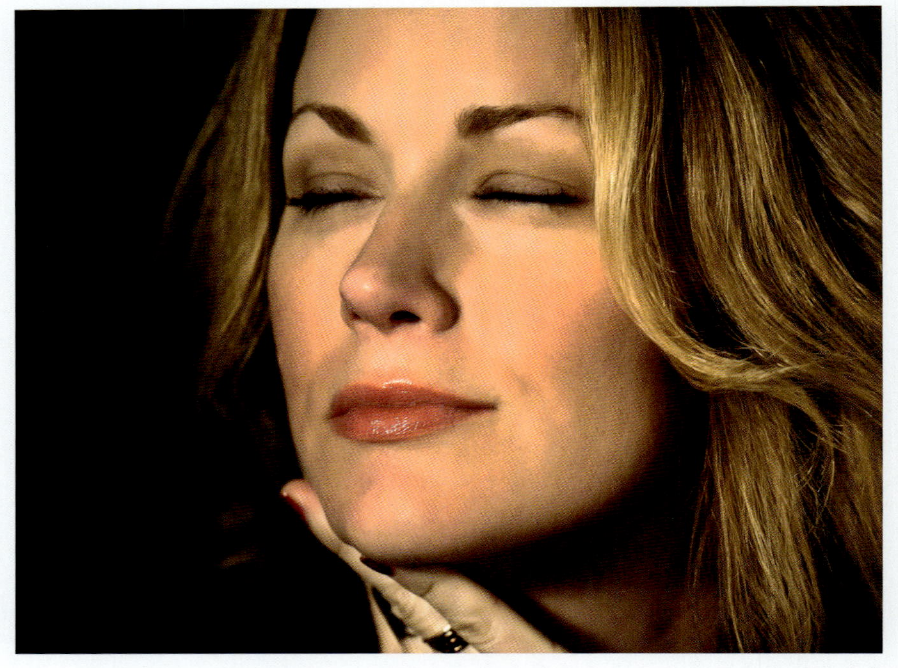

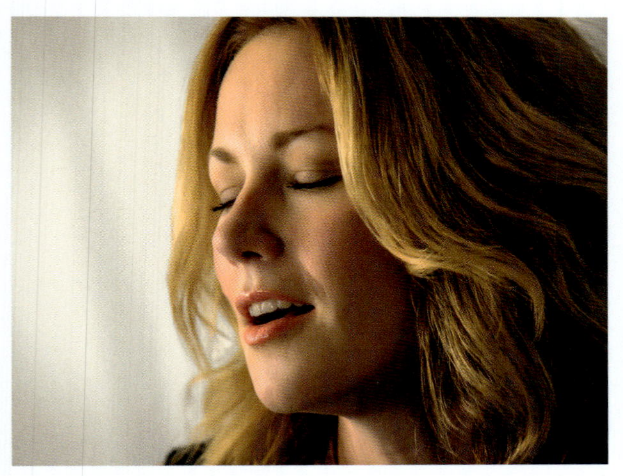

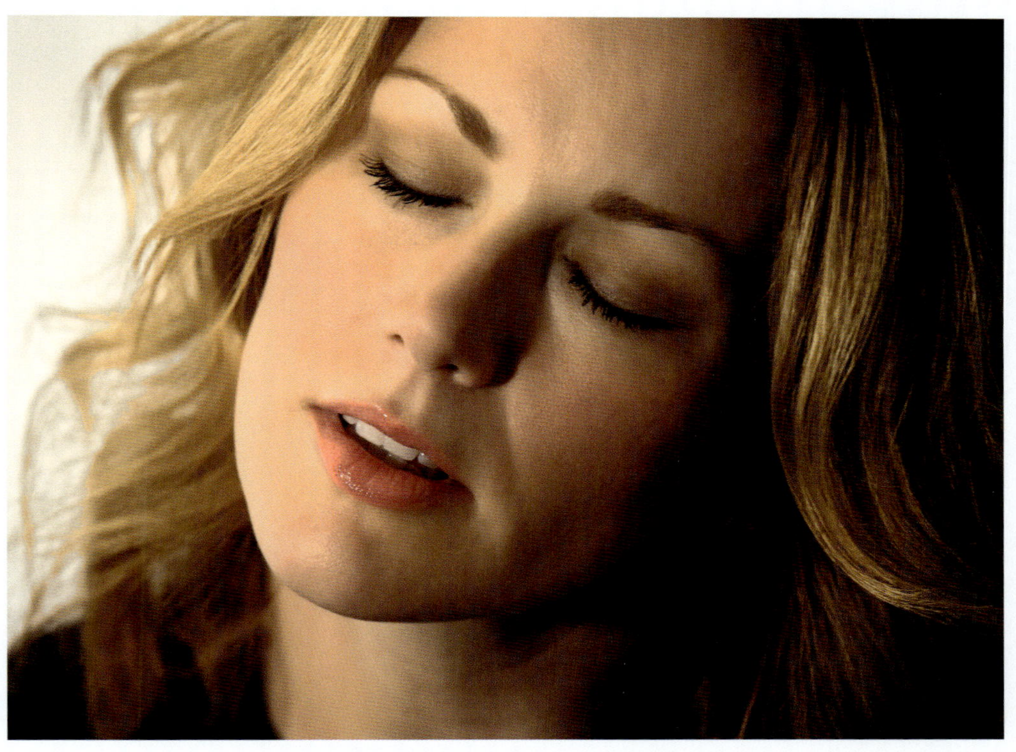

SIR GRAHAM NASH at home, Manhattan Beach, California, February 14, 2011

The Beatles – *A Day in the Life*
Jerry Lee Lewis – *Great Balls of Fire*
Gene Vincent – *Be-Bop-A-Lula*

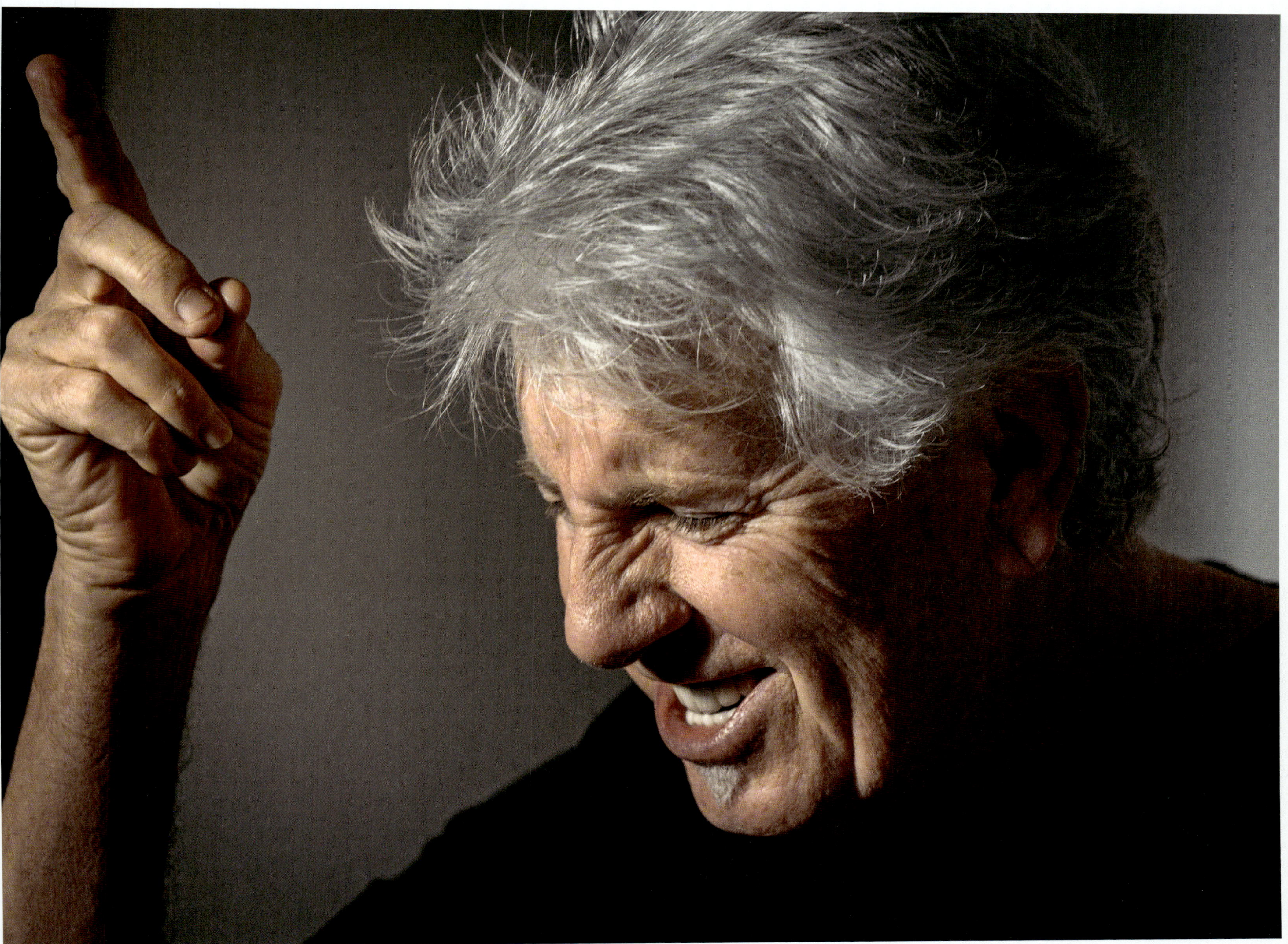

Graham Nash remembers rock and roll. He traded his lunch at school for a 78 RPM copy of "Be-Bop-A-Lula," the first record he ever owned. He and schoolmate Allan Clarke polished their Everly Brothers impersonation in their hometown of Manchester, England, years before they started The Hollies, one of the great groups of the original British Invasion. The Hollies played with The Beatles at Liverpool's Cavern Club and went on to create a series of memorable hits: "Bus Stop," "Stop Stop Stop," "Carrie Anne." Nash joined former members of The Byrds and Buffalo Springfield in Los Angeles in 1968 to start Crosby, Stills and Nash, joined a year later by Neil Young. As Crosby, Stills, Nash and Young, they played one of their first performances in front of a half million people at Woodstock. His song "Teach Your Children" would become a classic. Over the decades, Nash and Crosby—often with Stills, sometimes with Young, occasionally others—have become the hallmark of harmony in rock. A political activist, Nash helped found the antinuclear power organization MUSE in 1979. Nash has long explored his interest in photography, not only as a collector, but a museum exhibit curator and author. He is also a lifelong shooter himself. Known to his friends as Willy, one of rock's nicest guys, he always performs barefoot.

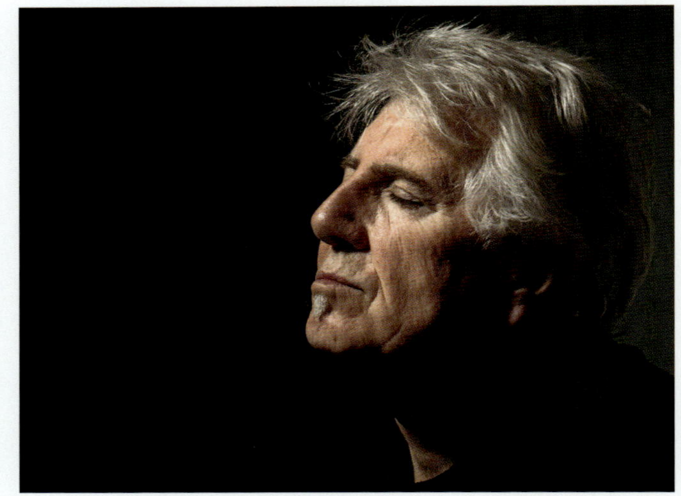

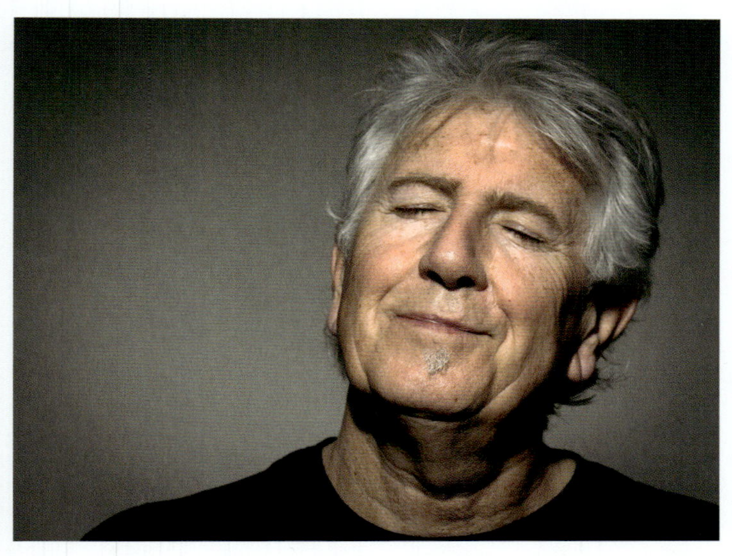

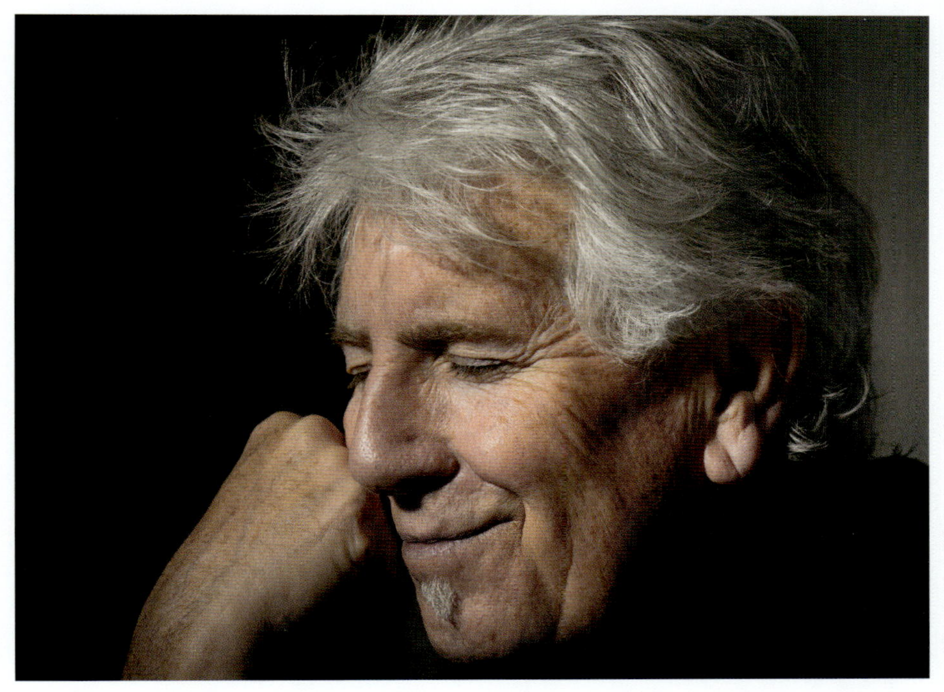

IGGY POP at home, Miami, Florida, February 3, 2015

Link Wray & His Ray Men – *Rumble*
Meade Lux Lewis – *Boogie Woogie*
Chrissy "Zebby" Tembo – *Trouble Maker*

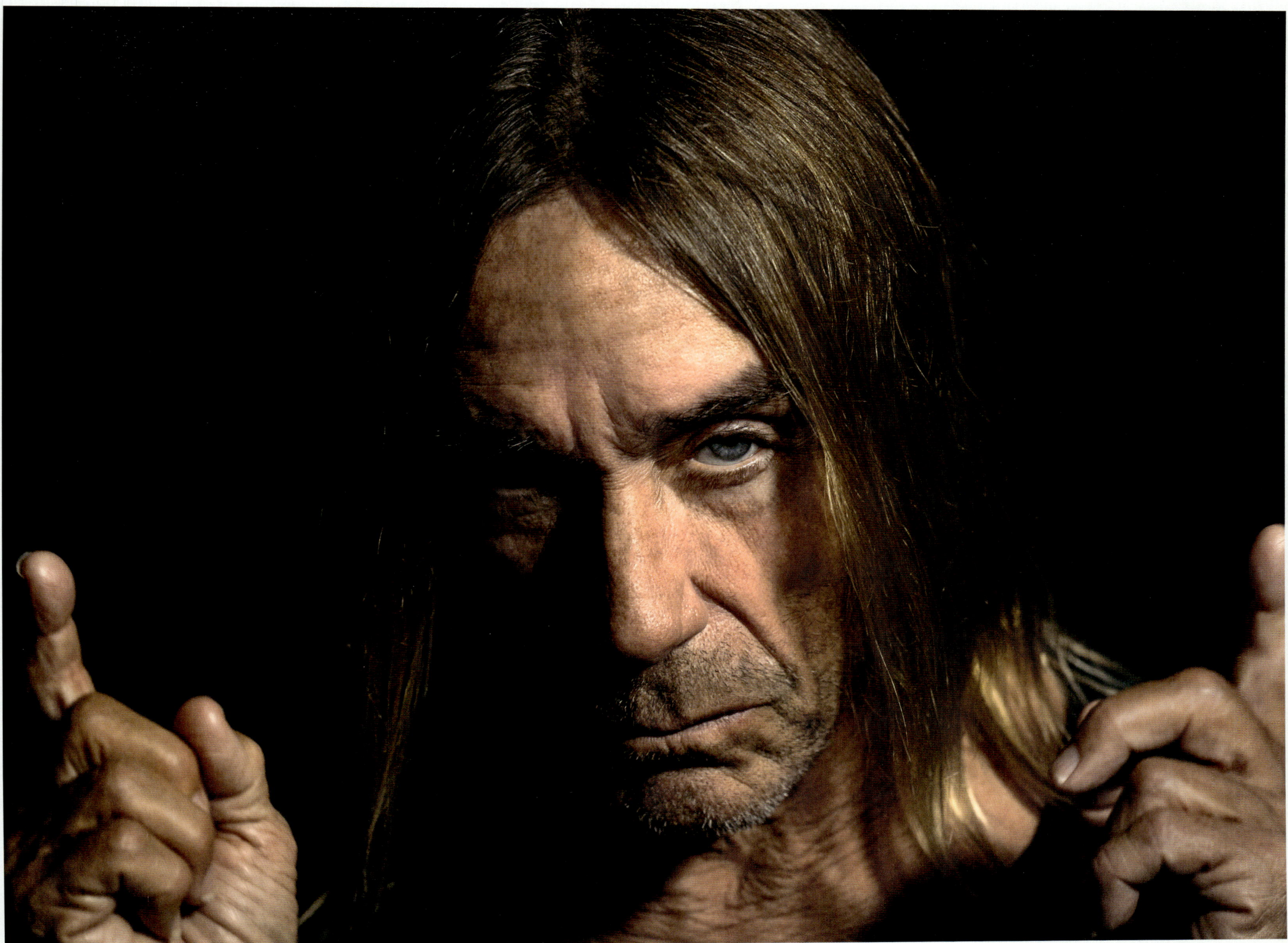

As his selections clearly indicate, Iggy Pop—born James Newell Osterberg Jr.—is one of rock's great primitives: guitarist Link Wray's 1959 epochal roar, pianist Lewis' train ride on the keys from the 30s, and cacophonous 70s Zamrock from Africa's urban jungle. As lead vocalist and incendiary front man of The Stooges, he pioneered an abrasive, aggressive hard rock sound on the post-psychedelic Detroit rock scene with songs like "I Wanna Be Your Dog" that eventually mutated into punk rock. His mid-70s collaborations with David Bowie produced some of the best work of both of their careers and, once he recovered from his long-running heroin addiction, he awakened to discover he had become one of the grand old men of punk, beloved beyond what The Stooges' slender sales figures might have suggested. His 1990 solo album *Brick by Brick* featured members of Guns N' Roses and the B-52s. He appeared in movies and TV shows, his songs were included on film soundtracks and he enjoyed celebrity collaborations such as his "Well, Did You Evah!" duet with Debbie Harry of Blondie on the AIDS fundraiser album *Red Hot + Blue*. A 2003 reunion by Iggy and The Stooges paved the way even for new recordings by the now celebrated band. Time has proven Iggy one of the incorruptible forces of rock, a man who made his own rules and stayed true to the code. He was inducted into the Rock and Roll Hall of Fame in 2010.

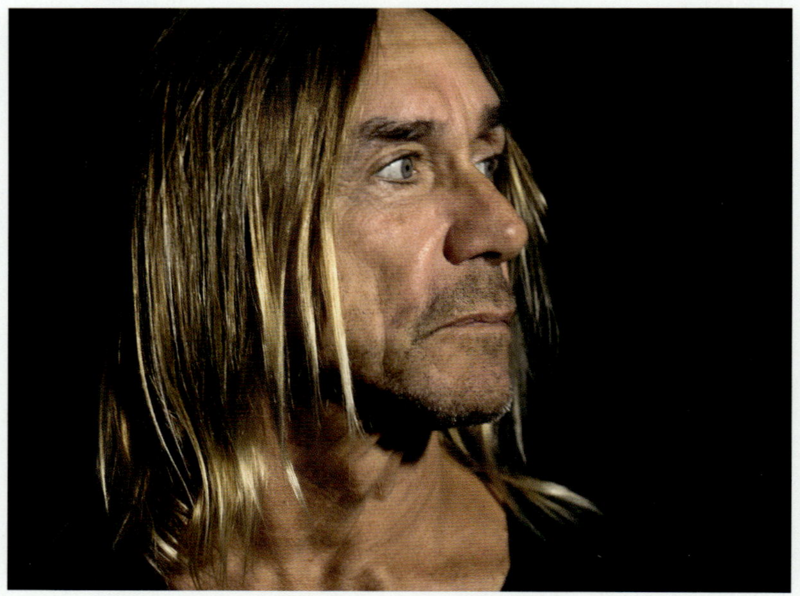

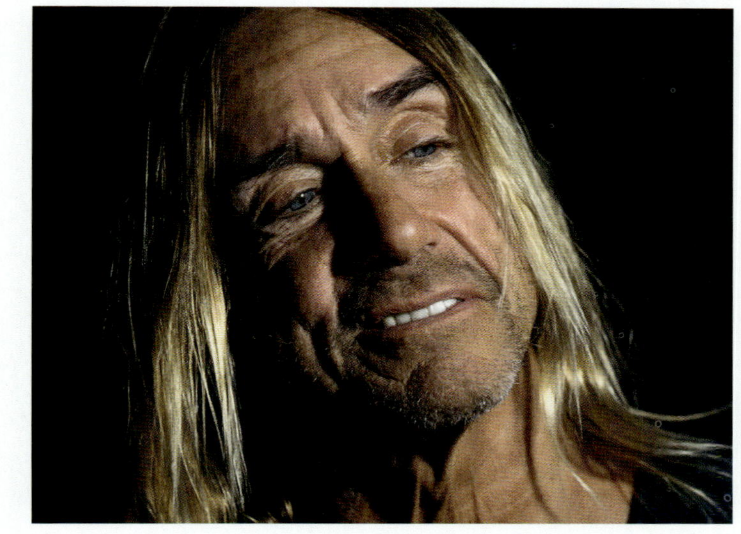

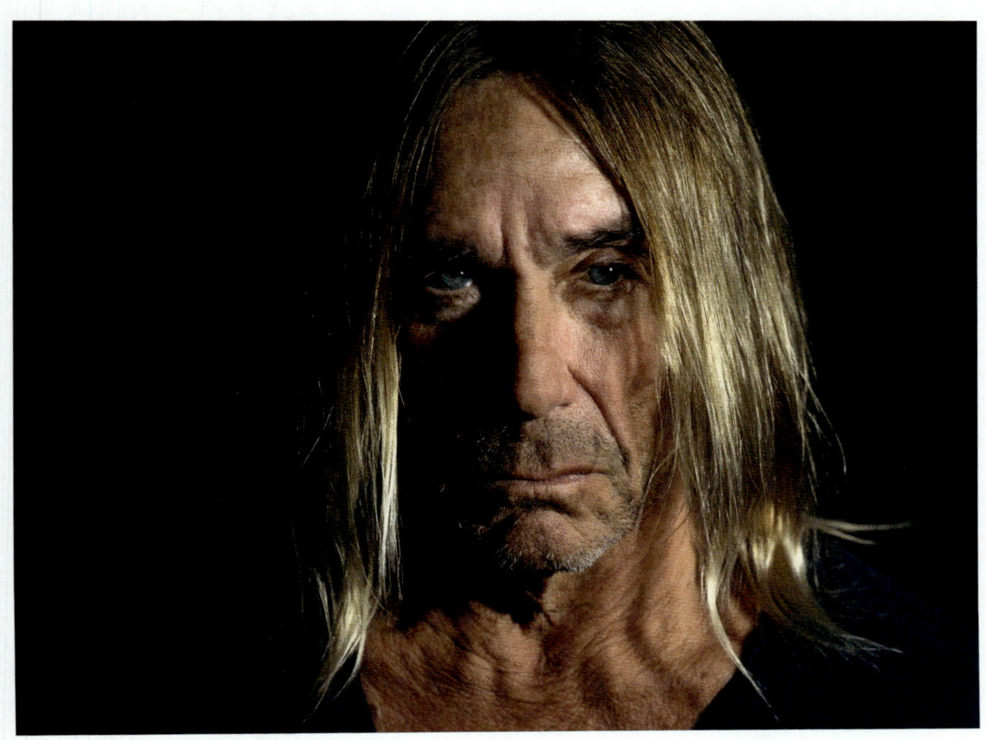

DIANNE REEVES at SFJAZZ Center, San Francisco, California, June 15, 2014

Laura Mvula – *She*
Dianne Reeves – *I Want You*
Dianne Reeves – *Suzanne*

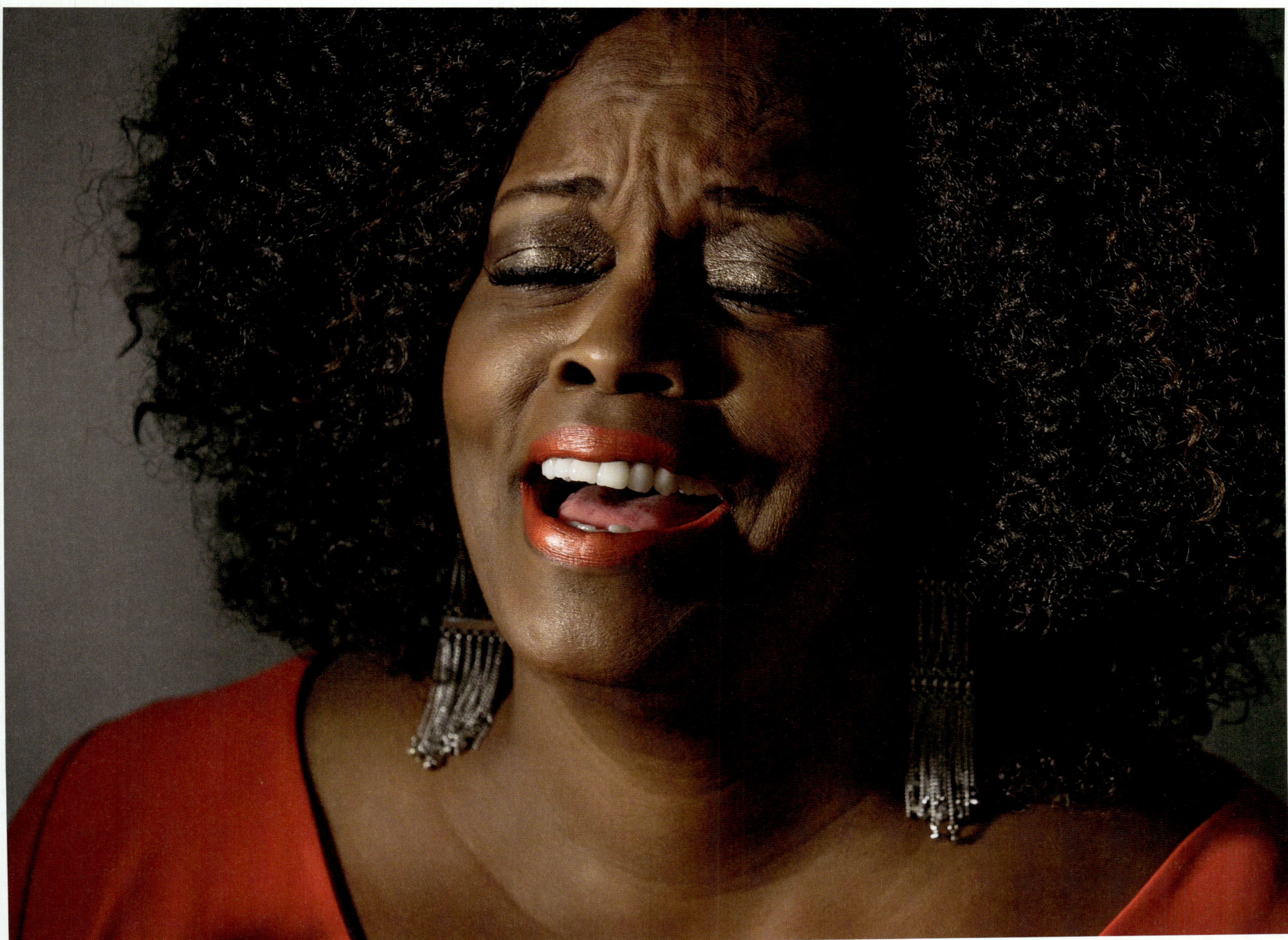

Winner of five Grammy Awards for Best Jazz Vocal Performance, Dianne Reeves may be one of today's leading ladies in jazz, but she dabbled in quiet storm smooth pop when she started out and straddled those worlds for many years before landing, once and for all, in the jazz camp. Raised in Denver, her uncle was a bassist with the symphony orchestra and introduced young Dianne to the great female jazz vocalists. Trumpeter Clark Terry discovered her when she was sixteen years old, and she moved to Los Angeles in 1976. She did Latin jazz with Caldera, sang smooth jazz with Billy Childs' Night Flight and toured with Sérgio Mendes. She performed with Harry Belafonte from 1983 to 1986, where she was exposed to African music and world beat. In 1987, she was the first artist signed to the re-activated Blue Note Records, and her career in jazz began in earnest. A seriously skillful scat singer and assertive song stylist, Reeves has become the living repository of the jazz vocal tradition of Ella Fitzgerald and Sarah Vaughan, appearing in the 2005 George Clooney film *Good Night, and Good Luck* as the classic 50s supper club singer. Her 2015 Grammy-winning album, *Beautiful Life*, featured a number of guests such as bassist Esperanza Spalding, percussionist Sheila E. and keyboardist George Duke, Reeves' cousin and lifelong musical collaborator, who died shortly after the album was completed.

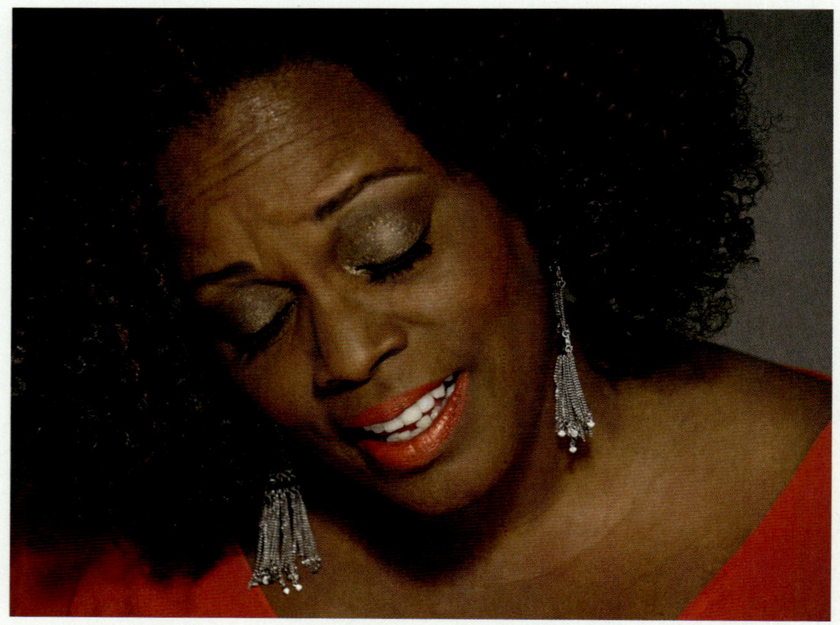

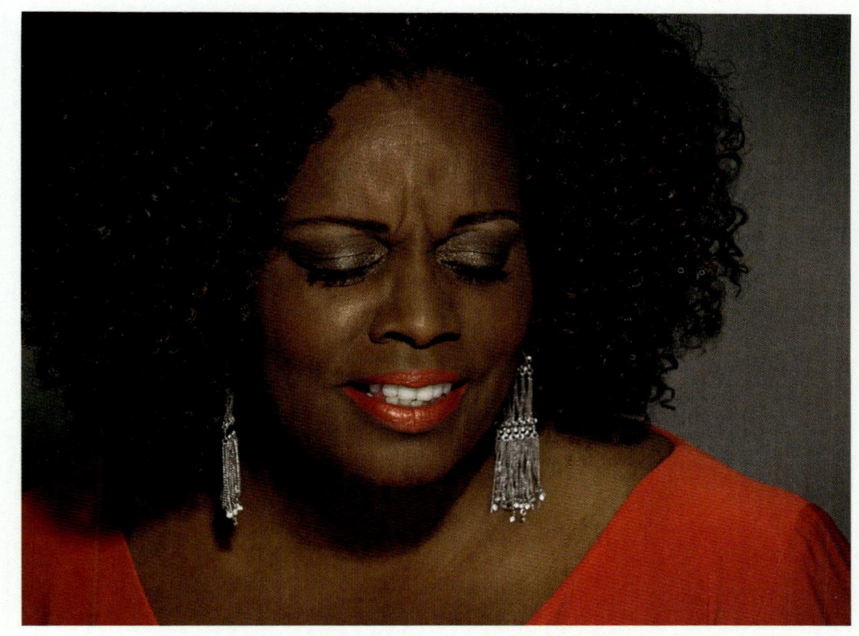

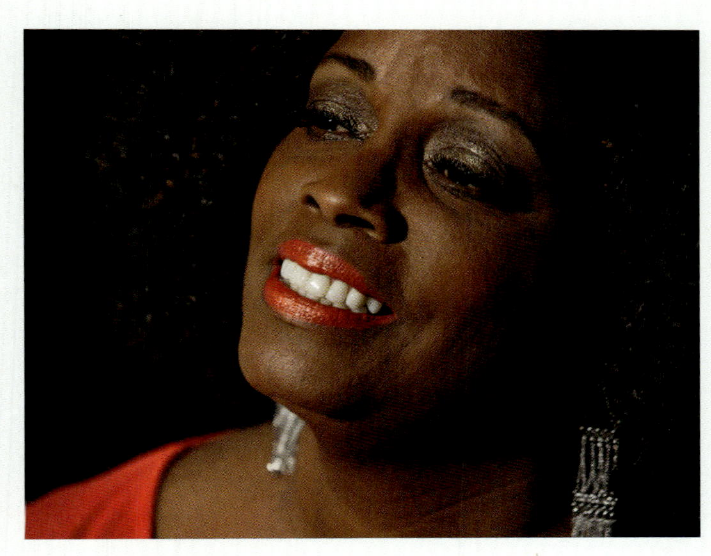

LEANN RIMES at home, Encino, California, May 15, 2014

David Hodges – *Falling Out of Love*
Ray LaMontagne – *Like Rock & Roll and Radio*
Patty Griffin – *Let Him Fly*

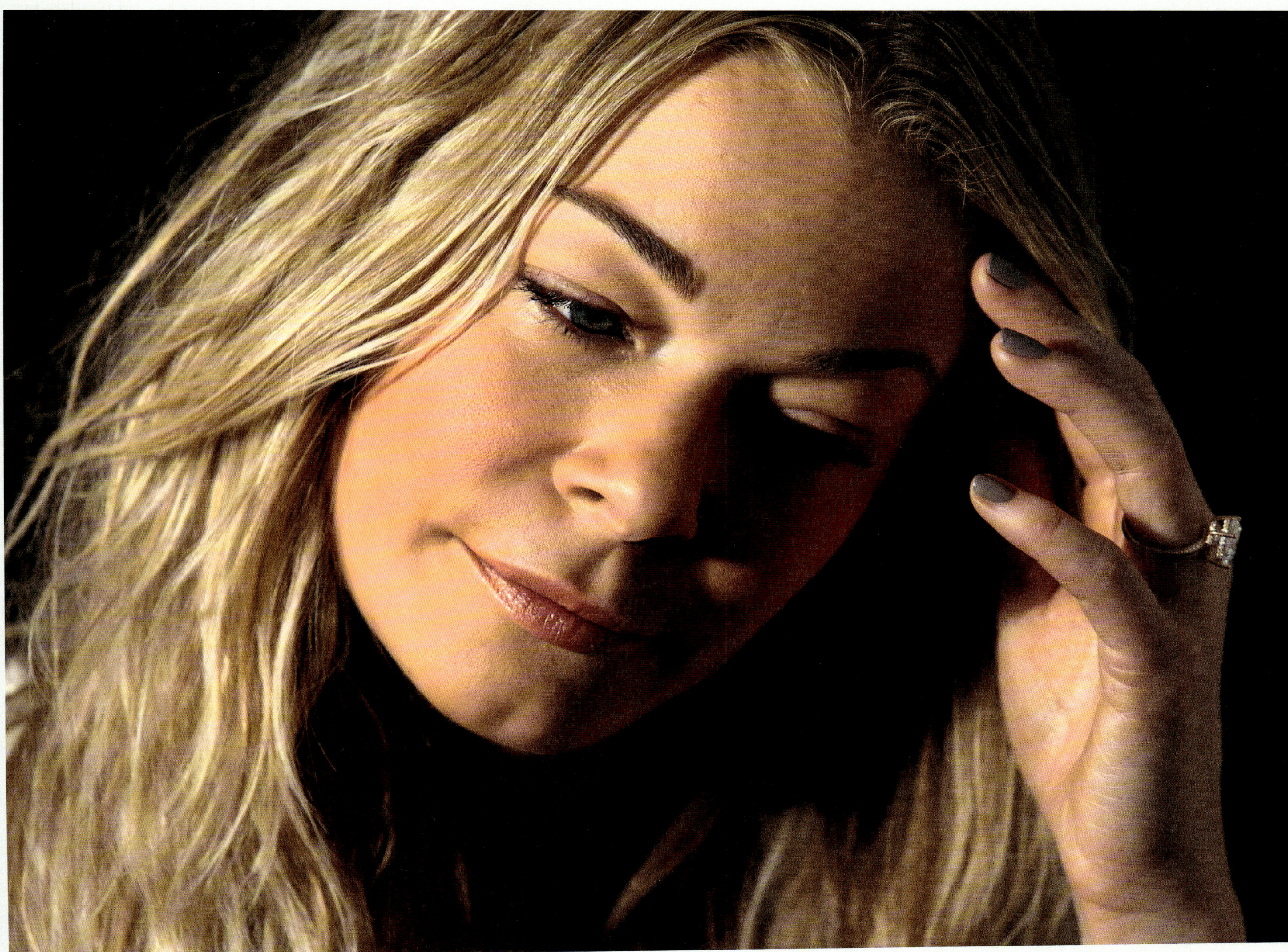

When she made her explosive 1996 debut at age thirteen singing "Blue," a song originally intended for country queen Patsy Cline before her death in 1963, LeAnn Rimes was widely seen as picking up the torch for old-fashioned country music, a welcome throwback to a classic style. But as soon as her second album, Rimes was broadening her horizons to bridge both country and pop fields. Rimes remains one of pop country's dependable figures, a remarkable voice who can find her place in a variety of material. Her father groomed her as an entertainer and she appeared on TV's *Star Search* when she was eight years old. With "Blue," she became the first country artist to win the Grammy Award for Best New Artist and the youngest country star since Tanya Tucker. With her 2000 power ballad "I Need You" from the soundtrack to the TV movie *Jesus*—a top ten smash on both pop and country charts—she had successfully mastered both realms. Her 2005 album, *This Woman*, was a deliberate return to contemporary country and lofted three hits on the country charts. But by her next album, she was back mixing pop and country, singing duets with Jon Bon Jovi, and blurring the lines again between the two.

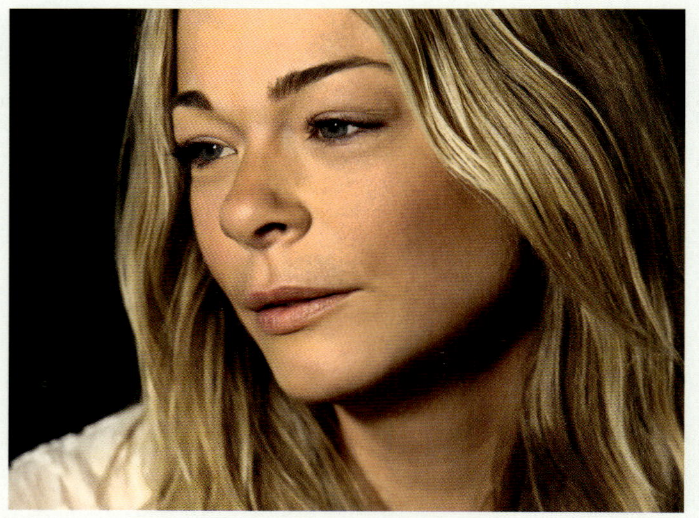

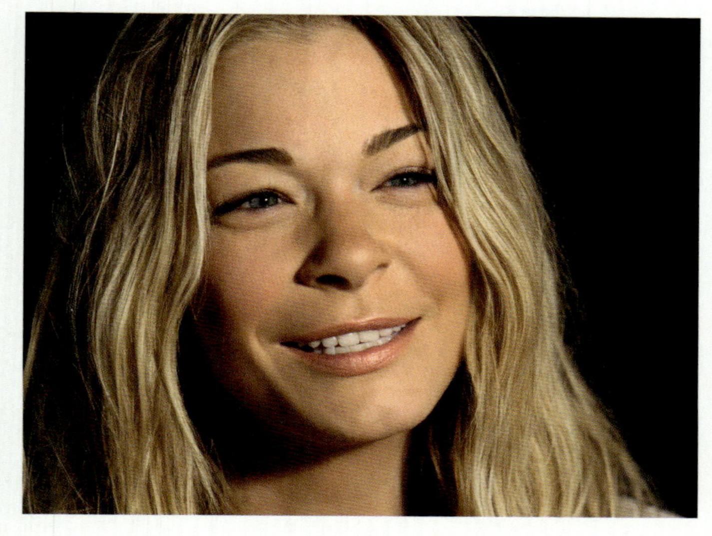

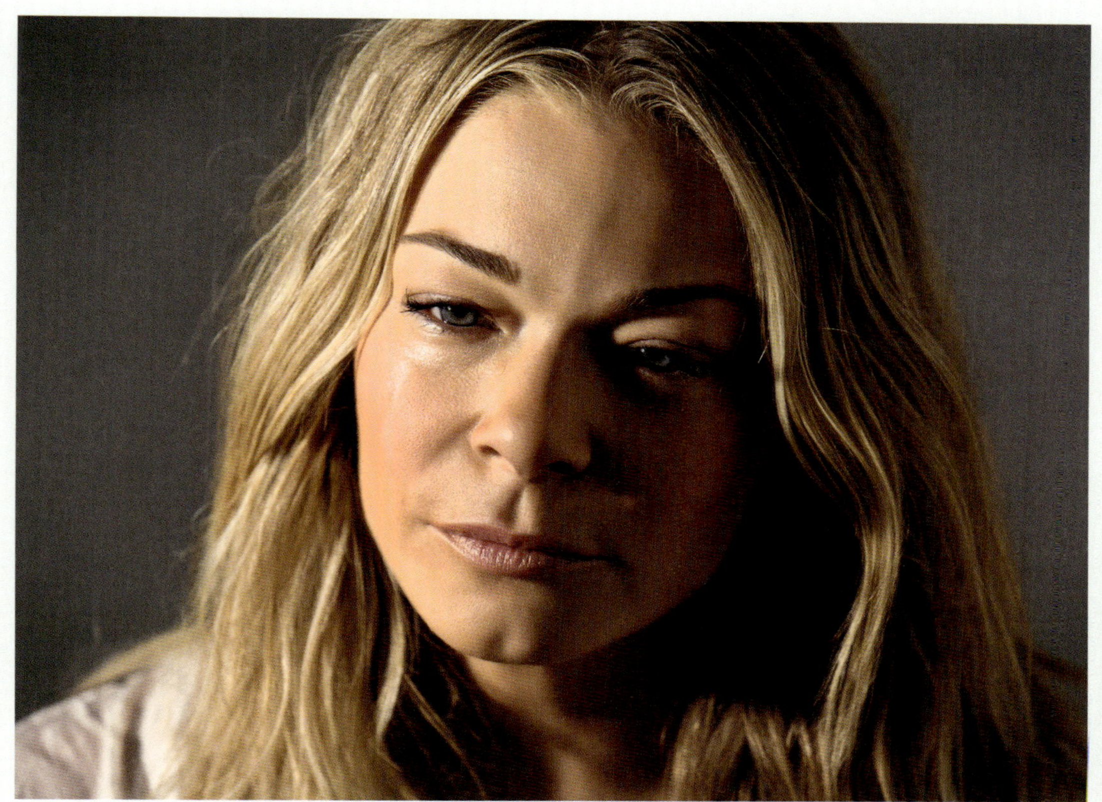

ROBBIE ROBERTSON at Village Studios, Los Angeles, California, February 11, 2011

Arsenal – *Far I Have Come*
Marvin Gaye – *Piece of Clay*
Dinah Washington – *This Bitter Earth*
Max Richter – *On the Nature of Daylight*

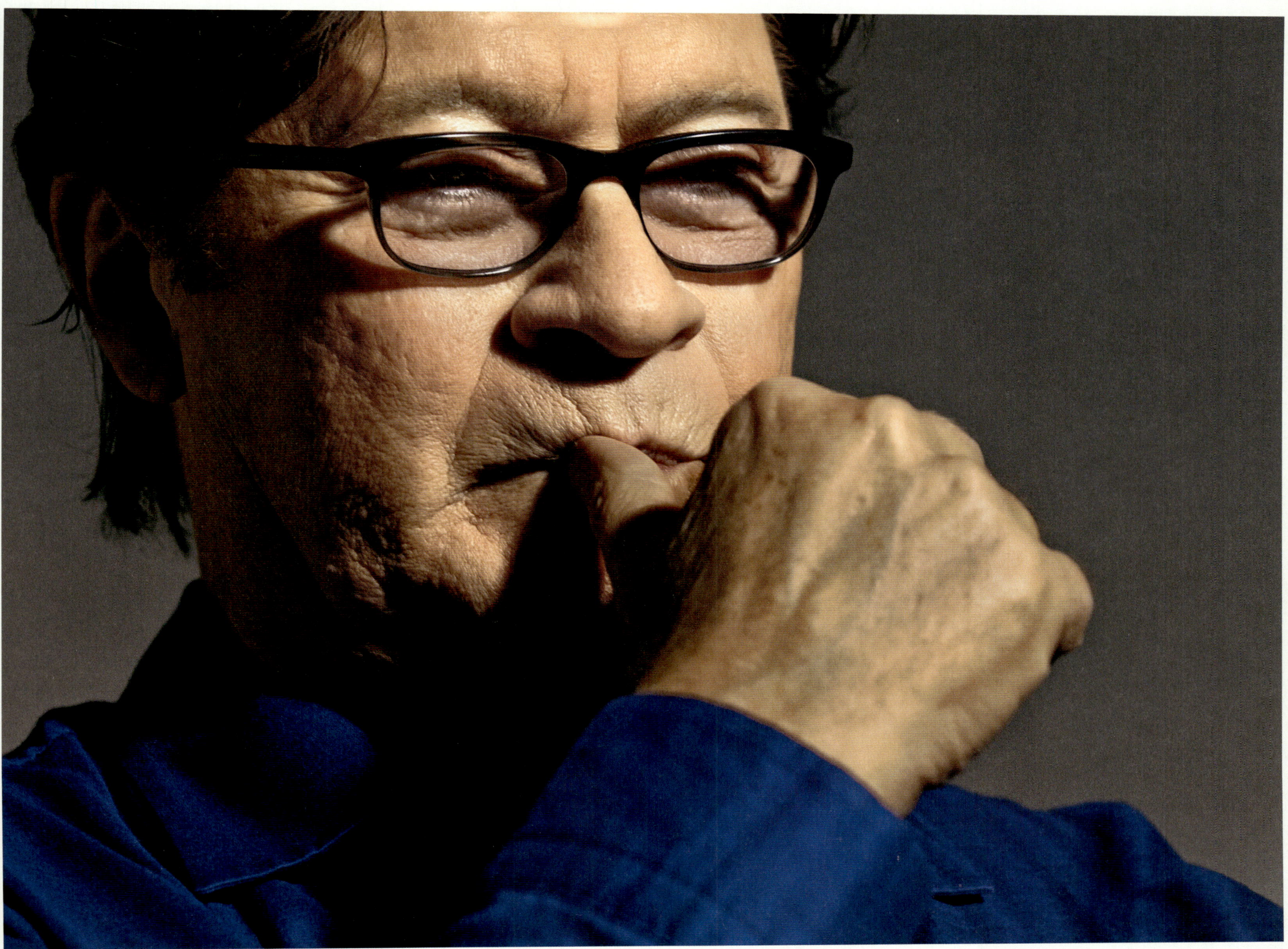

Since leaving a lifetime of the road behind him as guitarist of The Band, Robbie Robertson has worked extensively on music soundtracks for motion pictures with director Martin Scorsese. They first met when Scorsese directed the concert film of the epic 1976 farewell concert by the group, *The Last Waltz*, and Robertson has subsequently served as music producer on Scorsese films including *Raging Bull, Casino, The Wolf of Wall Street* and others, in addition to recording a handful of acclaimed solo albums. Robertson, who grew up in Toronto, joined the backup band for Arkansas wild-man rock and roller Ronnie Hawkins in 1960. After leaving Hawkins, the group performed as Levon and the Hawks and wound up backing songwriter Bob Dylan on his electric rock juggernaut. Their 1968 debut as The Band, *Music from Big Pink,* was one of the most influential rock albums of its time. For his selections, Robertson, displaying his arcane musical erudition, listened to the Belgian dance music group Arsenal; an obscure Marvin Gaye performance that went unreleased until a 1995 CD collection; and finally the 1960 hit by jazz vocalist Dinah Washington and a track from the 2004 second album by British contemporary classical composer Max Richter, *The Blue Notebooks*—two pieces Robertson previously effectively blended for the soundtrack of the Scorsese film *Shutter Island*.

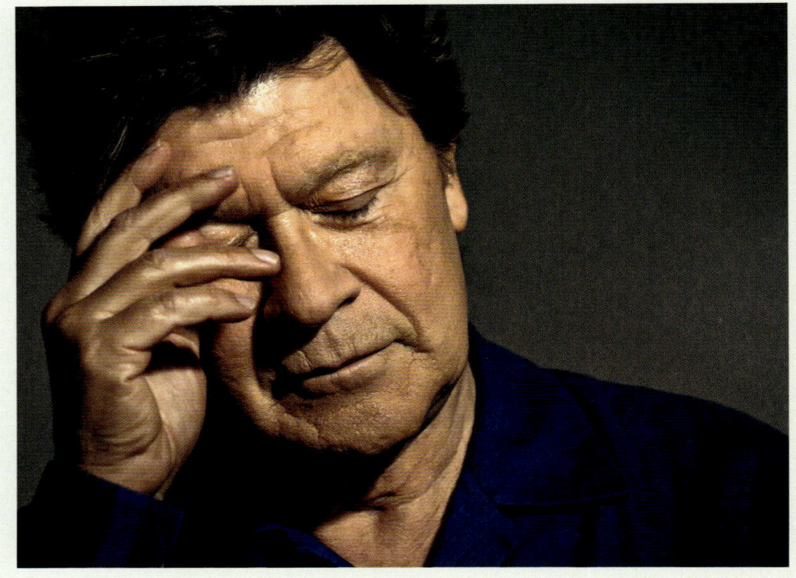

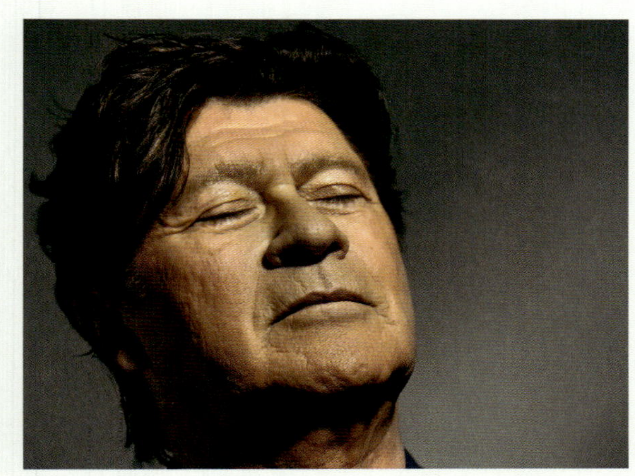

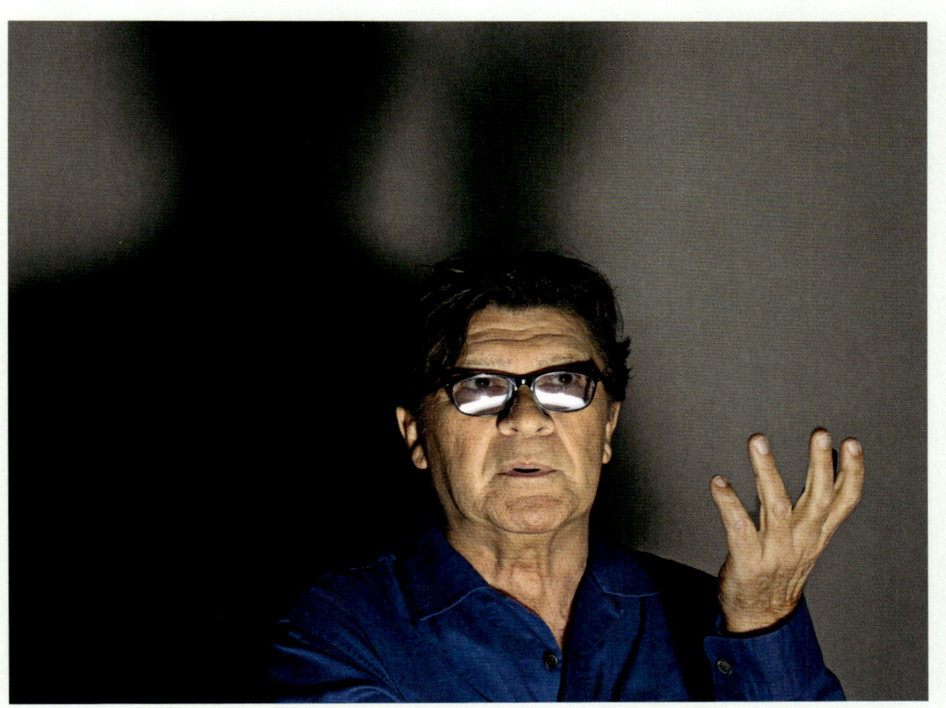

GAVIN ROSSDALE at home, Los Angeles, California, January 7, 2011

Jay Z – *99 Problems*
Gabriel Fauré – *Requiem in D minor*
Zola Jesus – *Trust Me*

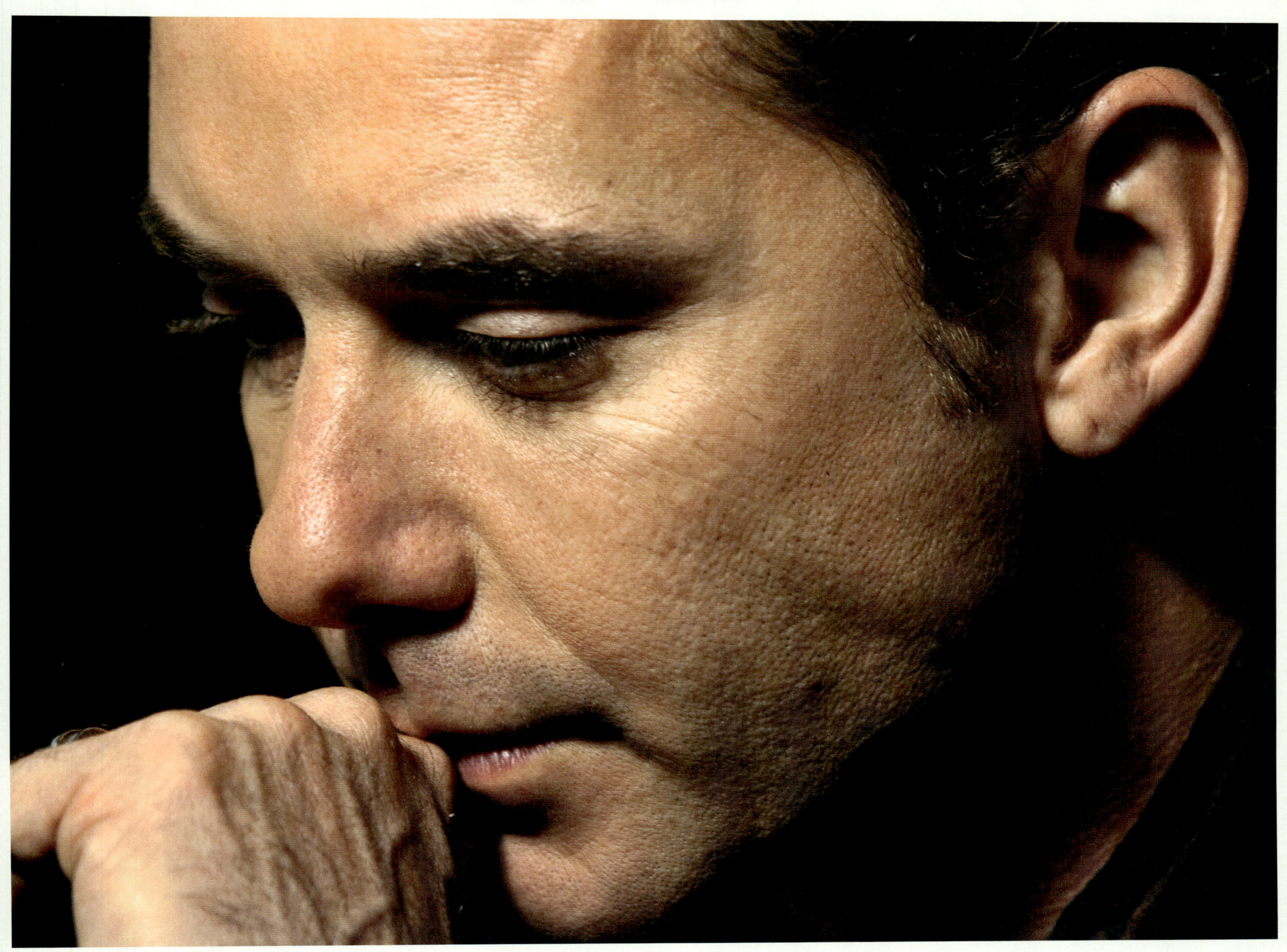

Gavin Rossdale's melodic, guitar-laced music with his rock band Bush may have represented the conservative end of the post-grunge movement led by Nirvana, Pearl Jam, NIN and others, but hits like "Machinehead" or "Swallowed" helped the band sell millions of albums. Rossdale parlayed movie-star good looks and his singular, resonant voice into one of the few enduring careers to emerge from that brief, evanescent pure-rock 90s outburst. After four albums, London-born Rossdale dissolved the band to re-emerge two years later with the abrasive hard rock of *Institute*, a more radical experiment that Rossdale later admitted was actually a solo album disguised as a group effort. His subsequent official 2008 solo debut, *Wanderlust*, featured a piano-led ballad, "Love Remains the Same," that became his first hit record of the new century. He reformed Bush after an eight-year hiatus in 2010, and the band has released two albums since. Rossdale, who has dabbled in film and television acting, has also worked on collaborations with theatrical troupe Blue Man Group and Finnish heavy metal band Apocalyptica. In 2014, he joined his wife Gwen Stefani as coach on the television talent show *The Voice*, a rare instance of the married couple mingling their professional lives since before they were married and Bush opened on tour for Stefani's band No Doubt. Married since 2002, they have three sons, Kingston, Zuma and Apollo, and recently announced their separation.

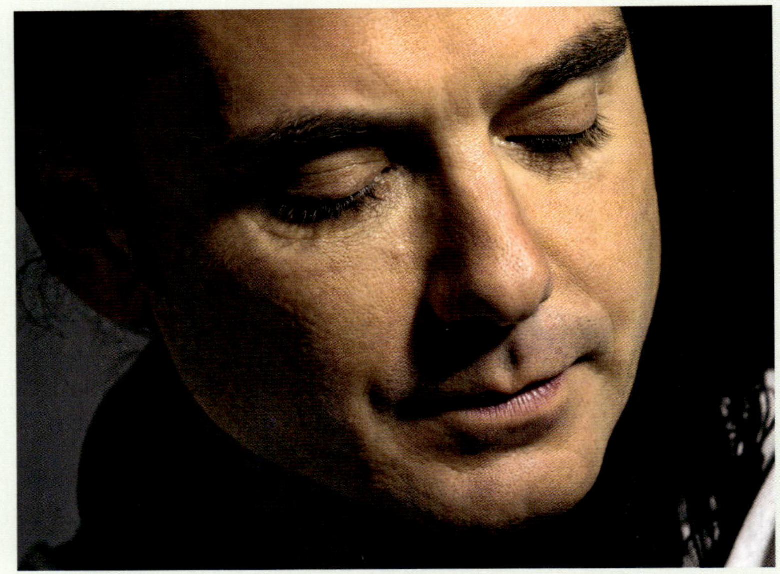

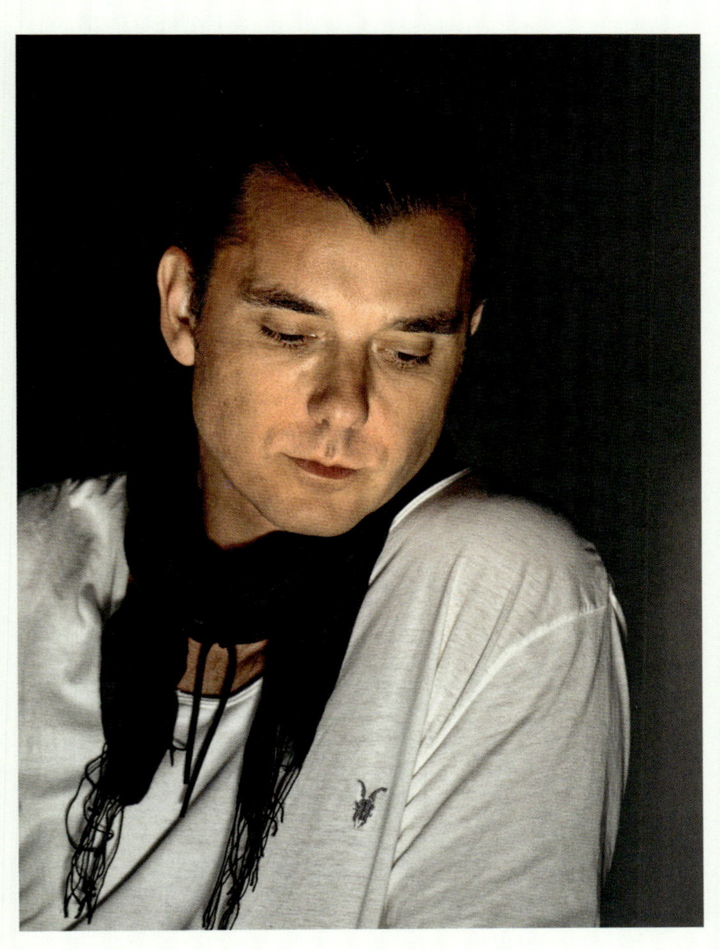

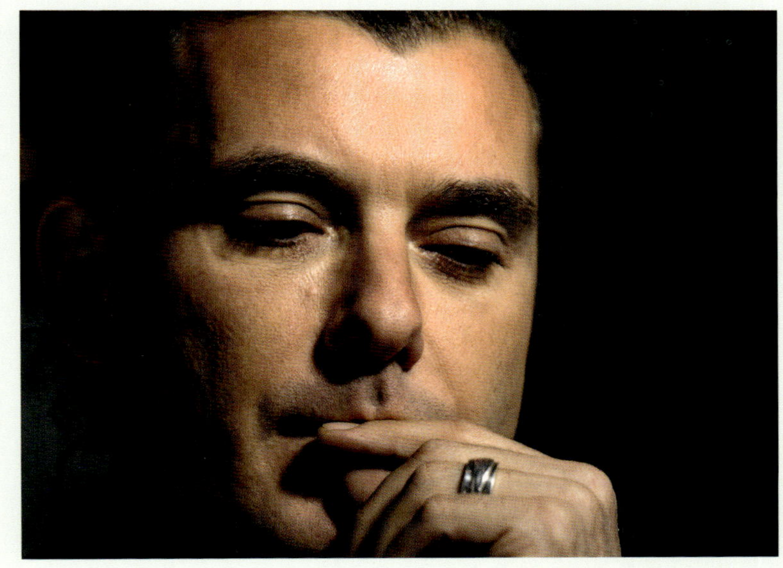

LEON RUSSELL at Le Parker Meridien, New York City, June 15, 2011

Sam Cooke – *Summertime*
Elvis Presley – *When My Blue Moon Turns to Gold Again*
George Jones – *He Stopped Loving Her Today*

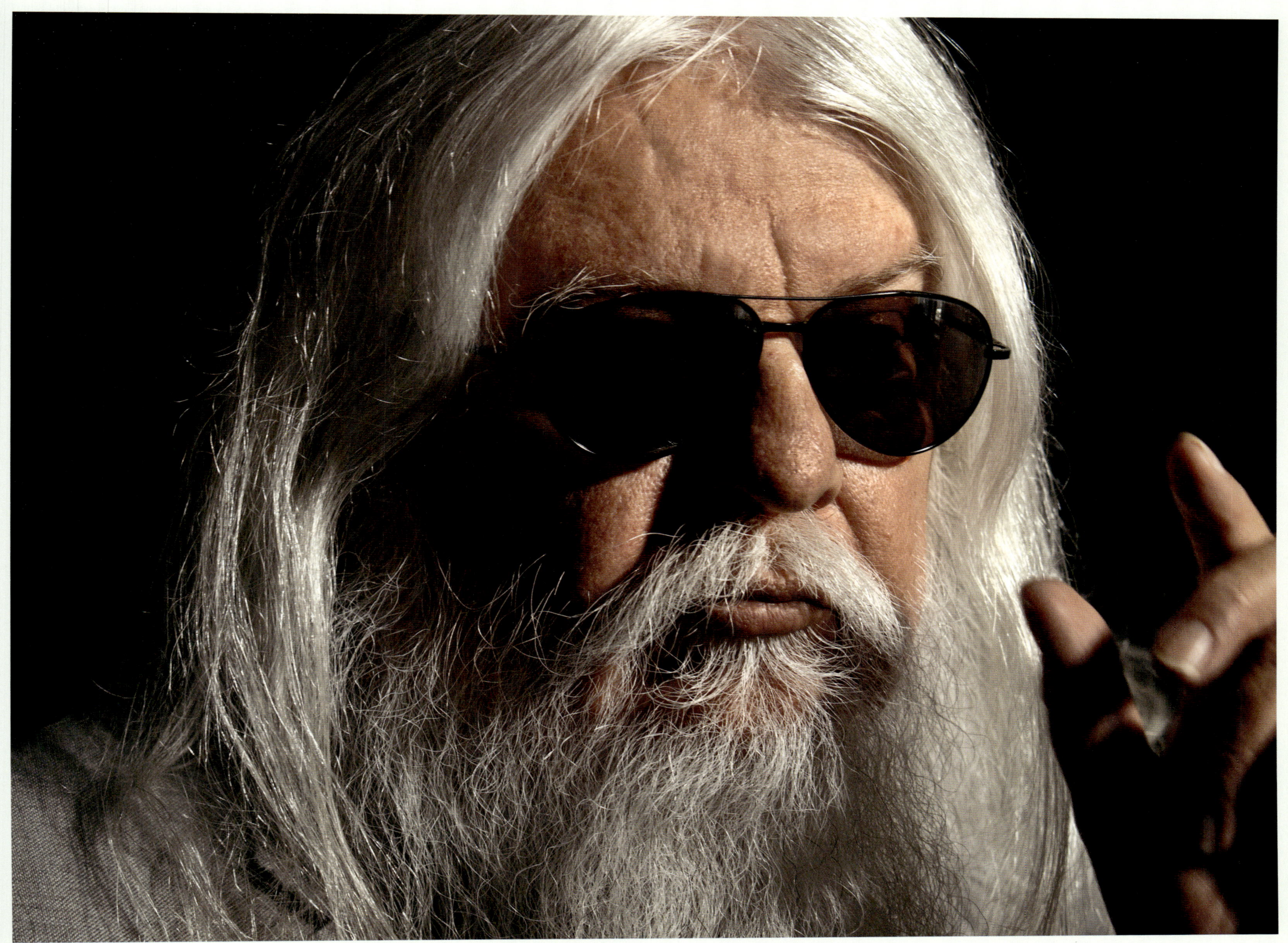

Leon Russell knows singers. His own idiosyncratic vocal style infused everything he sang, including his "A Song for You," a number eventually recorded by more than forty other singers, none of whom sang it the way he did. He started playing music as a teen in Tulsa, Oklahoma, but moved to Los Angeles, where he found success as a studio session pianist. He played on records by Jan and Dean, Glen Campbell, Gary Lewis and the Playboys, producer Phil Spector, and dozens more. As a member of Delaney and Bonnie and Friends, he traveled to England, where he recorded his 1970 debut album with a host of British rock royalty. He was musical director and ringleader of the 1970 Joe Cocker "Mad Dogs and Englishmen" tour. He produced records with Bob Dylan and blues guitarist Freddie King and sang duets with Willie Nelson, but disappeared from the scene. Russell saw his career rejuvenated by Elton John, who recorded a joint album with Russell, *The Union,* in 2009. Russell chose to listen to the sophisticated Sam Cooke version of the "Porgy and Bess" staple that appeared on the B-side of his first big hit, "You Send Me;" a track from the second Elvis Presley album that Elvis featured on one of his historic appearances on *The Ed Sullivan Show;* and the 1980 country weeper that instantly revitalized the moribund career of country music immortal George Jones.

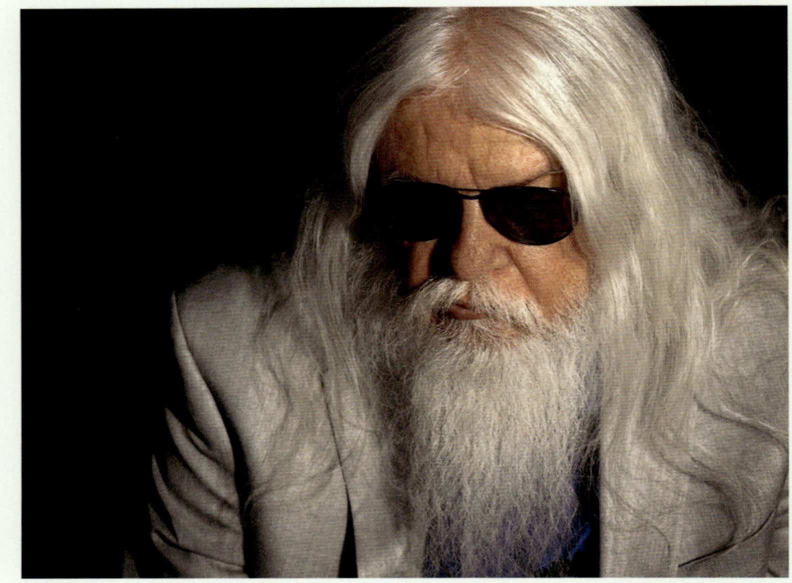

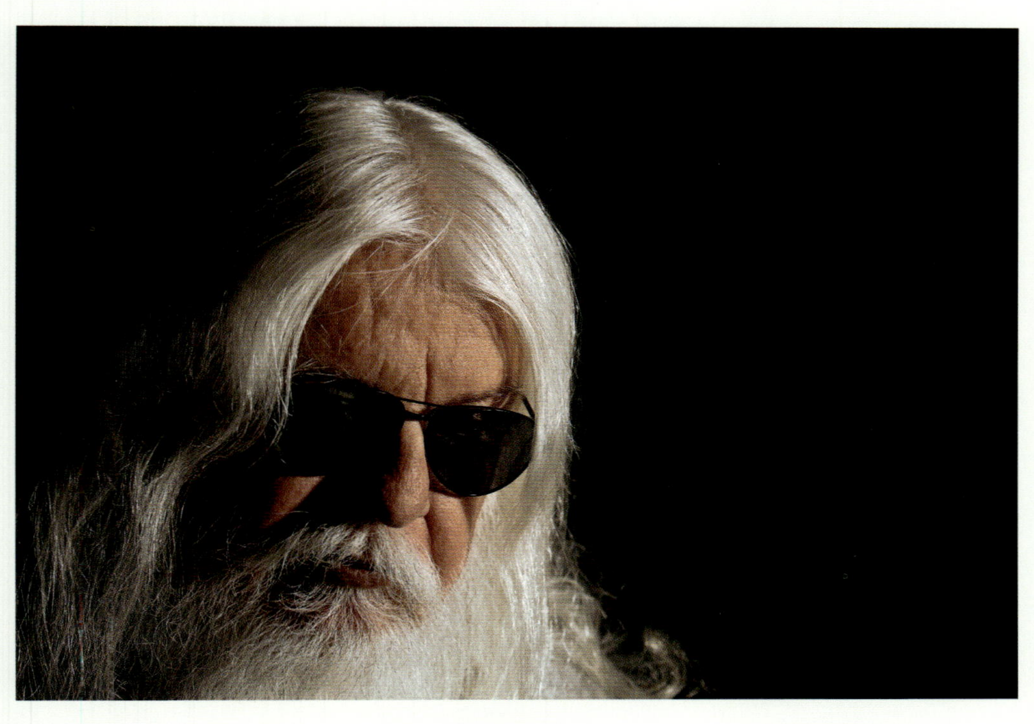

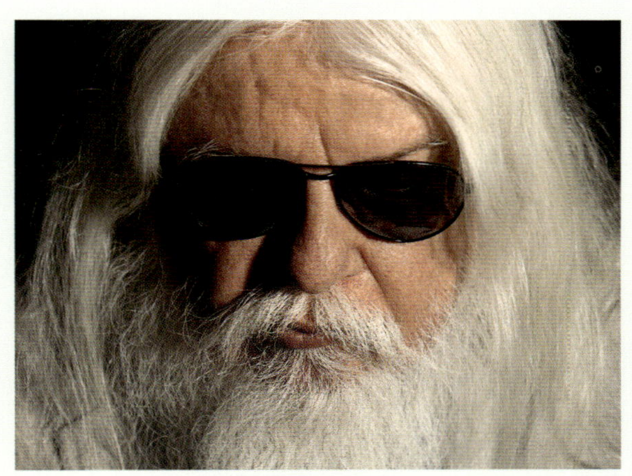

RZA at Shangri-La Studios, Malibu, California, February 9, 2014

Wu-Tang Clan – *C.R.E.A.M. (Cash Rules Everything Around Me)*

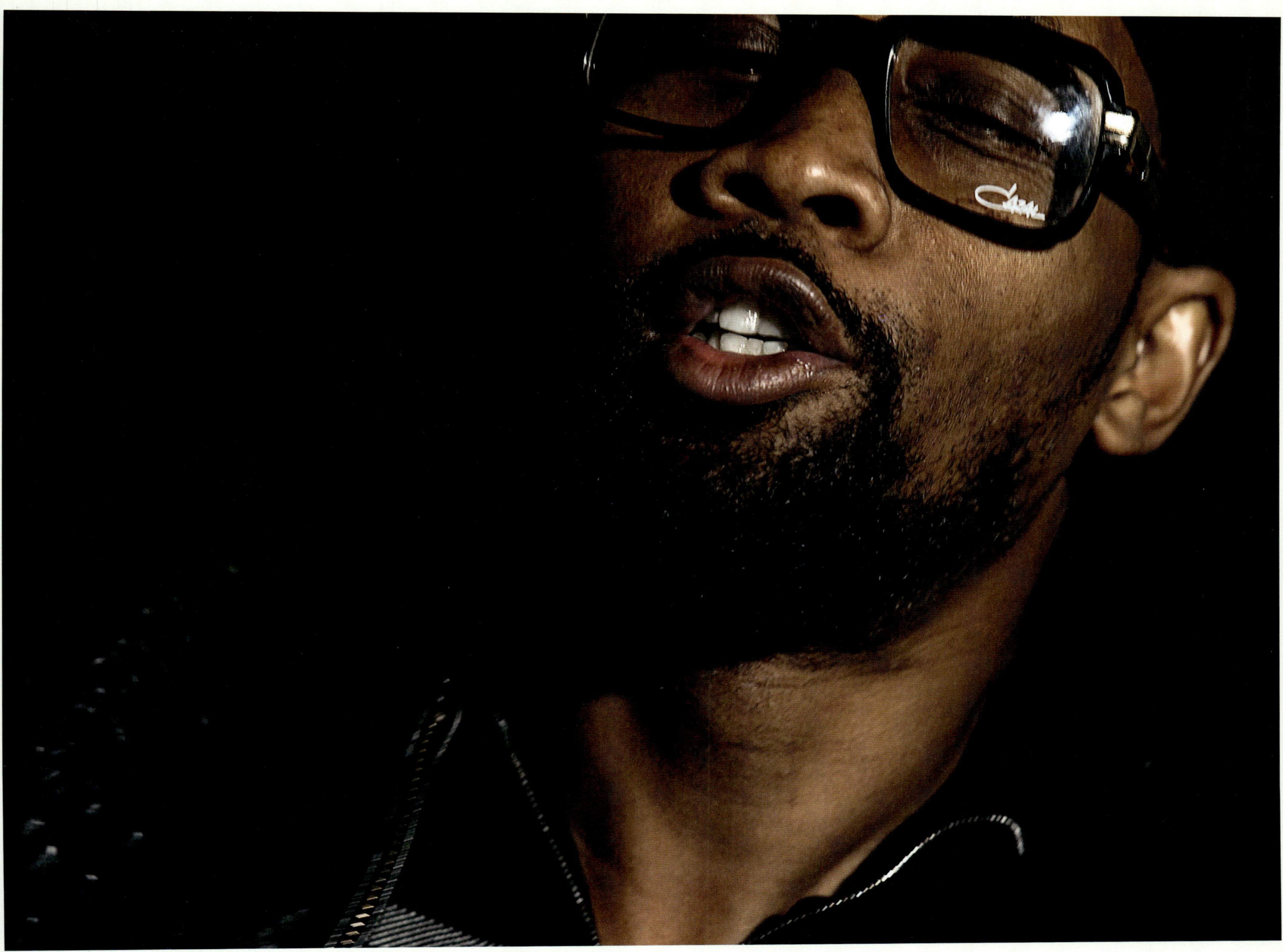

Robert Fitzgerald Diggs—named after both John F. Kennedy and Robert F. Kennedy—is known to one and all as RZA of the Wu-Tang Clan, the hip hop collective he ruled as producer, rapper, songwriter and chief cultural strategist, a position in the hip hop world whose importance cannot be underrated. The group started when a track RZA and his crew cut became an underground hit on the East Coast via mix tapes. He put together Wu-Tang in the early 90s with his cousins Ol' Dirty Bastard and The GZA with some other friends. They named the group after a martial arts movie. The 1993 debut album, *Enter the Wu-Tang (36 Chambers)*, became one of the cornerstone works of hip hop culture and vaulted the group to the front ranks of the field. RZA blossomed into a prodigious creative talent; producer of all the solo projects by Wu-Tang members, solo artist himself, soundtrack composer, business entrepreneur, occasional actor and, with the 2012 film *Man with the Iron Fists*, writer, director and star (with Russell Crowe) of his own fast-paced martial-arts action picture. His trademark production innovation of speeding up samples has been borrowed by Kanye West and many others. For his photo session, RZA selected the key track from his breakthrough masterpiece.

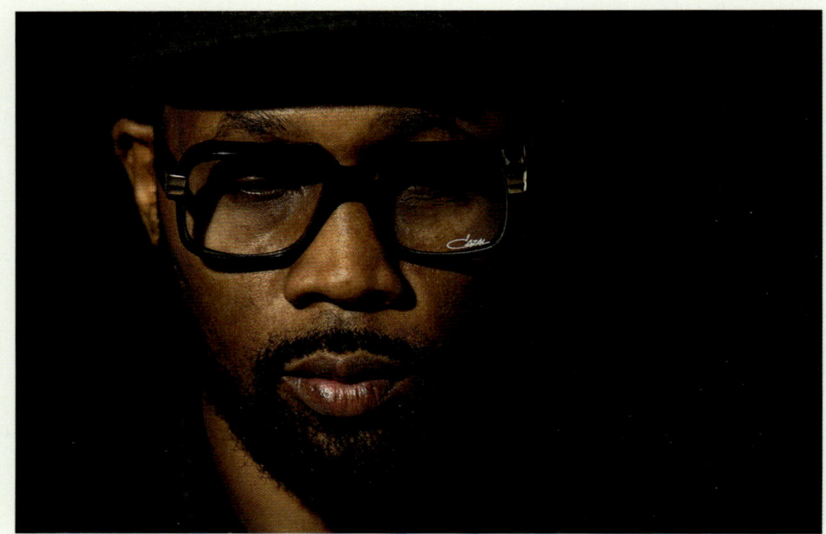

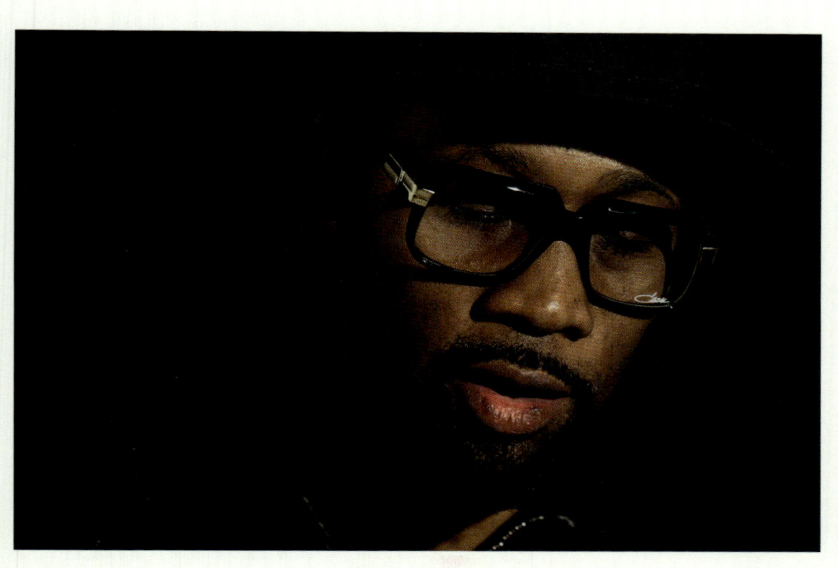

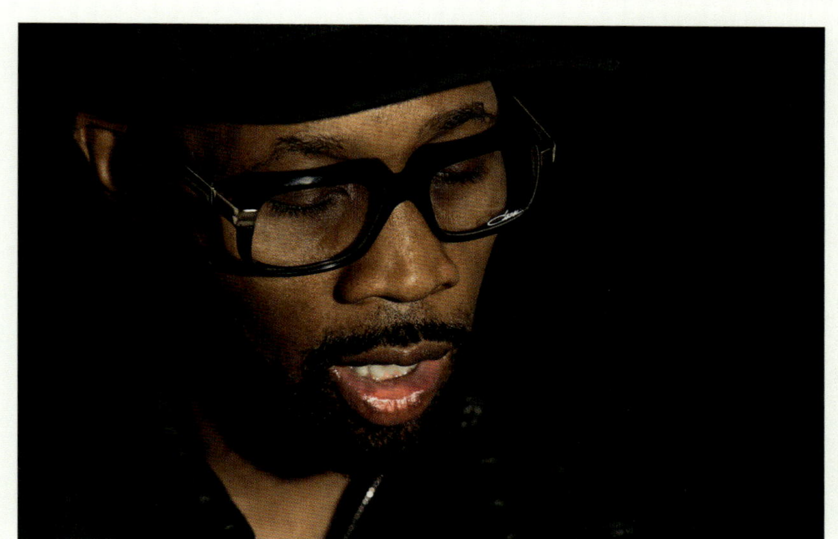

JOE SATRIANI at home, San Francisco, California, November 16, 2013

The Rolling Stones – *Casino Boogie*
The Jimi Hendrix Experience – *Voodoo Child*
The Beatles – *Across the Universe*

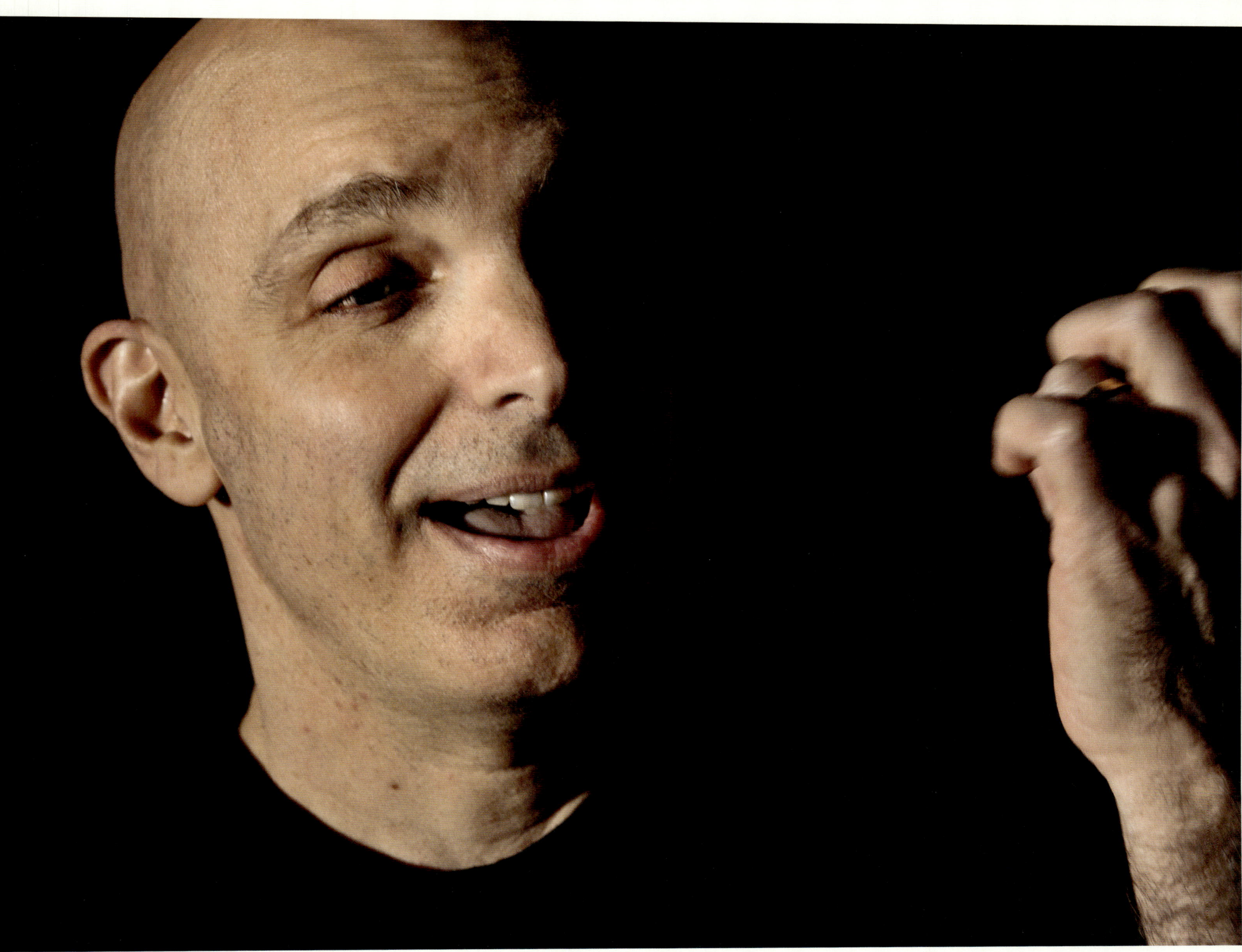

The face that launched a thousand guitar magazines, guitar whiz Joe Satriani has been widely regarded for his accomplished technique and flagrant virtuosity since he burst on the scene with his 1987 breakthrough *Surfing With the Alien*. The most successful guitar instrumentalist in the record business, Satriani took music lessons growing up in Long Island from bebop pianist Lennie Tristano. When he started teaching guitar himself, one of his first students was future rock virtuoso Steve Vai. After Satriani moved to Berkeley, California, in 1978, his students included Kirk Hammett of Metallica. Mick Jagger picked the unknown Satriani as lead guitarist on his 1988 solo tour. He replaced Ritchie Blackmore on a Deep Purple reunion tour. He has toured the world with other guitar greats such as ex-student Vai or Eric Johnson under the banner G3. He supplied lead guitar to Sammy Hagar's frontman bombast in the supergroup Chickenfoot. He continued all along to turn out a steady stream of flawless solo albums, including the track "If I Could Fly," which so closely resembled the subsequent Grammy-winning hit "Viva La Vida" that Coldplay quickly settled the copyright infringement action Satriani brought against the popular group. Whatever he does, his touch on the guitar is as identifiable as a fingerprint, his tone utterly precise and clear and, under his micrometrical control, his visions become flights of fancy.

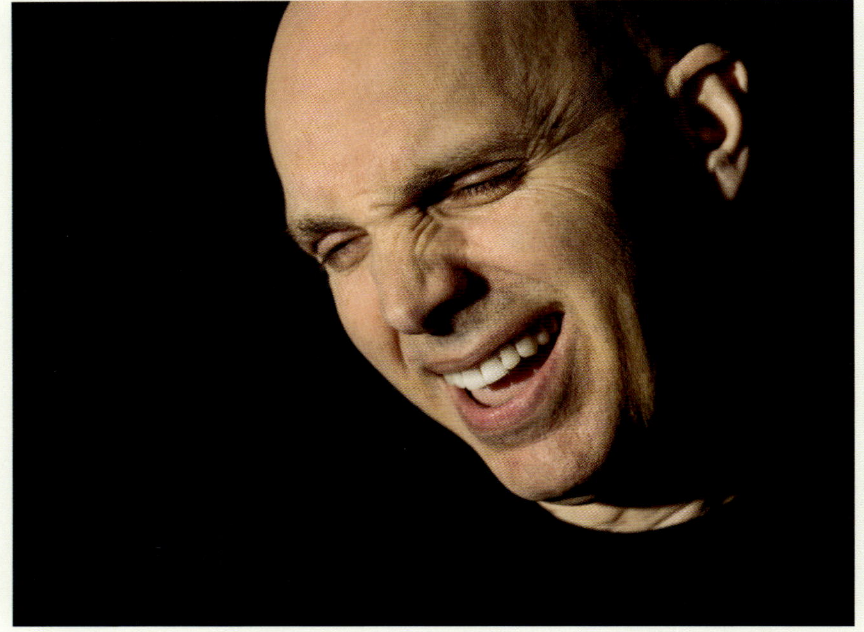

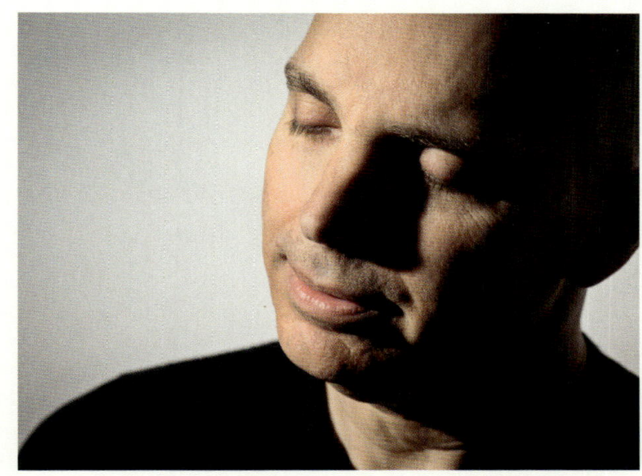

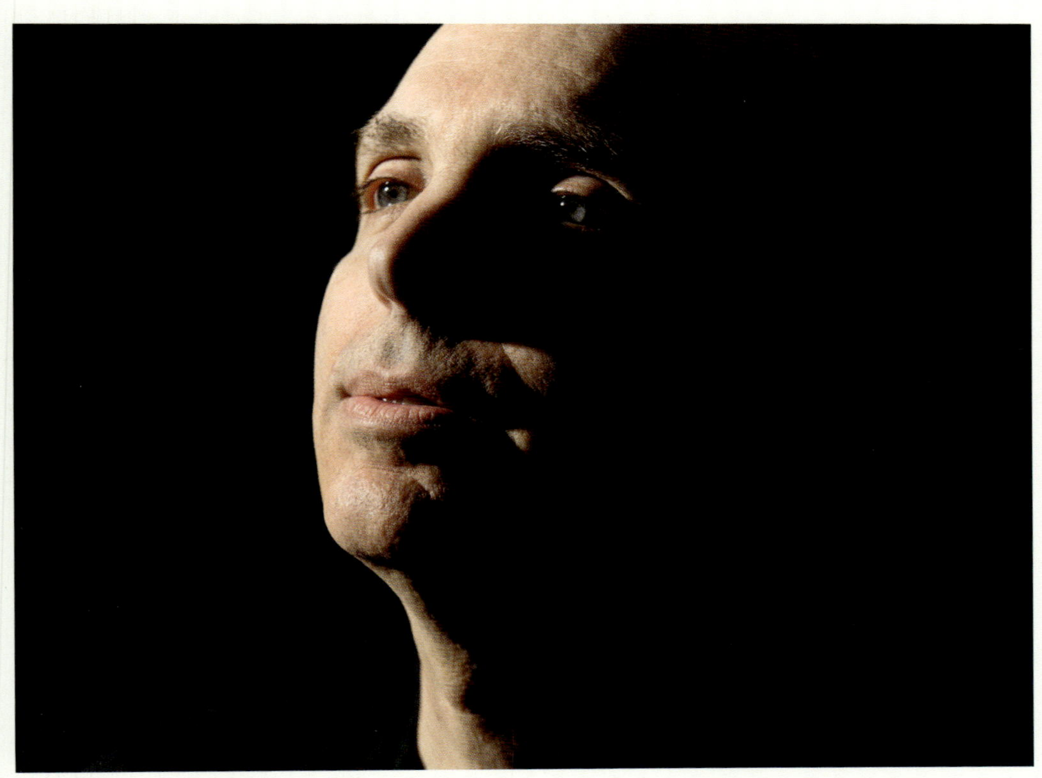

WAYNE SHORTER at home, Los Angeles, California, May 29, 2013

Wayne Shorter – *Forbidden, Plan-It!*

Royal Concertgebouw Orchestra – *Flagships*

Wayne Shorter – *Aurora Leigh* (performed by Renée Fleming and the St. Louis Symphony Orchestra)

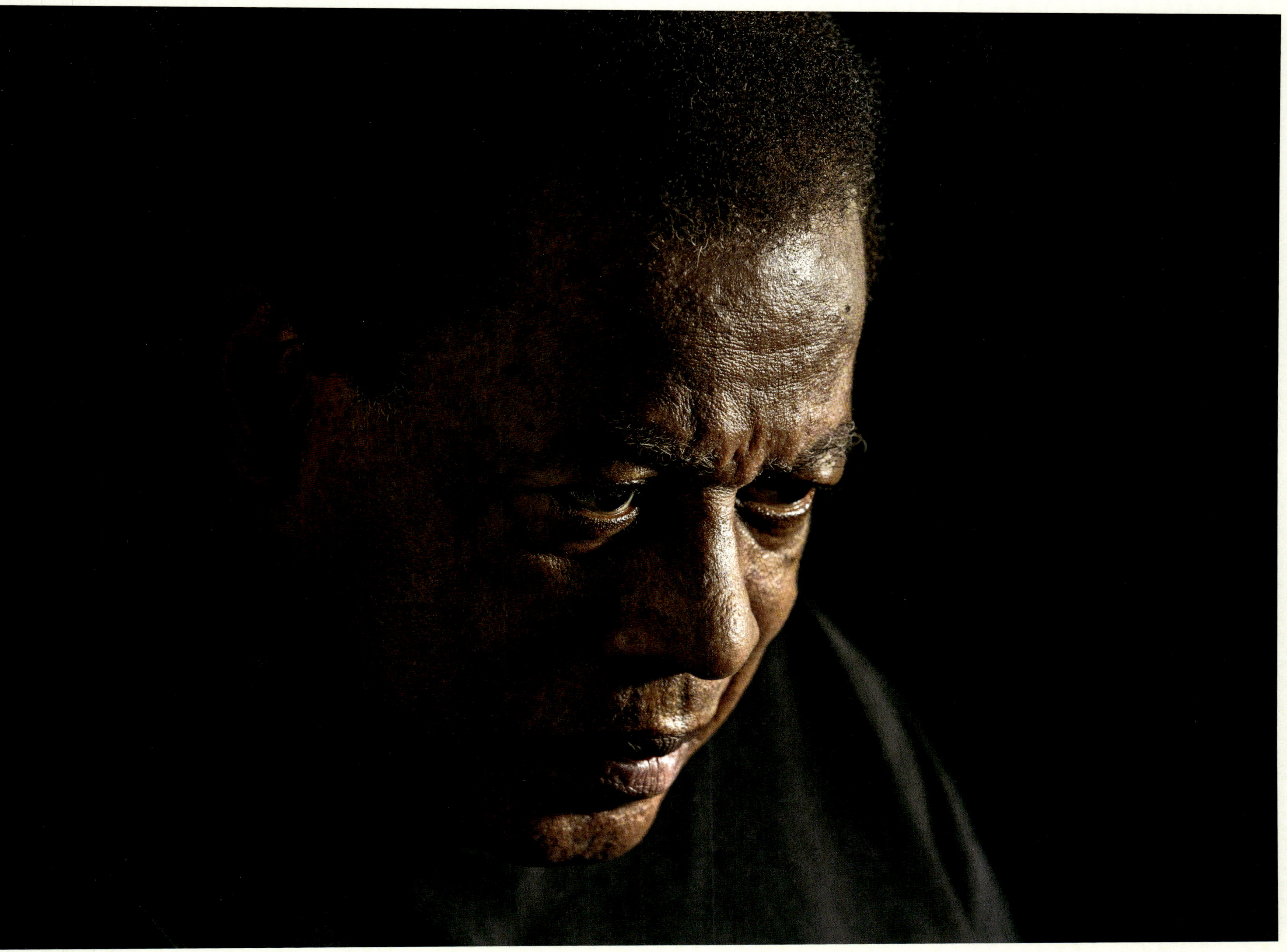

One of jazz' greatest composers and top improvisers, saxophonist Wayne Shorter brought the lyrical beauty and dramatic dynamics of big band jazz to small combos. He started out with Art Blakey and the Jazz Messengers in 1959 and soon was serving as the band's musical director. When John Coltrane left Miles Davis in 1960, he recommended Shorter as his replacement, but Shorter was unavailable. In 1964, Davis was able to convince Shorter to join what came to be called the Second Great Quintet, where he played with Davis alongside pianist Herbie Hancock, bassist Ron Carter and drummer Tony Williams for the next four years, producing some of the greatest work in Davis' epic catalog. After the quintet broke up, Shorter continued with Davis through the jazz fusion experiments *In a Silent Way* and *Bitches Brew*. He started the landmark jazz fusion group Weather Report in 1970 with keyboardist Joe Zawinul and produced a stunning series of provocative albums over the course of fifteen years. Shorter was also finding time to record solo albums, play as a sideman and reunite the classic Miles Davis quintet as V.S.O.P. He played on ten Joni Mitchell albums, recorded extensively with guitarist Carlos Santana, and played a lengthy solo on the title track to the album *Aja* by Steely Dan. In 2000, he formed the Wayne Shorter Quartet and was awarded a Lifetime Achievement Award by the Grammys in 2015, after winning his 11th Grammy. All the compositions he selected were written by Shorter.

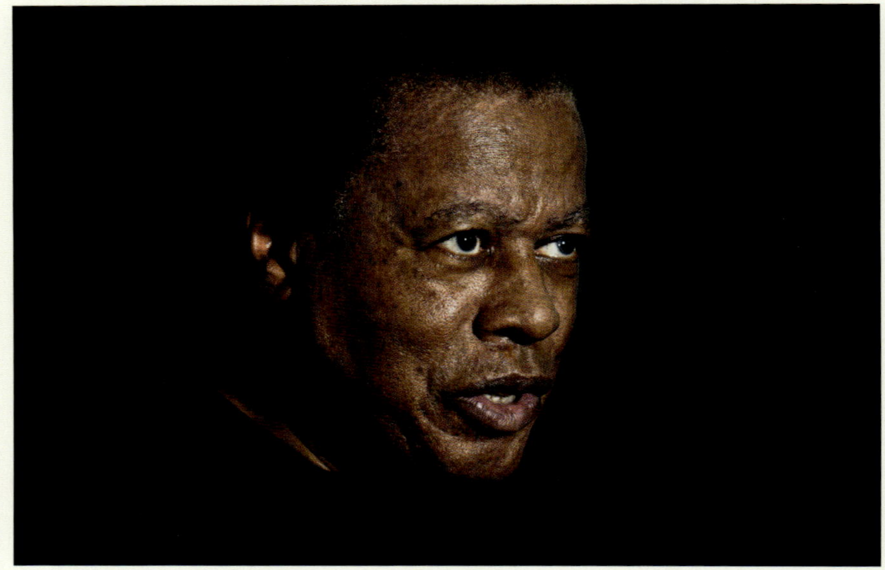

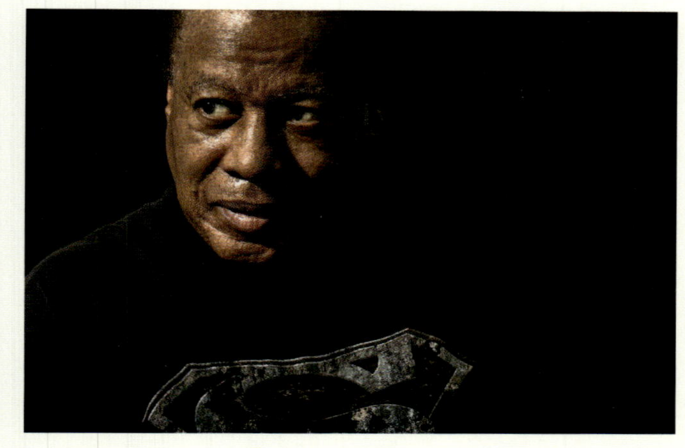

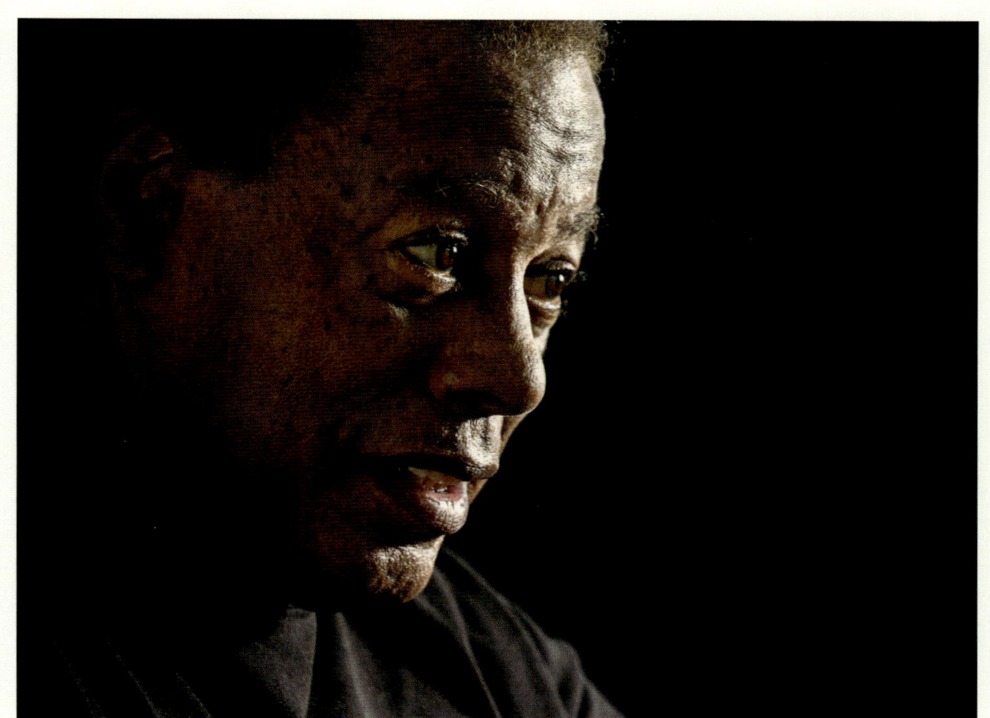

ESPERANZA SPALDING at The Fonda Theater, Los Angeles, April 27, 2012

Nina Simone – *Wild Is the Wind*
Nina Simone – *Lilac Wine*
Dmitri Shostakovich – *Piano Trio No. 2 in E minor, Op. 67*

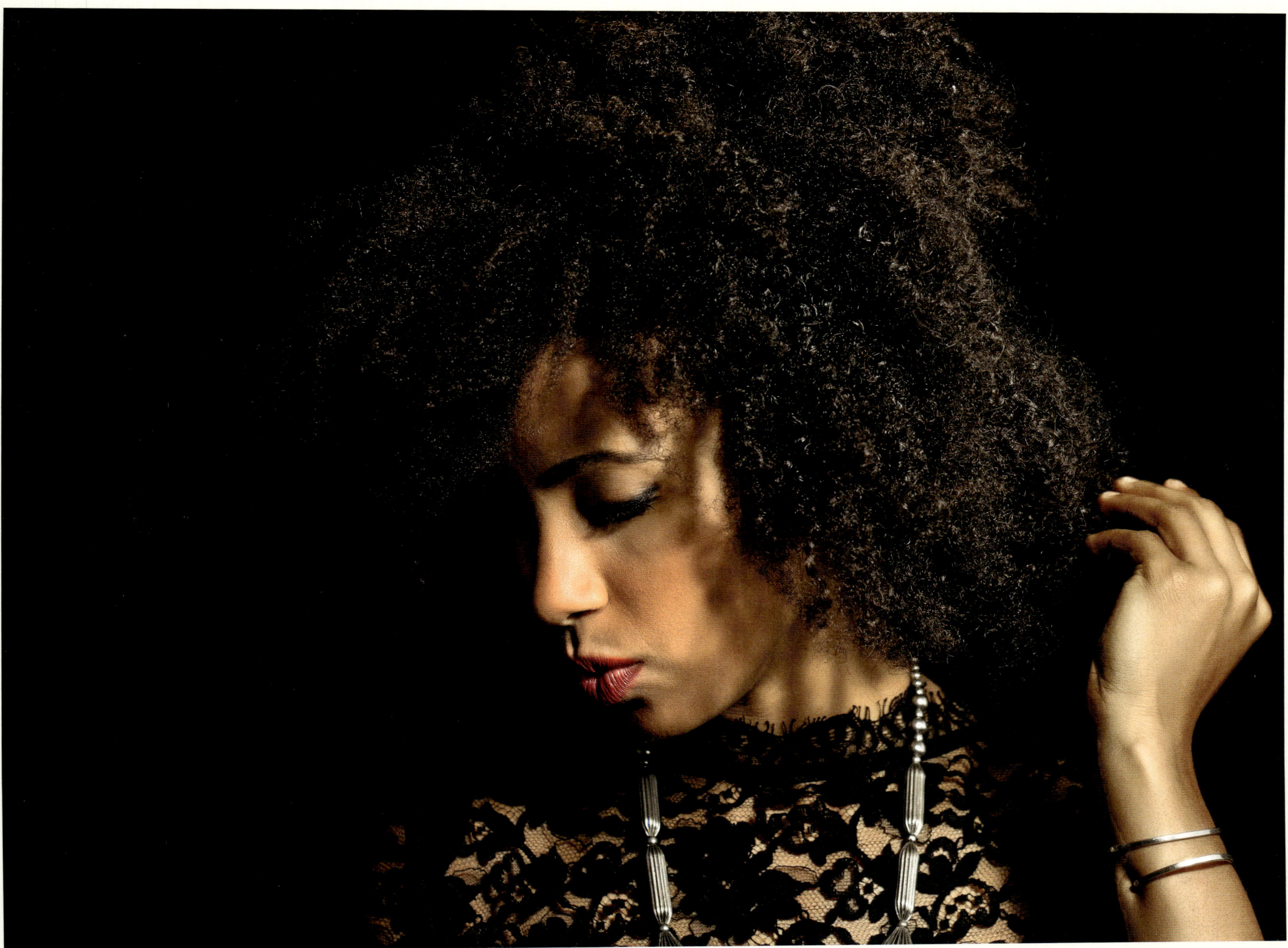

The most exciting new talent in jazz for years, wooly-haired Esperanza Spalding burst on the scene stealing the Best New Artist Award at the 2011 Grammys from the formidable likes of Justin Bieber, Drake, Florence + the Machine, and Mumford & Sons. Her light, airy voice and hard-charging melodic bass playing mark both her own music and collaborations; she has recorded duets with Janelle Monáe and Bruno Mars, among others. Her third album, *Chamber Music Society,* was the bestselling jazz record of 2011. President Obama invited her to perform at his Nobel Prize reception in Oslo. Raised by a part-Brazilian single mother in a hard-scrabble neighborhood of Portland, Oregon, she taught herself to play violin at the age of five after seeing Yo-Yo Ma perform on "Sesame Street." Although she earned a full scholarship to Berklee College of Music, financial hardships caused her to think about dropping out. Guitarist and Berklee faculty member Pat Metheny was one of the people who convinced her to stay. Vocalist Patti Austin hired her to tour while she was still in college, and eventually her touring commitments did lead her to leave school, while her career flourished. She sings in English, Spanish and Portuguese and describes her career as a cross between Madonna and Ornette Coleman.

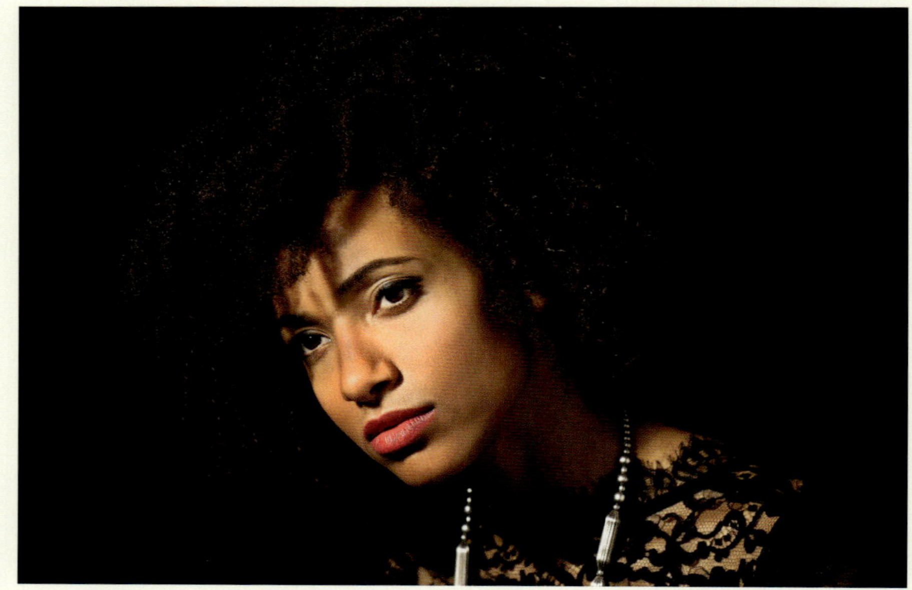

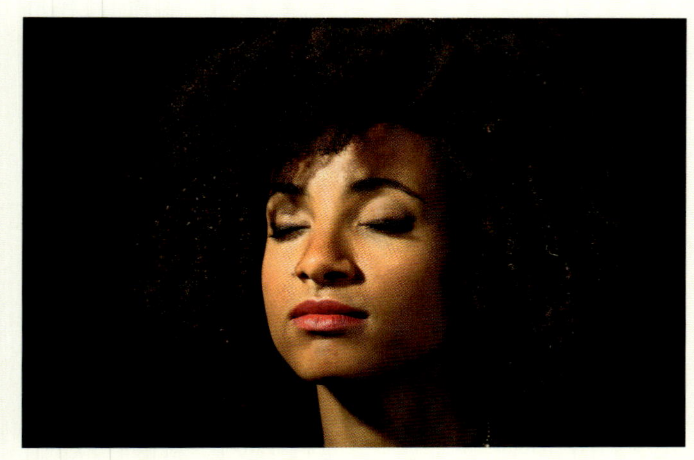

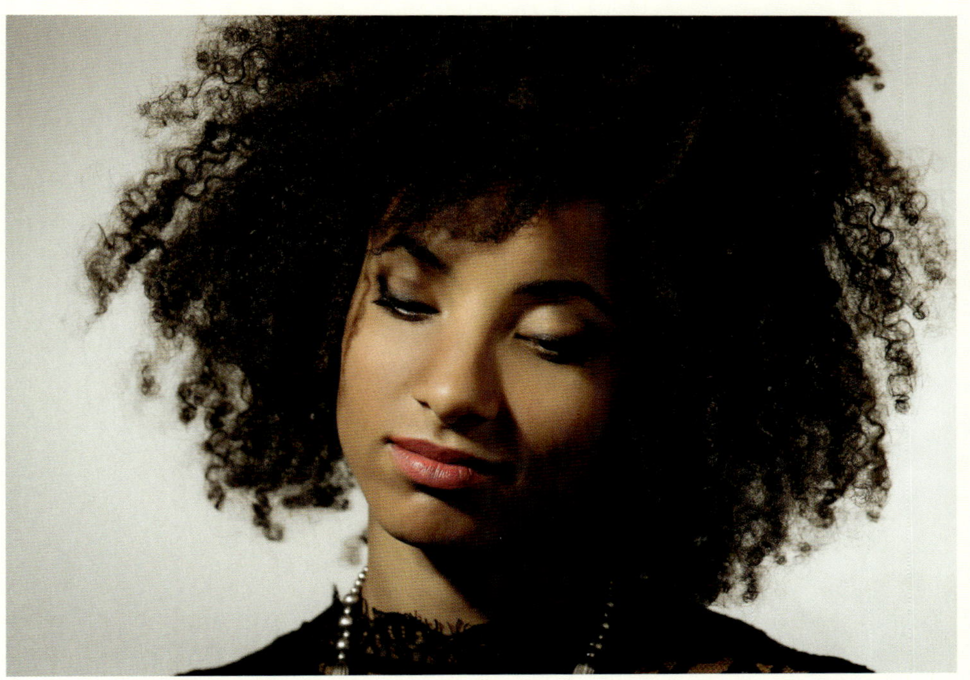

RINGO STARR at home, Los Angeles, California, March 10, 2012

The Beatles – *Come Together*
T. Rex – *Bang a Gong*

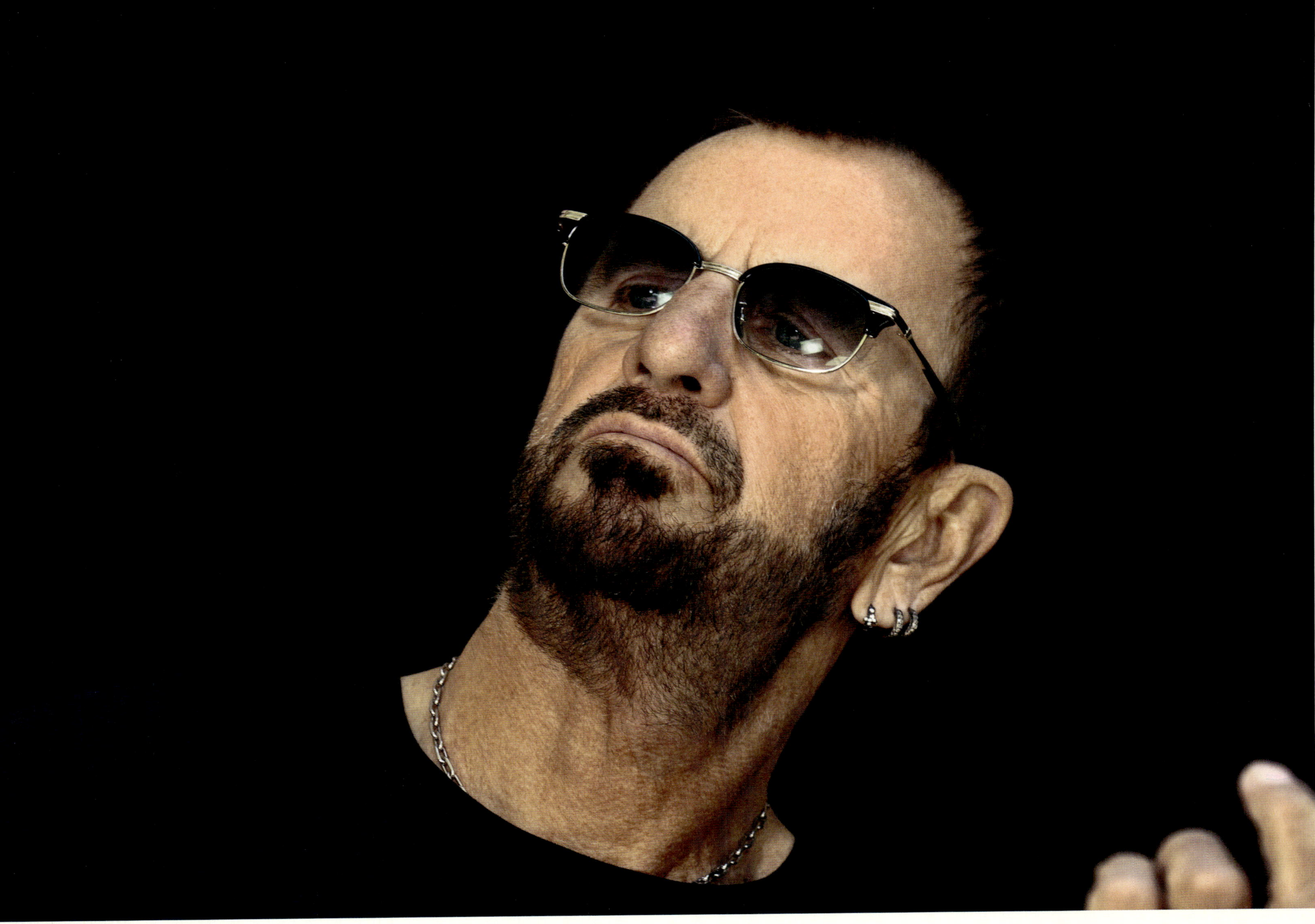

Richard Starkey, the once-and-forever Ringo Starr, was known to The Beatles as drummer for Rory Storm and The Hurricanes, a competing beat group on the early days of the Liverpool scene. He joined the band only a few weeks before The Beatles' first recording session, and became rock's most distinguished and beloved drummer. Since the demise of The Beatles, Ringo has made hit solo albums, appeared in films and TV and led a loose repertory group under the banner Ringo's All-Starr Band around concert stages of the world the past couple of decades. His dry wit, unblinking candor and wry good humor have made him one of rock's most appealing personalities, elfin and earnest enough to host a children's TV show, *Shining Time Station*, as well as be married to a former Bond girl. Ringo was one of the few subjects to listen to his own music for the photo session and it can hardly be surprising he picked "Come Together;" his rolling tom-toms are an important compositional element in the whole piece. It is a brilliant example of his collaborative gifts. As for T. Rex, Ringo once directed a documentary film about T. Rex star Marc Bolan. In 2015, he was the fourth member of The Beatles to be inducted into the Rock and Roll Hall of Fame twice, this time as an individual, the award presented by Sir Paul McCartney.

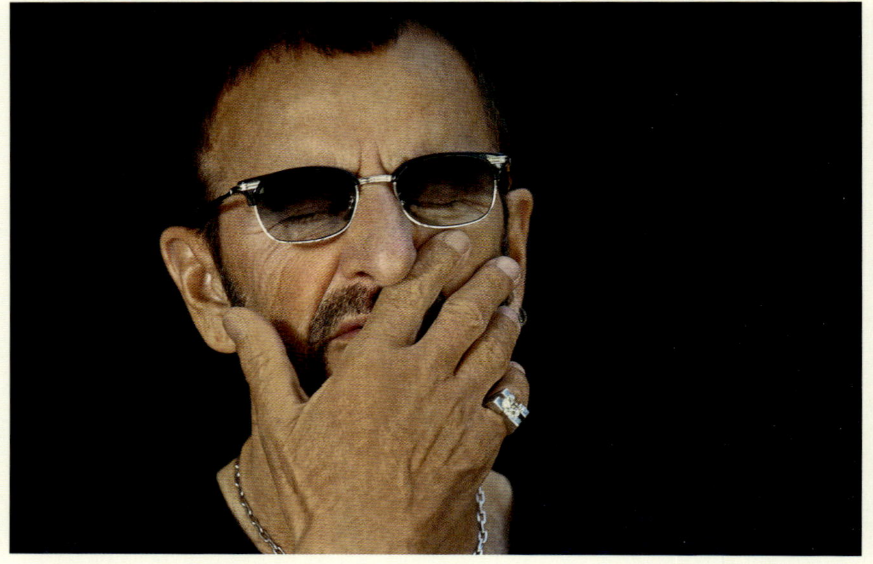

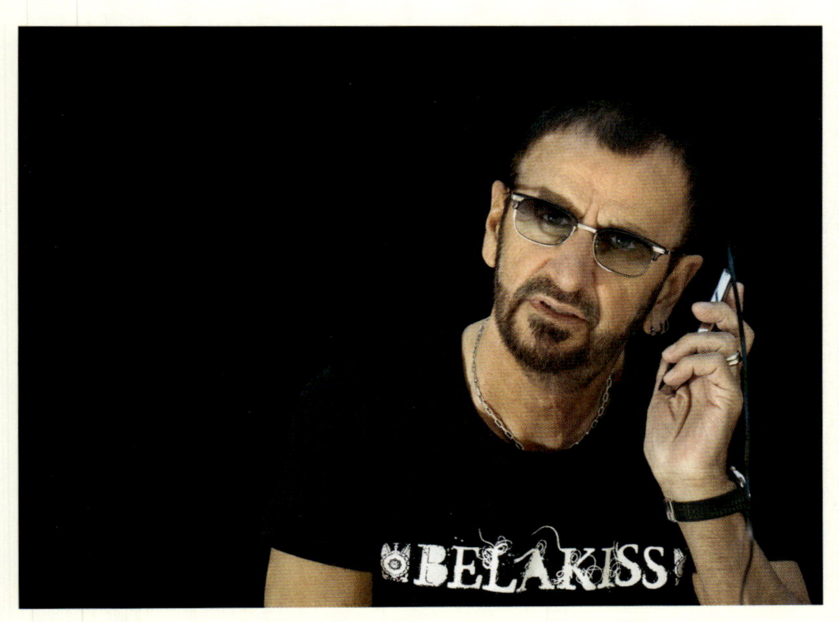
BELAKISS

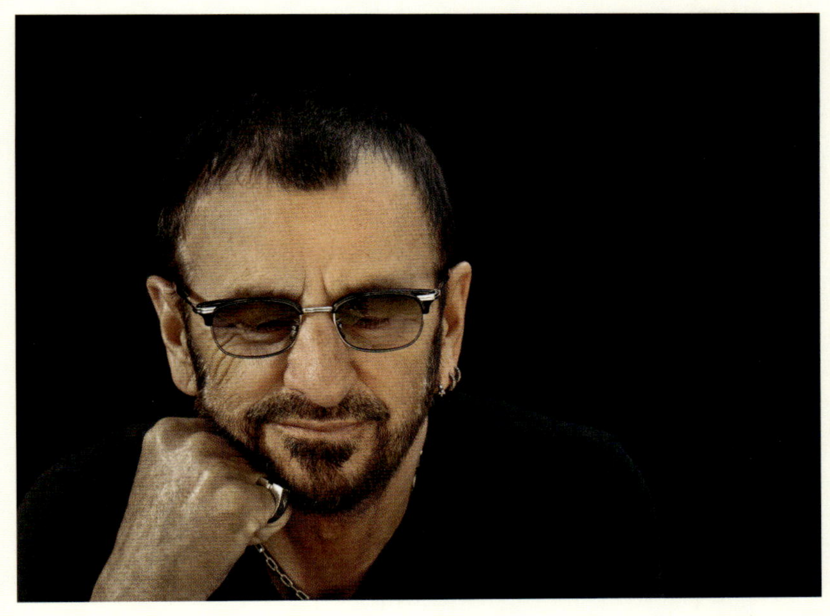

JEAN-YVES THIBAUDET at home, Los Angeles, California, September 10, 2014

Lana Del Rey – *Shades of Cool*

Beyoncé – *Haunted*

Frédéric Chopin – *Piano Concerto N° 2, second movement* (played by Arthur Rubinstein)

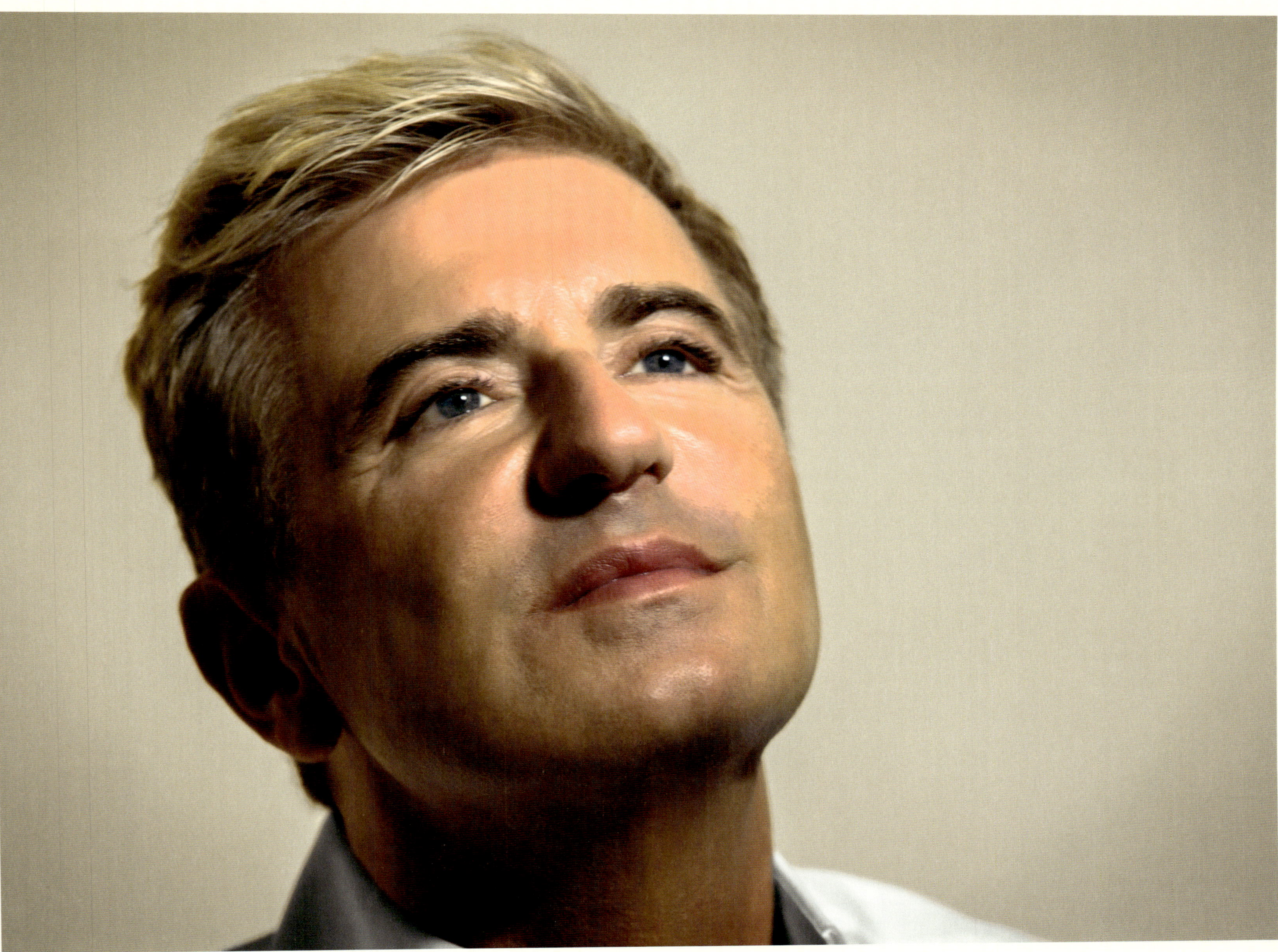

Not the standard starched-shirt variety classical music piano titan, Jean-Yves Thibaudet has rocked the arts and letters crowd for years with his fashion statements by punk designer Vivienne Westwood, excursions into the world of jazz and his own richly atmospheric film soundtrack compositions, not to mention his extraordinary technical command of the instrument. The French-born child prodigy began his musical studies at age five, gave his first performance at age seven and entered the Paris Conservatory at twelve. He has played with virtually every great conductor and symphony orchestra in the world, equally at ease with chamber music as orchestral works. In addition to being known for brilliant interpretations of Romantic composers like Chopin, Liszt, Rachmaninoff and Brahms or the French Impressionists such as Ravel and Debussy, Thibaudet has also recorded albums of Duke Ellington big band jazz, Bill Evans improvisations, and instrumental versions of a number of operas, many of which he transcribed himself. He has done much to promote and preserve the work of composer Erik Satie. His score for the 2005 film *Pride and Prejudice* was nominated for an Oscar. This mighty Frenchman is truly a modern classicist.

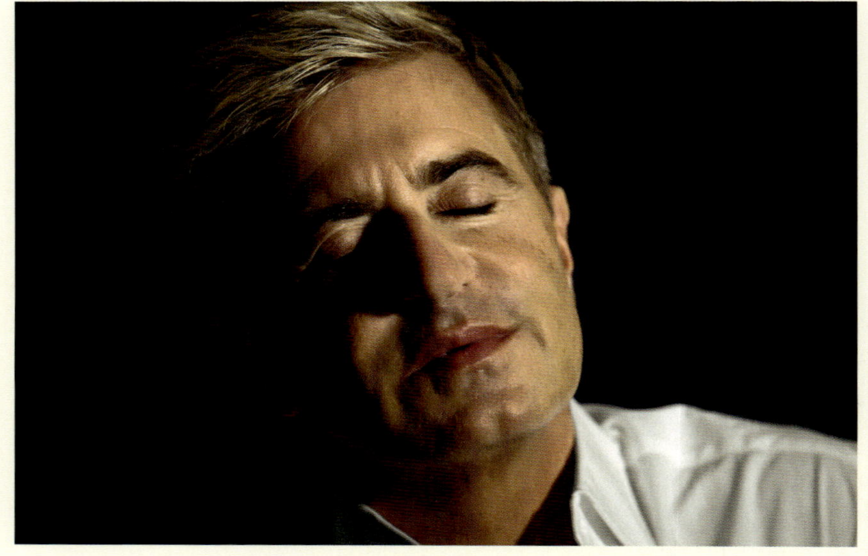

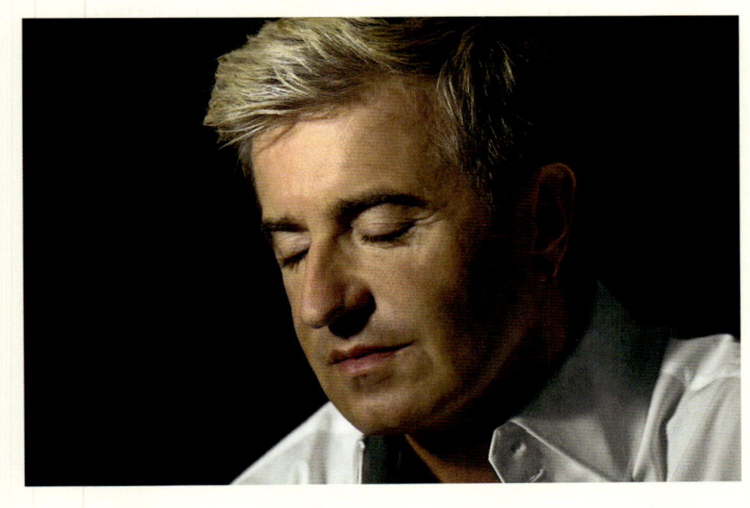

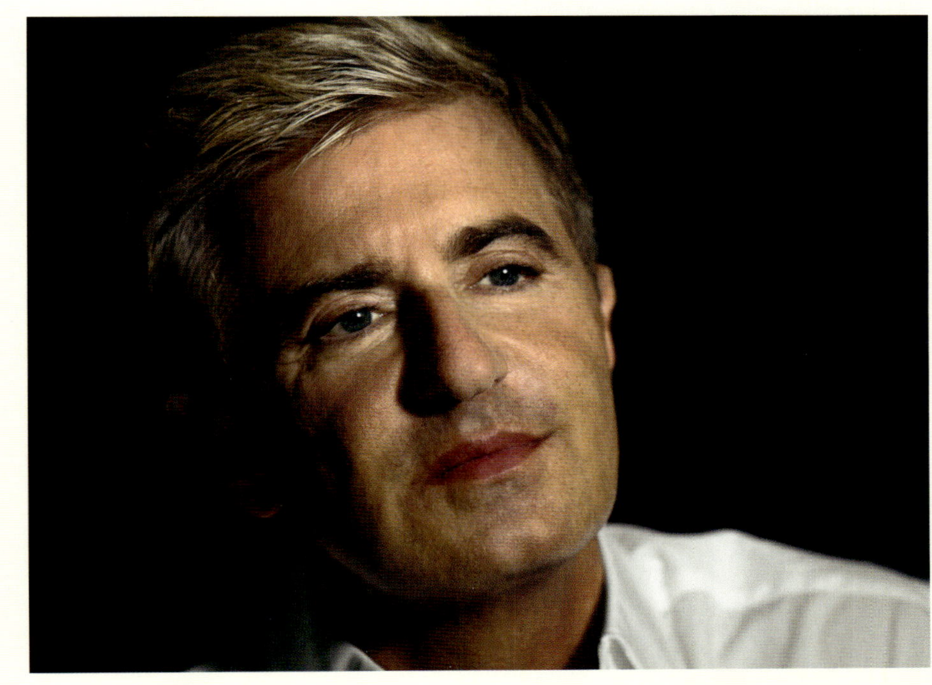

LARS ULRICH at Metallica Studio, San Rafael, California, November 18, 2013

Rage Against the Machine – *Killing in the Name*
Oasis – *Supersonic*
Diamond Head – *Streets of Gold*

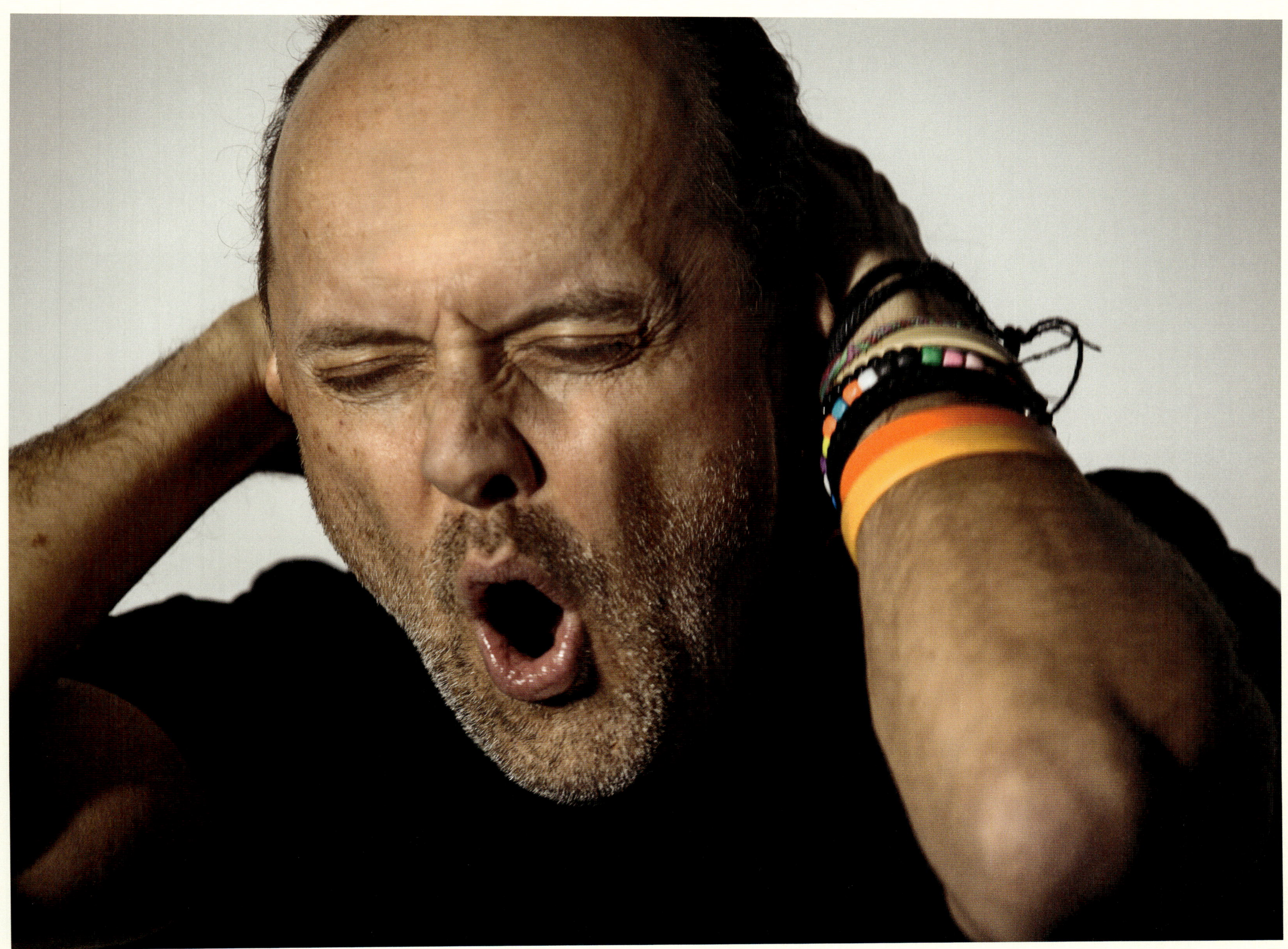

If Metallica founder and drummer Lars Ulrich had not been so successful at actually playing music, he could have been a first-rate rock critic. Ulrich has an encyclopedic knowledge and a voracious enthusiasm for all forms of heavy metal rock. He is not simply a performer; he is a fan. Son of a Danish tennis pro raised around the sporting lifestyles of Southern California, Ulrich attacked his profession with an almost maniacal passion. His drive coupled with the musical vision of guitarist and vocalists James Hetfield have been the twin engines of Metallica since day one. Emerging from the grimy rock underworld of subcultural metal bands, Metallica burst into the rock mainstream in 1988 with the band's fourth album, *And Justice for All,* and wound up taking their imaginative, deeply personal vision of music beyond borders nobody would have thought possible. The 1991 album *Metallica* (also known as "The Black Album") entered the charts at number one and established the band's complete dominance of the field behind a three-year run of constant touring and massive album sales. Surviving the band's brutal regimen and the turbulent internal personal conflicts documented unflinchingly in the 2004 film *Some Kind of Monster,* Metallica, the band that inspired an armada of other bands in their wake, settled into a comfortable, noisy seniority, relaxed enough for collaborations as unexpected as the San Francisco Symphony and Lou Reed.

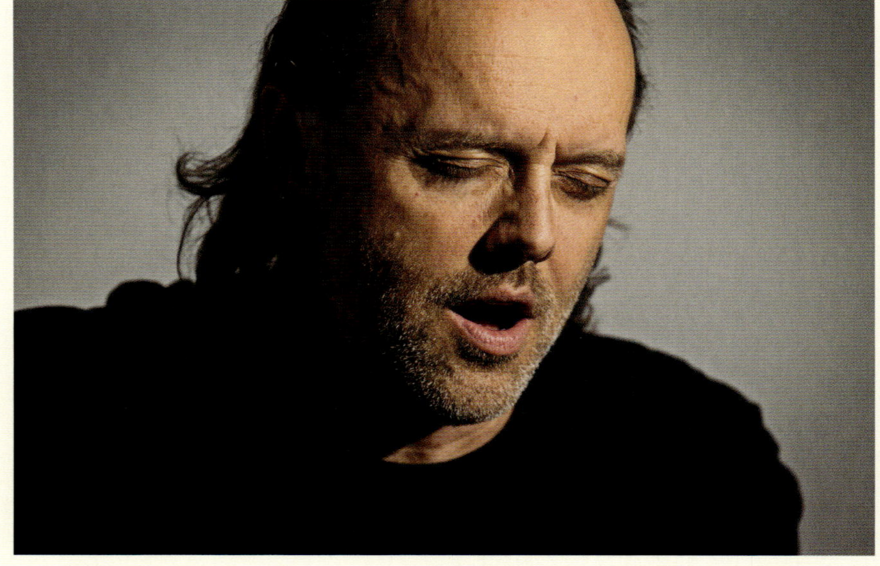

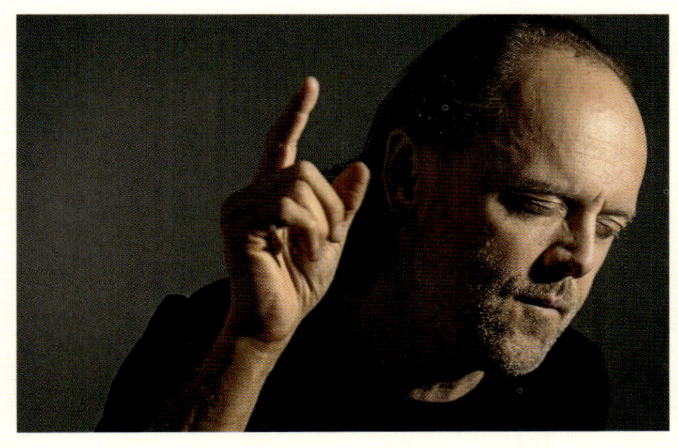

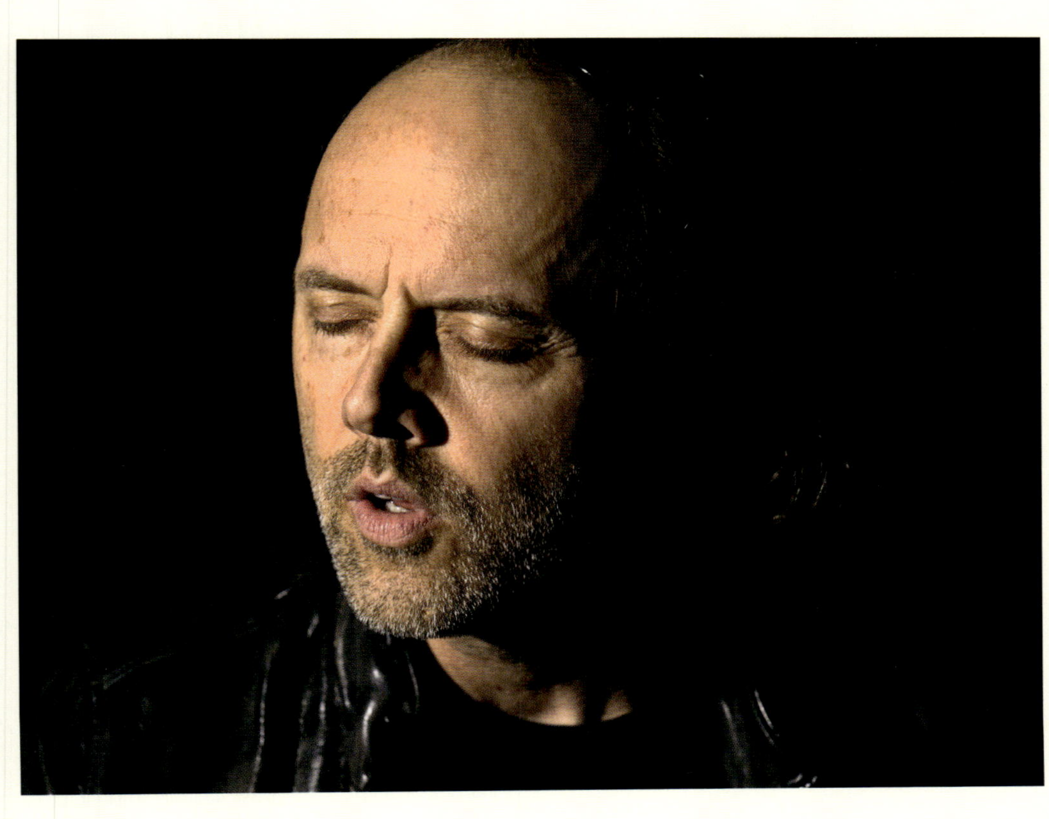

JOE WALSH at home, Bel Air, California, October 28, 2013

Albert King – *Personal Manager*
John Williams – *The Mission* Theme
Groove Armada – *At the River*

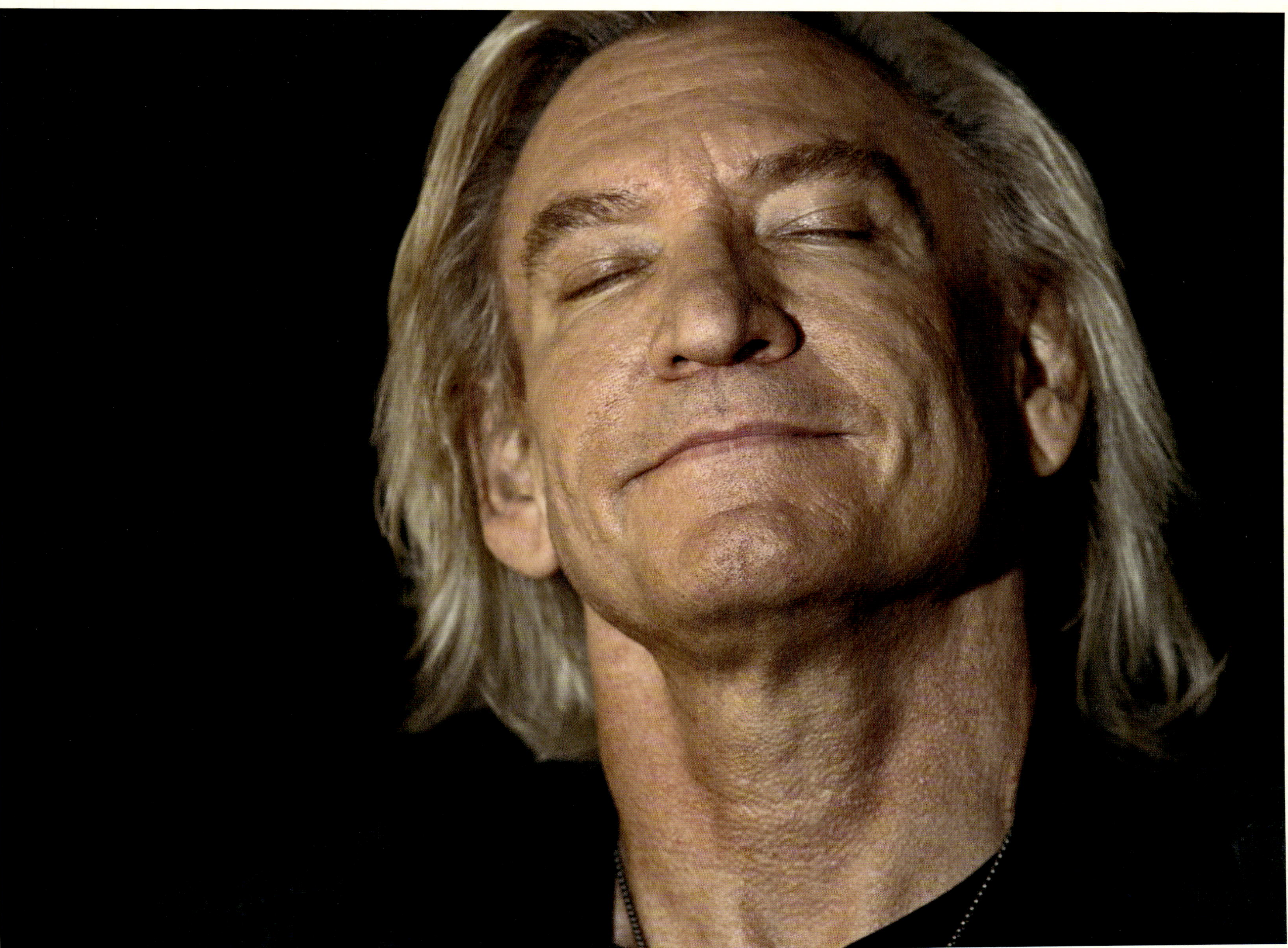

The comic relief among the leading men of The Eagles, Joe Walsh has always been a prankster and fun guy. From his early days in Ohio with the James Gang, "Rocky Mountain Way" and his other solo records, not to mention the occasional curve he throws with The Eagles, Walsh can be counted on for whimsical good humor, original perspectives and true zeal in everything he does. He may have been an unlikely choice to join the already established rock stars, but Walsh instantly cemented his position with his guitar solo on the title track to the band's next album, *Hotel California*. He has additionally lent his irreverent perspective to tours by Australia's The Party Boys and Ringo Starr and his All-Starr Band, briefly toured and recorded with a New Zealand reggae band called Herbs. He did *MTV Unplugged* with New Orleans keyboardist Dr. John. With Joe Walsh, expect the unexpected. Certainly his select-ions for the photo session reflect his unique, unpredictable character—a track from one of the great blues guitar albums of all time, *Born Under a Bad Sign*; the symphonic piece commissioned by John Williams as the TV theme song for "NBC Nightly News;" and a 1997 low-key electronica track from the British club music duo Groove Armada featuring a lazy trumpet solo over a loping electronica beat and a sample from the Patti Page song "Old Cape Cod."

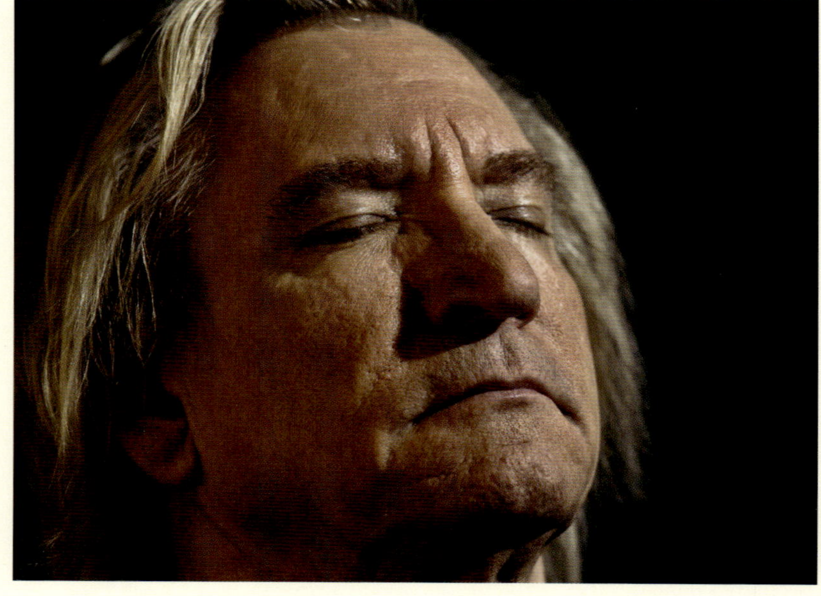

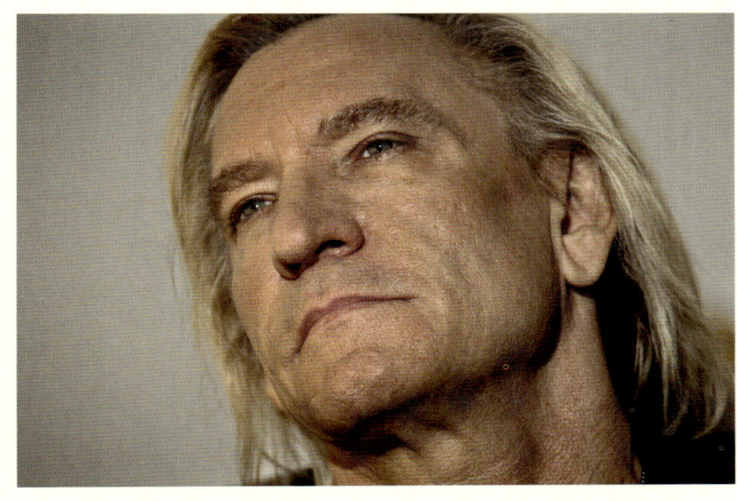

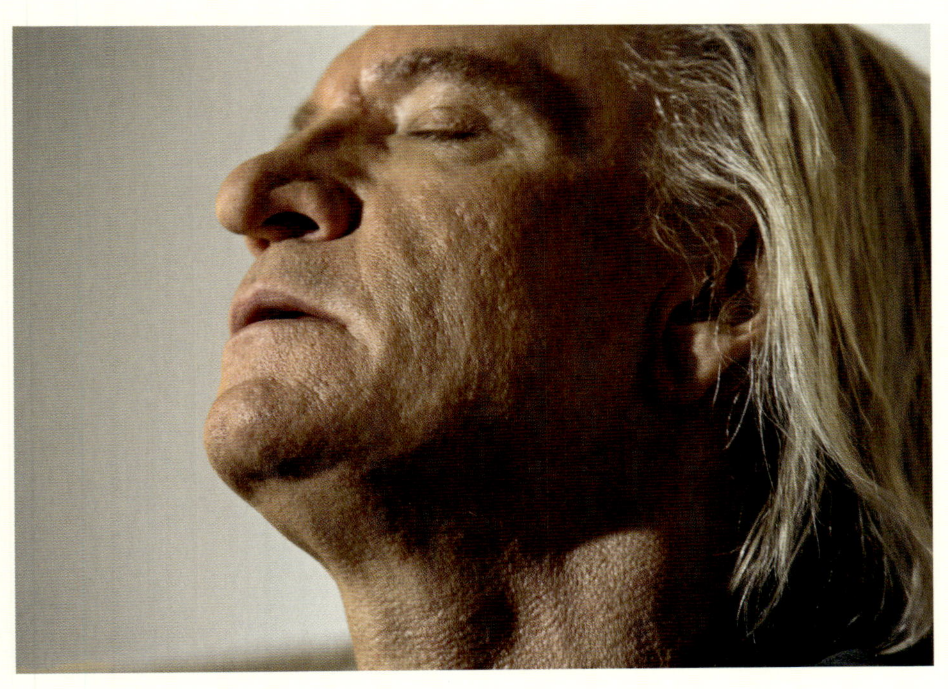

VERDINE WHITE at home, Los Angeles, California, February 5, 2011

James Brown – *Papa's Got a Brand New Bag*
The Beatles – *Come Together*
Miles Davis – *Kind of Blue*

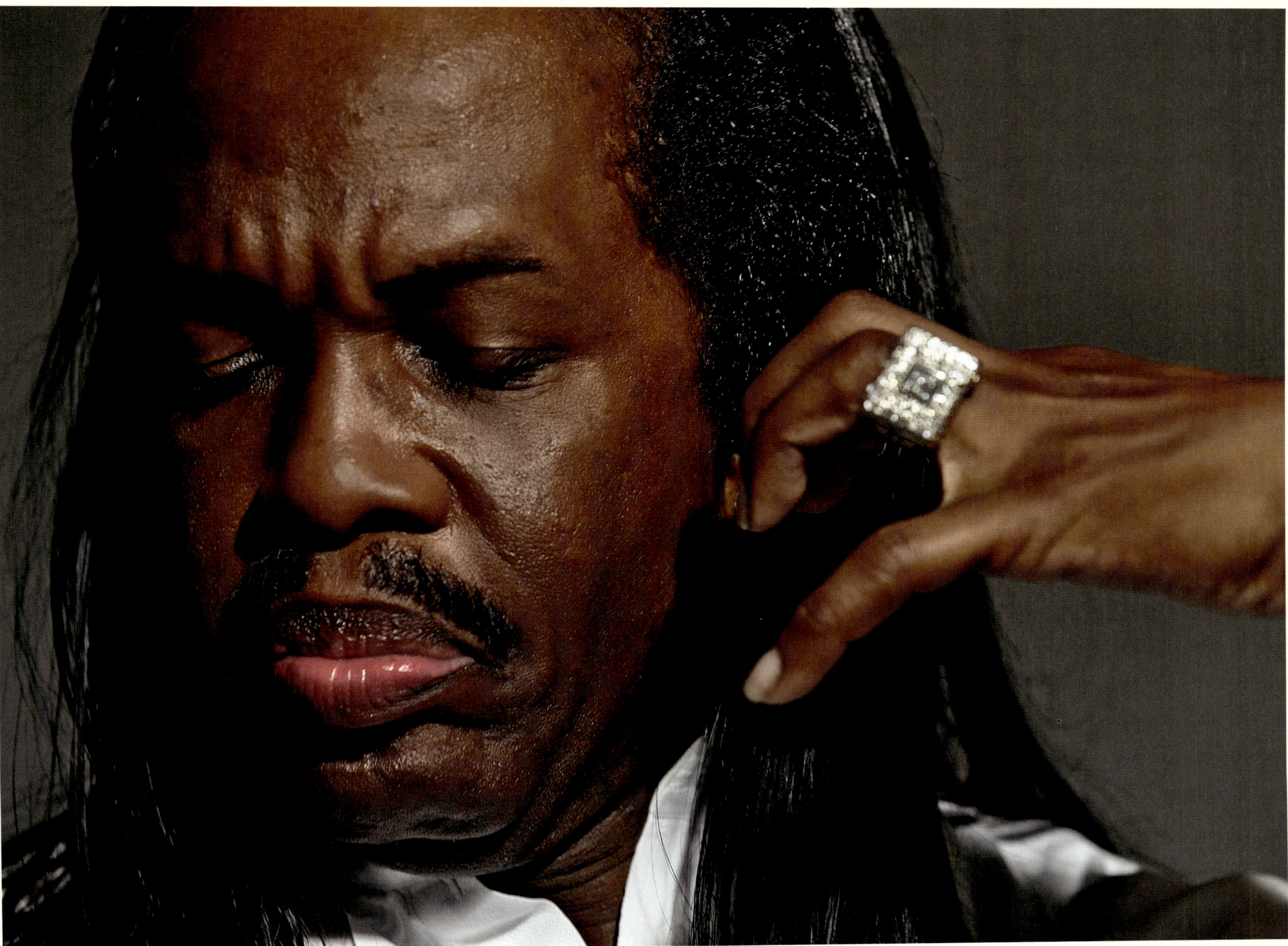

As the only bassist in the history of pioneering R&B group Earth, Wind & Fire, Verdine White helped write the vocabulary of the instrument in funk. One of the two or three most influential instrumentalists in his field, White has played on every one of the band's twenty-one albums. He has been awarded six Grammys, been inducted into the Rock and Roll Hall of Fame, and entertained at the White House. He had been playing in local clubs around Chicago when his older brother Maurice White, drummer with the Ramsey Lewis Trio and Chess Records sessions, moved to Los Angeles and changed his group's name to Earth, Wind & Fire in 1970. Verdine never looked back. Although the band was slow to develop a wide audience for the daring, exciting new sound, after "Shining Star" hit number one in 1975, Earth, Wind & Fire punched out a string of pop smashes—"Sing a Song," "Boogie Wonderland," "After the Fire Is Gone." The group's cover of The Beatles' "Got to Get You into My Life" was the bright, shiny highpoint of the 1978 Bee Gees/Peter Frampton cinematic rendition, *Sgt. Pepper's Lonely Hearts Club Band*. He lives with his wife of thirty-five years, Shelly Clark of the vocal group Honey Cone. Music runs in the family. His father was a doctor who played saxophone. His teenaged granddaughter is already a gifted vocal student.

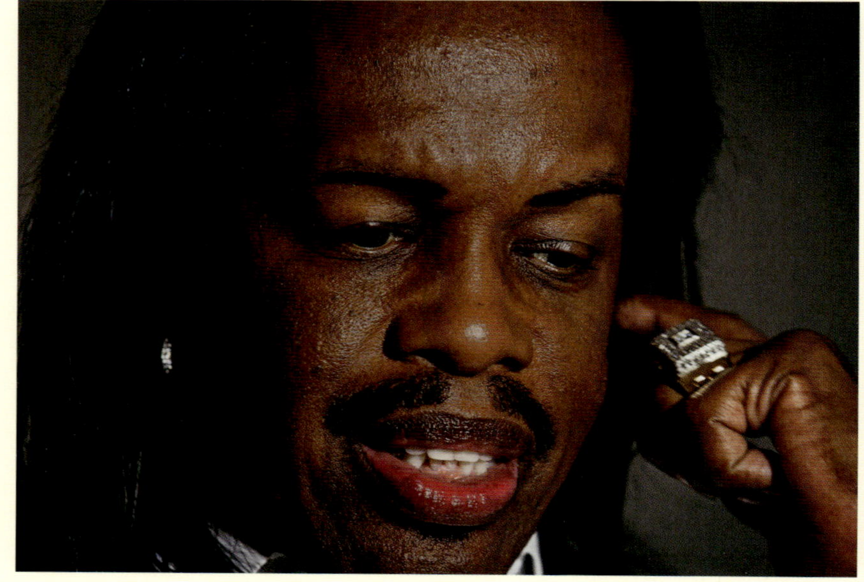

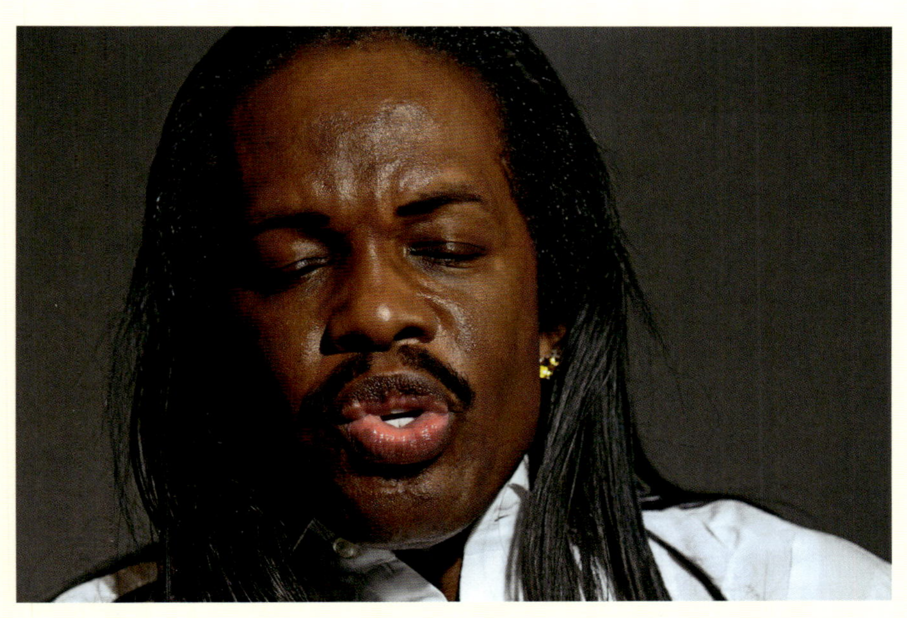

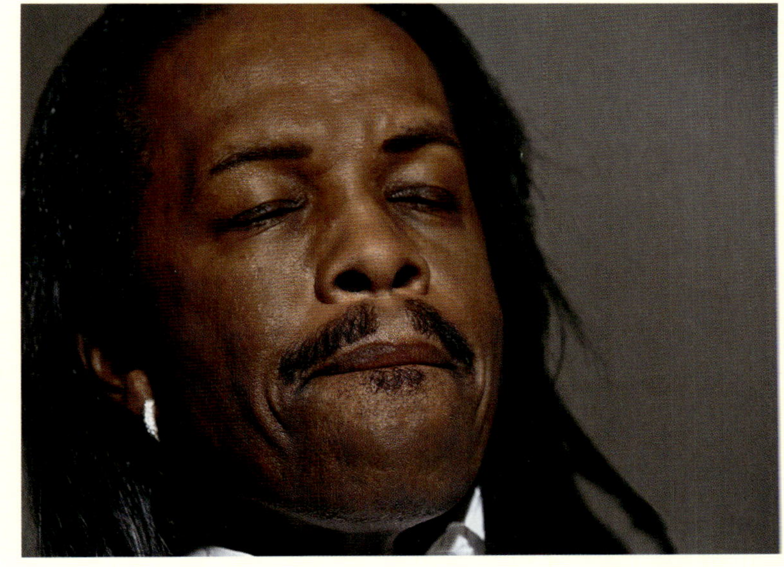

GERALD WILSON at studio, Encino, California, July 17, 2012

Gerald Wilson – *Blues for Yna Yna*
Wayne Shorter – *Footprints*

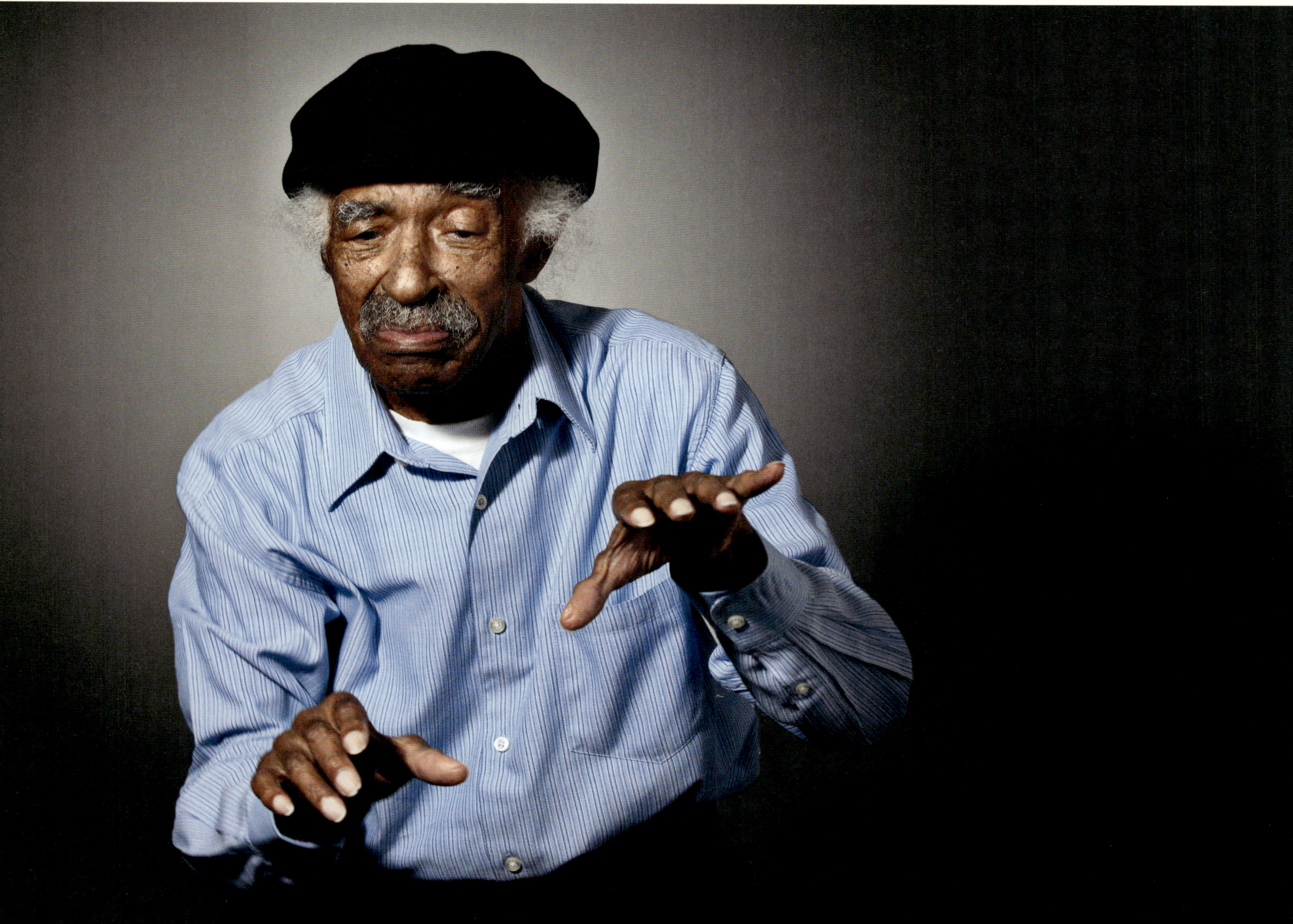

The perennially underrated Gerald Wilson passed away at age ninety-six, less than two months after his session, an arranger whose distinguished work reaches back to the Swing Era, who never received his due recognition during his lengthy lifetime. He joined the Jimmie Lunceford band in 1939, replacing arranger Sy Oliver on trumpet. After the war, he played and arranged for Count Basie, Duke Ellington and Dizzy Gillespie, as well as starting his own band. He dropped out of jazz during the early 50s to work in the grocery business, but started another band and gradually returned to full activity. He was married for more than fifty years to a Mexican-American woman, Josefina Villasenor Wilson, and many of his compositions feature a Spanish flavor, including his "Viva Tirado," which was a smash hit for the Latin rock group El Chicano. He often named pieces after his children and grandchildren and frequently featured on recordings his son Anthony Wilson and son-in-law Shuggie Otis (son of R&B great Johnny Otis) on guitars. For his photographs, Wilson listened to the bracing seven-minute leadoff cut to his great 1961 album, *You Better Believe It*, with the seventeen-piece band romping with reedman Harold Land and organist Richard "Groove" Holmes. The song, originally written for a TV crime drama, was named for his pet cat. He also listened to "Footprints," the 1966 jazz standard by saxophonist Wayne Shorter, made famous in a recording by Miles Davis.

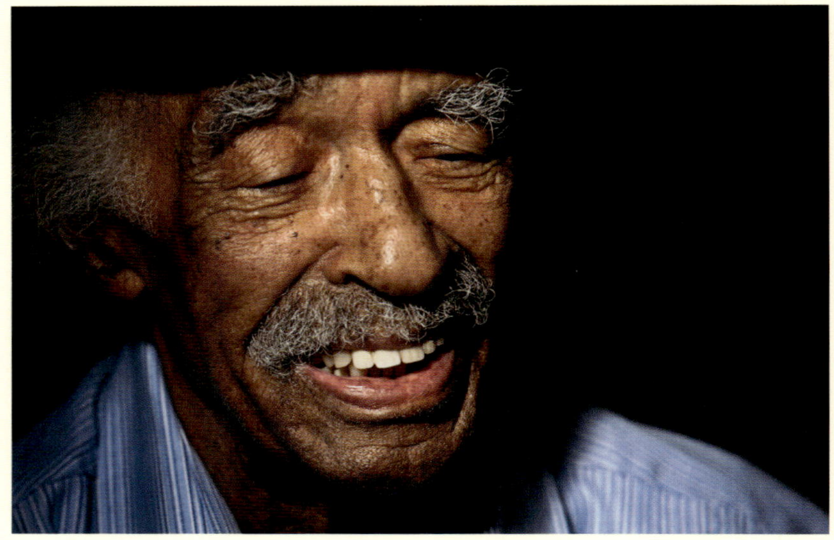

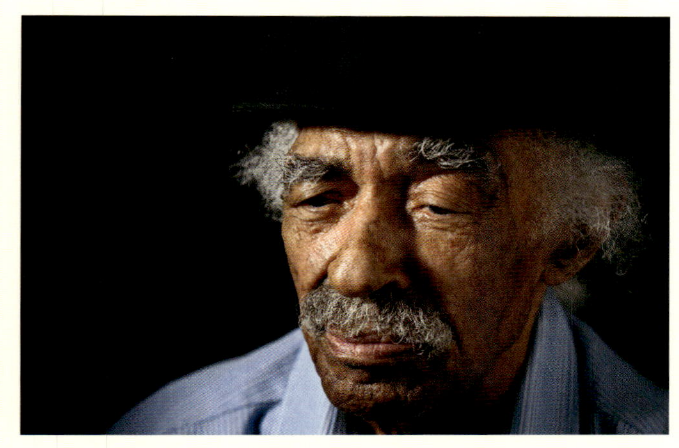

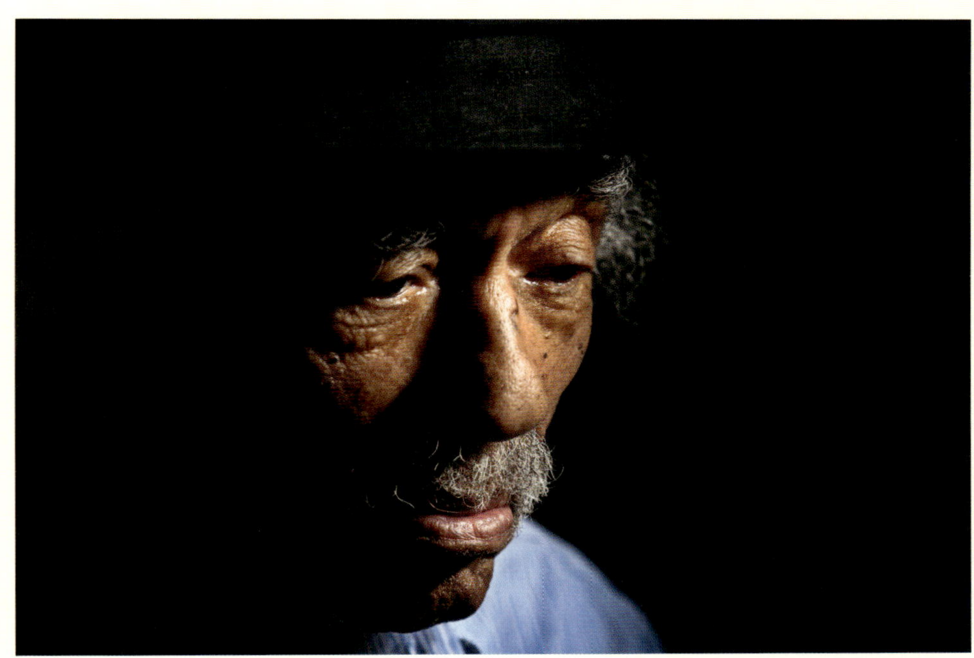

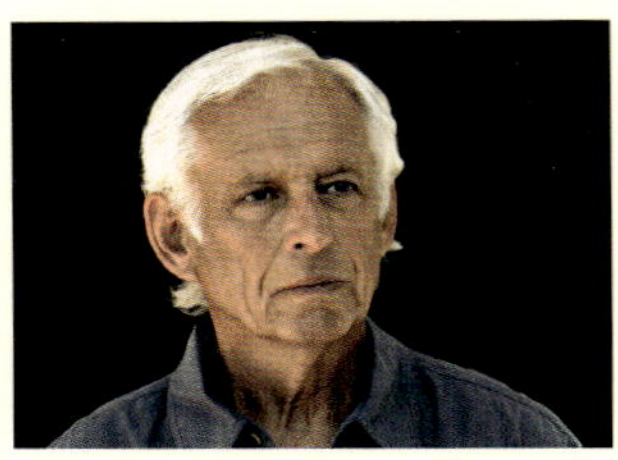

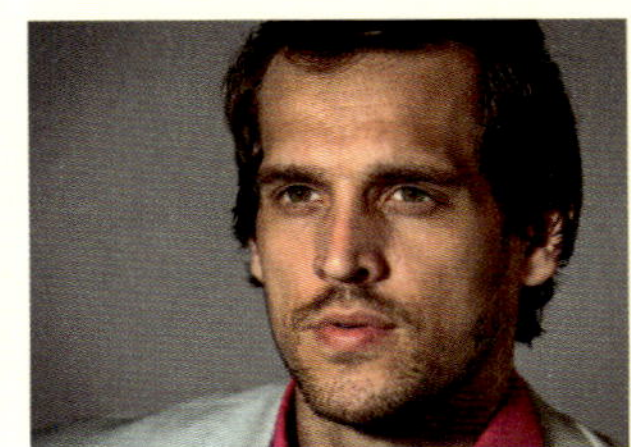

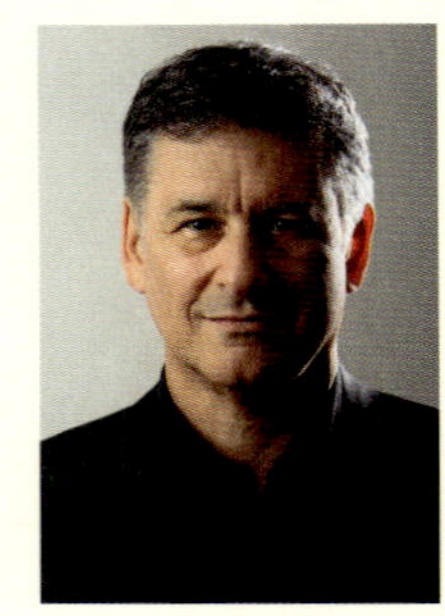

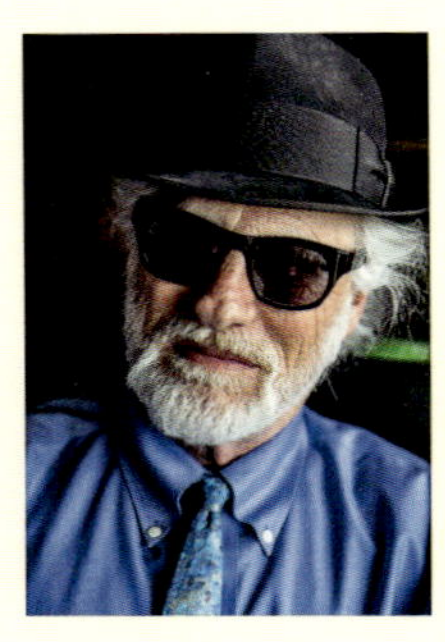

RICHARD M. EHRLICH was born in New York City and resides in Los Angeles. Since 2001 his fine art photographs have been held in the permanent collections of nineteen museums, including Smithsonian National Museum of American History, Los Angeles County Museum of Art, UCLA Hammer Museum, The George Eastman House, Denver Art Museum, and Santa Barbara Museum of Art.

Ehrlich was the first to photograph the Holocaust Archives in Bad Arolsen, Germany. The project is part of the permanent collections of the United States Holocaust Memorial Museum, Yad Vashem in Jerusalem, The Jewish Museum New York, The Jewish Museum Berlin, and Musée d'Art et d'Histoire du Judaïsme, Paris, as well as others.

Ehrlich has participated in over thirty gallery shows, and his books include: *The Forbidden Zone: Images from Namibia*, *Anatomia Digitale*, and the recently published *The Other Side of the Sky* and *Reverie*.

LUCAS ASHER, this book's project organizer, is president at Street Invasion, Inc., handling all artist relations. He is also the lead singer and songwriter of the alternative rock band Faulkner who is collaborating with Wu-Tang Clan founder RZA at Rick Rubin's Shangri-La studios. And he is a technology entrepreneur, has worked with many leading acts in music, and is based in Venice, California, and New York.

DANIEL J. LEVITIN is Dean of Social Sciences at The Minerva Schools at Keck Graduate Institute and James McGill Professor of Neuroscience and Music at McGill University. He is the author of three consecutive bestsellers, *This Is Your Brain On Music*, *The World in Six Songs*, and *The Organized Mind: Thinking Straight in the Age of Information Overload*. He is credited with fundamental discoveries about the nature of music processing in the brain, including the role of the brain's dopaminergic system in mediating musical pleasure. Levitin is also a professional musician (guitar, bass and saxophone) and has played with Bobby McFerrin, Rosanne Cash, David Byrne, Sting, Rodney Crowell, Victor Wooten, Ben Sidran and Mel Tormé.

JOEL SELVIN, who started covering pop music for the San Francisco Chronicle in 1970, is the author of fourteen books, including his bestselling history of Haight-Ashbury rock, *Summer of Love*, the New York Times bestseller *Red: My Uncensored Life in Rock* which he co-wrote with Sammy Hagar, and his acclaimed biography of songwriter Bert Berns, *Here Comes the Night*.

ACKNOWLEDGMENTS

This project is dedicated to R. Mac Holbert, master of light, shadow, color and nuance, whose contribution and long-term friendship remained central to the realization of this project.

I am indebted to Lucas Asher for his uncanny ability to make many of the artists realize the wisdom of participating and in gaining their acquiescence—a Herculean effort that was the backbone of this project.

My deep appreciation to Dan Levitin for his insightful comments and encouragement to continue. His knowledge of music and neuroscience is unparalleled and was indispensable.

Joel Selvin captured the essence of these forty-one artists with imaginative and beautifully written notes, no small task given the diverse and complex nature of the group. He was also responsible for capturing five artists for the project for which I am very grateful.

Ming Tshing, as always, provided superb technical and special assistance.

To my indefatigable assistants: Richie Knapp, Tyson Smyer, Jeffrey Beard, Ryan Burke, Nick Fahey—all maestros of lighting.

Major indebtedness to Fred Chandler, as well as Irving Azoff, Kenny Burrell, Anastasia Brown, Eduardo Del Barrio, Danielle Diego, Irit Ehrlich, Gary Fishman, Judie Garnett, John Houlihan, Lani Hall, Chris Knight, Arlie Manuel, Melanie Merians, Stan Moress, Rique Patire, Rebecca Rothstein, Tom Schnabel, Carolina Shorter, and Becky Mancuso-Winding for their dedication and persistence in acquiring artists.

Very special kudos to Manfred Heiting for his counsel and advise on design and layout and unwavering support without which this publication would not have been brought to fruition.

To Gerhard Steidl and associates for their very special artistic endeavors in the final realization of this project.

Richard Ehrlich

First edition published in 2015

Book design: Gerhard Steidl and Duncan Whyte
Copy editor: Max Herren
Separations by Steidl's digital darkroom

Production and printing: Steidl, Göttingen

Steidl
Düstere Str. 4 / 37073 Göttingen, Germany
Phone +49 551 49 60 60 / Fax +49 551 49 60 649
mail@steidl.de
steidl.de

ISBN 978-3-86930-966-8
Printed in Germany by Steidl